JUDAISM IN THE FIRST CENTURIES OF THE CHRISTIAN ERA THE AGE OF THE TANNAIM

VOLUME III. NOTES

LONDON : HUMPHREY MILFORD
OXFORD UNIVERSITY PRESS

JUDAISM

IN THE FIRST CENTURIES OF THE CHRISTIAN ERA
THE AGE OF THE TANNAIM

BY

GEORGE FOOT MOORE

PROFESSOR OF THE HISTORY OF RELIGION
IN HARVARD UNIVERSITY

VOLUME III

CAMBRIDGE
HARVARD UNIVERSITY PRESS
1930

PRINTED AT THE HARVARD UNIVERSITY PRESS

CAMBRIDGE, MASS., U. S. A.

PREFACE

By "Judaism in the first centuries of the Christian Era, The Age of the Tannaim" I mean the religion which has acquired an historical right to the name "Judaism" in its own definition of it. In the Preface (Vol. I, p. vii) I defined the scope of the volumes as I proposed it to myself: "The aim of these volumes is to represent Judaism in the centuries in which it assumed definitive form as it presents itself in the tradition which it has always regarded as authentic." "The aim of the present work is to exhibit the religious conceptions and moral principles of Judaism, its modes of worship and observance, and its distinctive piety, in the form in which, by the end of the second century, they attained general acceptance and authority" (Vol. I, p. 125). "These primary sources come to us as they were compiled and set in order in the second century of the Christian Era, embodying the interpretation of the legislative parts of the Pentateuch and the definition and formulation of the Law, written and unwritten, in the schools, in the century and a half between the reorganization at Jamnia under Johanan ben Zakkai and his associates, after the fall of Jerusalem in the year 70, and the promulgation of the Mishnah of the Patriarch Judah" (Preface, Vol. I, p. vii).

The succession of the authoritative teachers who are called "Tannaim" may, for our purposes, be regarded as beginning with Shammai and Hillel and their schools in the time of Herod. In the historical Introduction I have endeavored to show how this type of Judaism gained the ascendency, while its exclusive supremacy was attained only after the fall of Jerusalem. "The older and younger contemporaries of Gamaliel II and their disciples, with their successors in the next generation, are the fundamental authorities of normative Judaism as we know it in the literature which it has always esteemed authentic" (Vol. I, p. 87, cf. 86).

The learned study of the Law is, however, much older, as is shown in the chapter on the Scribes (Vol. I, pp. 37–47), where the importance of Sirach (Ecclesiasticus, ca. 200 B.C.) as a landmark is recognized. The continuity of this development of Judaism with the Scriptures and its progress beyond them in some directions are evident. In numerous places I have endeavored to illustrate this in particulars by references to uncanonical writings from the two centuries preceding the Christian Era, emphasizing the appropriation and assimilation of the prophetic teaching (Vol. I, p. 113, cf. pp. 15 f.).

Until the supremacy of the type of Judaism represented by the Tannaim was achieved — before the fall of Jerusalem and the reorganization at Jamnia, Lydda, and in Galilee, — as I have recognized in various connections, Judaism was much less homgeneous than it appears in the Tannaite sources; parties, sects, schools, or looser groups differed and contended over points of major and minor importance. I have frequently directed attention to these diversities, but except for the controversies between the Sadducees and the Pharisees little or nothing is known about the parties by which these differences were cultivated. The recent discovery in the Cairo Genizah of parts of a Hebrew book proceeding from an organized schismatic sect in the region of Damascus leads to the surmise that the groups that sloughed off or were extruded may have been more numerous and more significant than we should have suspected.

Fortunately, for the task I have set myself the continuity and the progress of the main current of what is called rabbinical Judaism — I should prefer the name "normative Judaism" — with the Scriptures at one end and the Tannaite sources of the second century at the other is of greater importance than the diversity and dissent; and it is as evidence of continuity and progress that I have chiefly employed the writings of the preceding centuries from Sirach on.

I should perhaps have evaded some misunderstandings if I had said explicitly at the outset what I did *not* propose to do.

First, then, I did *not* propose to write on the history of the Jews in their wide dispersion and the multiplication of "Jews" by conversion, nor of the effects of contact with alien civilizations, religions, philosophical theologies, and superstitions, and the resulting varieties. What I have attempted to describe is the Judaism of Palestine in a limited period, which in its main features furnished the norms of worship, morals, charity, piety, and observance, for all subsequent times.

Second, I have *not* attempted a descriptive account of Judaism in New Testament times. Neither the Christian era nor the completion of the New Testament marks an epoch in the history of Judaism. The religion in which Jesus was brought up in Galilee, or Paul grew up at Tarsus and in which he pursued his studies "at the feet of Gamaliel" in Jerusalem, is the proper subject of investigations which would demand a different selection and critical evaluation of sources and an altogether different method.

The investigation of the religious environment of Jesus has acquired factitious importance in the modern turn of Christian theology and consequent direction of its apologetic. For this theology, revelation is not primarily the content of a body of inspired Scriptures comprised in the Old and the New Testaments, but the person of Jesus Christ, who was himself the supreme, if not the sole, revelation of the character of God, the Father in heaven, who is love. The "Kingdom of God" is the "regulative principle" of Christian theology; in it, as Jesus defined it, was revealed God's own purpose in the world, the final cause of creation, history, revelation, and redemption; and it is as a citizen of the Kingdom of Heaven that man is saved. The "essence" of Christianity is therefore to be sought in the religious and moral teaching of Jesus as the expression of his own religious life, or as might be said nowadays, his "religious experience."

The older apologetic found the essential peculiarity of Christianity in its doctrines of the divine nature of Christ and of redemption through his atoning death, appropriated by faith and communicated in the sacraments, which distinguished Christianity from Judaism and from all other religions that presented themselves as ways of salvation; the new apologetic seeks such a difference in the teaching of Jesus by word and example contrasted with the religion of the contemporary Scribes and Pharisees. As a system of professedly orthodox Protestant theology this may be called modern, but in so far as the "essence" is sought only in the teaching and example of Jesus it has precursors from the age of the Reformation down. It must suffice here to repeat that into this inquiry I have not transgressed.

Third, I have not meant to become involved in "Religionsgeschichtliche Probleme," the question when, where, and how the Jews got some of the notions which others seem to have entertained before them. In the period with which I have essayed to deal the most important of these notions had already been amalgamated, if not fully assimilated; the rabbis found them in their Scriptures and accepted them on the authority of revelation without any suspicion that they had any other origin. Some of these problems are very interesting and I have for years been much engaged with them; but the comparisons belong to the general history of religions, not specifically to Judaism. A general observation on the subject of borrowings in the sphere of ideas is expressed in Vol. II, pp. 394 f.

I have no intention of using the present supplementary volume for discussion of subjects which lie outside the scope of my work as defined above. Nor shall I fulfil in these Notes the desire or expectation that I give an "authority" for every statement. On the contrary, I have resisted the temptation to multiply references to the sources beyond the selection given in the foot-notes. For vast collections made for a wholly different purpose the reader may resort to Strack-Billerbeck, Kommentar zum Neuen Testament aus Talmud und Midrasch (4 volumes, 1922–1928); but he should be warned that the critical sifting of this miscellany devolves upon him who uses it for any particular purpose.

In the text of the volumes on Judaism I frequently had to pronounce a positive opinion on points on which I am well aware that the evidence is not of a nature to warrant confident assertion, or is susceptible of other interpretations. I think I have never delivered such an opinion without having weighed all the evidence or without acquaintance with the modern discussions; but as I have neither the right nor an inclination to conclude the argument with an *ipse dixit* I have taken occasion to present in the Notes at some length the views of scholars who entertain other opinions, for instance, on the Great Synagogue, or the membership and presidency of the Sanhedrin, or on the continuity of development in Judaism before and after the fall of Jerusalem, with the reasons adduced for them. On the other hand, I have made no attempt to give a bibliography of these controversies nor to enter into them, and it is not unlikely that some important contributions have been omitted.

For the rest, the Notes are supplementary to the text. Two classes of possible readers have been in mind, and I must crave the indulgence both of those to whom some of the notes seem superfluous and of those who find desired explanations lacking. Many notes not foreseen in Vol. I have been introduced, and some of those then contemplated will not be found in the present volume, generally because it seemed preferable consolidate the treatment of larger topics rather than to disperse it among many references.

Finally, I have availed myself of the opportunity to make numerous corrections. A second printing of the two volumes was necessary so soon after the first that there was time only to eliminate obvious typographical errors, and some even of such escaped notice. In the emendations in the Notes I have profited most by a detailed review by Professor Chaim Tschernowitz in two numbers of the periodical שבילי החנוך (1928), and by the extensive annotations of Professor Louis Ginzberg, kindly communicated to me in writing, some of which I have taken the liberty of inserting with his initials appended. To many other reviewers and correspondents I must content myself here in behalf of myself and my readers with a general acknowledgment of obligations.

Professor Louis Finkelstein of the Jewish Theological Seminary in New York has been so good as to verify in the library of the Seminary references to books and periodicals not accessible to me here; and, as in the previous volumes, my colleague, Professor H. A. Wolfson, has gone over the references to the Talmuds and Midrashim and called my attention to places where the statement in the text or the Note seemed to be inexact or not to be clear, for all of which I am most grateful.

The captions of the Notes are designed to make it possible to use for them the general indexes in Vol. II; to facilitate finding some of the longer detached notes I have subjoined here an indication of the pages of this volume on which they may be looked for.

CONTENTS

LONGER NOTES AND DISCUSSIONS

NOTES

NOTES

I, 4 l. 23f.

Not in Judaea and Jerusalem alone. The broad commission is in accordance with ancient principles of jurisdiction (Vol. I, p. 18). E. Meyer, Entstehung des Judenthums, p. 66; Ursprung und Anfänge des Christentums, II, 126. Josephus, Antt. xii. 3, 3 § 142.

I, 5 l. 12–14

On these documents see Note on Vol. I, 23 l. 14 ff. (below, p. 5).

I, 6 N 1

In the Yalkuṭ (II, § 1068) the extract from Seder 'Olam exhibits a somewhat different text and enumeration, giving three Persian kings and one Median. Artaḥshasta (our "Artaxerxes") was taken to be a royal title borne by all these kings whatever their personal names, and thus confusion was worse confounded.

I, 8 n. 3

For G. A. Box *read* G. H. Box and make the same correction in the Index.

I, 8 N 2

See also the Epistle of Sherira (Spanish recension; ed. Lewin, p. 73):
וכיון שעלה עזרא וזרובבל מבבל והגולה עמהם ובנו בית המקדש | והיו שם ראשי סנהדרין
כגון שמעון הצדיק ואנטיגנוס איש שוכו ושאר אותן הזוגות וגו׳.

I, 8 n. 4

It is doubtful whether 4 Esdras 14 can be dated late enough to take in the whole Tannaite literature in such exact enumeration.

I, 9 l. 1f.

The revelation to Moses of all that the prophets after him would say, and of the contents of the Ketubim (including Esther), as well as the whole Unwritten Law (Vol. I, p. 239, 245, 254 f.; also Jer. Megillah 74d), is not an exact parallel, and it is hardly to be supposed that this was in the author's mind.

I, 9 n. 1

Besides the extracts from the Fathers, Fabricius gives (p. 1157 n.) references to the literature, especially to Huet, Demonstratio Evangelica, Propositio iv, p. 536 seq. The earliest patristic testimony is probably that of Irenaeus, iii. 21, 2 (the Greek is preserved by Eusebius, Hist. Eccles. v. 8, 15).

I, 16 N 3

On the Tannaite, or Halakic, Midrash, see Vol. I, pp. 125 ff.; 132–134; 135–149.

I, 18 l. 10–13

In Rome, for example, there were distinct jurisdictions for cases between citizens, and between foreigners, or citizens and foreigners — praetor urbanus and praetor qui inter peregrinos ius dicit (praetor peregrinus).

I, 19 l. 2–4

Cf. Vol. II, pp. 142, 150. — Abot 2, 12, Abot de-R. Nathan 17, 1–2 (ed. Schechter, f. 33a); Bacher, Tannaiten, I, 67 n. 6, R. Jose (ha-Kohen); Abot 2, 10, Abot de-R. Nathan 15 (ed. Schechter, f. 30a): Bacher, Tannaiten, I, 96, R. Eliezer (b. Hyrcanus).

I, 20 l. 7 ff.

See also Encyclopaedia of Religion and Ethics, s.v. 'Marriage' (Greek), especially VIII,445 A; Pauly-Wissowa, XIV, 2259 ff.

I, 21 l. 13 ff.

The separateness of the Jews from people of other races and religions was probably made more distinctly a religious principle in the hellenistic crisis and by the Pharisees when they came into power, and, secondly, by the larger dispersion in heathen environment, where they could not exclude the rest of the population, but only keep themselves apart from them. According to the Books of Ezra and Nehemiah its remoter antecedents were in the attitude of the returning Babylonian Jews (גולה) to the "people of the land," as subsequently the Jews of strict observance held aloof from the ignorant and negligent to whom they extended the same name, "people of the land" (עמי הארץ).

I, 23 l. 14 ff.

Zeitschrift für ägyptische Sprache und Altertumskunde, XLVI (1910), 1–61. Sachau, E., Aramäische Papyrus und Ostraka aus einer jüdischen Militär-Kolonie zu Elephantine, Leipzig, 1911. Cowley, A. E., Aramaic Papyri of the Fifth Century B.C., Oxford, 1923 [including those in Sayce and Cowley, Aramaic Papyri discovered at Assuan, London, 1906].

I, 23 l. 27 ff.

Montgomery, J. A., The Samaritans, the Earliest Jewish Sect, Philadelphia, 1907 (with full bibliography). Gaster, M., The Samaritans, Their History, Doctrines and Literature, London, 1925.

I, 24 n. 5

The Jews called the adherents of the sanctuary on Gerizim "Cuthaeans," insinuating that as descendants of the colony brought by Shalmaneser from Cuthah and established in the cities of Samaria (2 Kings 17, 24) they were at least half-heathen (2 Kings 17, 33 ff.). Josephus, Antt. ix. 14, 3 § 290: *οἱ κατὰ μὲν τὴν Ἑβραίων γλῶτταν Χουθαῖοι, κατὰ δὲ τὴν Ἑλλήνων Σαμαρεῖται.* Cf. xiii. 3, 4 § 74 *Σαμαρεῖς, οἳ τὸ ἐν Γαριζεὶν προσεκύνουν ἱερόν.*

I, 26 l. 13

E.g. under Ptolemy Philometor, Josephus, Antt. xiii. 3, 4 § 74 ff. Each side claimed to have the true and only legitimate temple, and the advocates they put forward staked their lives on proving it from the Law. The king, after hearing the arguments, decided in favor of the temple in Jerusalem, and put to death the representatives of the Samaritans who had lost their wager.

I, 26 l. 15 f.

"Seir" is the reading of the Latin version (qui sedent in monte Seir), supported by the Syriac (גבל, Peshitto 2 Chron. 25, 11, 14 for הר שעיר; cf. Psalm 83, 8 Heb.). The Greek version, without variants, *ἐν ὄρει Σαμαρείας.* *Γεβαληνή* as a name for Idumaea or a region in it is frequent in the Onomastikon of Eusebius, e.g. *Ἰδουμαία . . . ἔστι δὲ ἡ ἀμφὶ τὴν Πέτραν Γεβαληνὴ καλουμένη.* (See Lagarde's Index.) Narrating the expedition of Amaziah king of Judah against Edom (2 Chron. 25, 5 ff.) Josephus writes, Antt. ix. 9, 1 § 188: *διεγνώκει γὰρ τοῖς Ἀμαληκιτῶν ἔθνεσι καὶ Ἰδουμαίων καὶ Γαβαλιτῶν ἐπιστρατεύεσθαι;* cf. Antt. ii. 1, 2 § 5 f.: *οὗτοι κατῴκησαν τῆς Ἰδουμαίας τὴν Γοβολῖτιν λεγομένην* καὶ τὴν ἀπὸ Ἀμαλήκου κληθεῖσαν Ἀμαληκῖτιν. See Reland, Palaestina, i, c. 12 (De regione Edom), i, c. 15 (De Gebalene). — Modern Jebal ('mountainous tract,' south of Kerak); Robinson, Biblical Researches (1841), II, 551 ff. The Hebrew Sirach has יושבי שעיר ופלשת וגוי נבל הדר בשכם. In Sirach's time Seir (the Idumaeans) is more probable as the name of a hated 'people' than Samaria. The intrusion of the Edomites into old Judaean territory moved more than one of the later prophets to bitter words. See C. C. Torrey, "The Edomites in Southern Judah," Journal of Biblical Literature, XVII (1898), 16–20. — In Asmonaean times Hebron was an Idumaean town (Josephus, Bell. Jud. iv. 9, 7 § 529, captured by Simon, cf. § 534–537); on the forcible Judaizing of the Idumaeans by John Hyrcanus, see Vol. I, pp. 336 f.

I, 26 n. 2

ὁ λαὸς ὁ μωρὸς ὁ κατοικῶν ἐν Σικίμοις. Cf. Test. XII Patriarchs, Levi 7, 2: ἔσται γὰρ ἀπὸ σήμερον ἡ Σίκημα λεγομένη πόλις ἀσυνέτων (LXX Deut. 32, 21). — "The third is no people"; see Midrash Tannaim on Deut. 32, 21 (ed. Hoffmann, p. 196); "these are the Cuthaeans," — proof text Ezra 4, 1; cf. ibid. on 32, 41 (p. 203). Cf. Sifrè Deut. § 331.

I, 29 l. 13–16

With the change in the alphabet attributed to Ezra may be compared the official adoption of the Ionic alphabet in Athens in the archonship of Eukleides (404/403 B.C.), superseding the local alphabet previously used in Attica. — The list of letters liable to be erroneously interchanged on account of their similarity in Sifrè Deut. § 36 (on Deut. 6, 9, ed. Friedmann f. 75a; Midrash Tannaim, p. 28) applies to the so-called "square alphabet"; it shows also, as would be expected, that the form of some of the letters was not exactly that with which we are best acquainted, especially in print, where the type-founders, partly from necessity, partly for what they probably regard as aesthetic considerations, have produced new varieties of the Hebrew alphabet, as they have in other cases, notably in Greek. Of interest in this passage are also the names of some of the letters, formed by reduplication.

I, 29 N 3

The Taḳḳanot of Ezra (nine) are found in Jer. Megillah 4, 1 (f. 75a), accompanied by the motives for some of them, and in a list of ten in Baba Ḳamma 82a, where the motives and some discussions follow in the Talmud. The two lists agree in the main. They are given here from the Palestinian Talmud. Moses had ordained that the Israelites should read from the Torah (Pentateuch) on the Sabbaths and Holy Days (ימים טובים) and New Moons, and the secular days of the festival (חולי של מועד), as it is written, 'And Moses proclaimed to the Israelites the appointed seasons of the Lord' (מועדי יהוה, Lev. 23, 44); Ezra ordained that they should read lessons (also) on Mondays and Thursdays, and on the Sabbath at the afternoon service (מנחה). He prescribed for those who had had an emission (בעלי קריין), an ablution before reading in the Law.[1] The courts should be in session in the towns on Mondays and Thursdays. Peddlers (of cosmetics, perfumes, and the like) should make their rounds in the towns "on account of the honor of the daughters of Israel" (that the woman may make themselves fine). Clothes should be washed on Thursday on account of the honor of the Sabbath (on which everybody ought to be dressed in clean clothes). Bread should be baked (early) on Friday, that the piece to be given to the poor may be ready. People should eat garlic on Friday night (as an aphrodisiac). Women in the latrines should talk with one another (to avoid suspicion). A woman should wear a girdle (סינר), front and back. A woman should rub and comb her hair three days before her purification (the reason is explained in the Talmud; cf. Niddah 67b).

I, 31 N 4

On the Great Synagogue (or Assembly), see W. Bacher in Jewish Encyclopedia XI (1905), 640–643; E. Schürer, Geschichte des jüdischen Volkes, u. s. w., II, 354 f. (literature ibid.).

On the nature of this assembly opinions are sharply divided. The question is involved with the identification and date of Simeon the Righteous, who according to Abot 1, 2 was one of the (last) remaining members of the Great Assembly, and with the whole chronology of the Persian period. A survey of the views of mediaeval rabbis is given by Azariah dei Rossi, Me'or 'Enayim, Imrè Binah c. 22 (cf. ibid. c. 37). For a modern statement of the problems and the opinions about them, see S. Krauss, "The Great Synod," Jewish Quarterly Review, X (1898), 347–377.

1. In the Babylonian Talmud it is understood that Lev. 15, 16 applies only to eating Terumah or sacred food (i. e. only to priests); Ezra extended it to "the words of the Law" (and thus to laymen). See Maimonides, Keri'at Shema' 4, 8, according to which it had never been generally observed, was impracticable, and in his day disregarded.

So long as Jewish scholars operated with the chronology of the Seder 'Olam and the Talmudic references to the Great Synagogue, it seems to have been the accepted opinion that it belonged to one generation; the Bet Din of Ezra is what is called Keneset ha-Gedolah, to which many Taḳḳanot are ascribed.[1] Serious difficulty arose, however, when Josephus with his Simeon the Righteous and his succession of high priests came to their knowledge, and attempts were made to reconcile Josephus, and eventually other chronological data derived from Greek sources, with the Talmud. These difficulties were perceived by Azariah dei Rossi, who cited not only Josephus but a Breviarium de Temporibus, which he took for what it professed to be, a work of Philo of Alexandria (in reality a forgery published, with other supposititious writings, by Annius of Viterbo). He observes that some therefore put Simeon the Righteous in the eighth generation from Joshua, the high-priest of the restoration (namely, the five successors of Joshua named in Neh. 12, 10, followed by Onias son of Jaddua, and Simeon son of Onias, as in Josephus, Antt. xii. 2, 5); see Me'or 'Enayim, Imrè Binah, cc. 22 and 37.

There is a voluminous modern literature on this subject, revolving principally about the two Simons and the high priest who met Alexander the Great. References to the authors who participated in the discussion from Jost (1839) to Graetz (1857) may be found in Leopold Löw, Gesammelte Schriften, I, 399 n., and the further history of opinion is to be followed in Kuenen's monograph (1876) cited below. In the periodical Ben Chananja, I (1858), Löw published a series of articles under the title, "Die grosse Synode, ihr Ursprung und ihre Wirkungen," which are reprinted in his Gesammelte Schriften, 1889, I, 399–449, by the pages of which citations are made here.

His thesis is that the Simeon the Righteous of Abot 1, 2 was neither the Simon (I) of Josephus nor the Simon (II) of Ben Sira, but Simon the Asmonaean, and the Great Assembly that described in 1 Macc. 14, 25–49 (see vs. 28: ἐπὶ συναγωγῆς μεγάλης τῶν ἱερέων καὶ λαοῦ καὶ ἀρχόντων ἔθνους καὶ τῶν πρεσβυτέρων τῆς χώρας), on the 18th of the month Elul, in the year 172 of the Seleucid era (140 B.C.) As Löw notes, the possibility that the honorific "ha-Ṣaddiḳ" belonged to this Simeon had occurred to Azariah dei Rossi (Me'or 'Enayim, Imrè Binah, c. 22, end). With him Löw (p. 413 ff.) identifies the Talmudic Simeon the Righteous. The assembly of 1 Macc. 14 came to be called

1. Authors who held this view are enumerated by Löw, Gesammelte Schriften. I, 401.

the Great Assembly, "da in der Folge die Volksversammlungen ausser Brauch kamen." The numerous prophets who according to the Talmuds belonged to the Great Synagogue make a difficulty which Löw recognizes, since they cannot be imagined to be of the generation of Haggai, Zechariah, and Malachi, with whom according to tradition prophecy ceased, all the more in view of 1 Macc. 14, 41 (the Jews and the priests voted that Simon should be ruler and high priest *εἰς τὸν αἰῶνα, ἕως τοῦ ἀναστῆναι προφήτην πιστόν*). On this point he cites (p. 419) Krochmal, Moreh, 1851, p. 111 f.

This date would evidently remove the difficulty of having to stretch the succession (Antigonus of Socho and the Pairs who transmitted the tradition down to Hillel and Shammai) over two or even three centuries; and it had already been noted by Zunz (Gottesdienstliche Vorträge, p. 37, ed. 2, p. 40, n.) that the appointment of "pairs" (זוגות) is attributed to John Hyrcanus, the son and successor of Simon the Asmonaean (Jer. Ma'aser Sheni, f. 56d, below, and the parallel, Jer. Soṭah, f. 24a, below). Jose ben Jo'ezer was probably one of these appointees (Löw, op. cit., p. 421–423). — John Hyrcanus' "pairs" were, however, apparently inspectors of tithing whose scrutiny made it unnecessary for even the most scrupulous to raise any question about Demai. Except that they made their tours of inspection in couples, they seem to have nothing in common with the successive "Pairs" of whom the Mishnah (Ḥagigah 2, 2) makes the president and vice-president of the Sanhedrin respectively (Vol. I, p. 45, n.). And plainly the assembly of 1 Macc. 14, even if we imagine that its existence was continued as a kind of council under Simon, would be something very different from what Jewish tradition supposes its Great Synagogue to have been and done. It has indeed been supposed by Zunz and others that the Great Sanhedrin was organized in this period, with the "Pairs" at its head (see Löw, p. 431 ff.), to which Megillat Ta'anit, c. 5, on the 24th of Ab (probably 170 A. S.), תבנא לדינא, is referred by Löw, and it might accordingly be imagined that from the time of Hyrcanus on the Sanhedrin succeeded to the functions of the Great Assembly. But aside from the uncertainty of the combinations by which this date is arrived at, it is pertinent to repeat an observation which has frequently been made, namely, that while many and various things are attributed in our sources to the *Men* of the Great Synagogue, enactments of the Great Synagogue itself are not recorded, as would be natural if it were thought of as an assembly, a council, or a high court like the Sanhedrin.

In an article, שמעון הצדיק וכנסת הגדולה in the periodical נר מערבי, 1924, pp. 137–142, S. Zeitlin offers a different explanation: The Great Synagogue was not limited to the first generation or two after the return of the Golah, nor was it a permanent body with regular sessions perpetuating itself through two or three centuries by co-optation or appointment, but an assembly called together as need was on occasions of national importance from the days of Ezra and Nehemiah on, or to pass important ordinances. [A somewhat similar hypothesis is considered by Krochmal, Moreh, 1851, p. 102b, cf. p. 52, who mentions Jabneh and Usha.] Such an occasion arose when it was necessary to decide whether Judaea should side with the Seleucid Antiochus III, or should remain loyal in its Ptolemaic allegiance; in this crisis, about 200 B.C., Simeon the Righteous (Simeon II, the high priest of Sirach's time) took a leading part. Another was that recorded in 1 Macc. 14, in 141 B.C., when Simon the Asmonaean was recognized as hereditary high priest and political ruler (see Löw's theory above). A third was in the year 65 A.D., on the eve of the war with Rome (Josephus, Bell. Jud. ii. 20, 3, cf. Vita c. 38 § 190–194), when the high priest Annas (Ananos) and Simon son of Gamaliel were leading figures. The objection that might be made on the ground of Abot 1, 2, where Simeon the Righteous is called "one of the (last) survivors of the Great Assembly," Zeitlin sets aside by a conjectural emendation of the text: for משירי כנסת הגדולה he would read מרישי כה"נ, "one of the heads (presidents) of the Great Assembly." [It may be observed that Sherira, ed. Lewin, p. 73, speaks of Simeon the Righteous and Antigonus of Socho as "heads of the Sanhedrin," like the following "Pairs."] The emendation is graphically easy, and in Zeitlin's opinion rendered historically necessary by the chronological impossibilities of the actual text.

Skepticism about the existence of such a body as the "Great Synagogue" of rabbinical tradition developed among Christian writers over the part attributed to this body in the definition of the canon of Scripture (Morin, Richard Simon), and especially after the antiquity of the vowel-points and accents and the whole tradition of the text (Massorah) became a controversial issue among Protestants. The most considerable monograph of this period is J. E. Rau, Diatribe de Synagoga Magna, Utrecht, 1727. Rau makes the most of the fact that Ezra and Nehemiah have no mention of such a body, nor does any other writer in or near the time in which it is supposed to have been active. On the traditional side it is sufficient to refer to Buxtorf, Tiberias (1620), especially cc. 10 and 11.

Among modern critical investigations of the whole question the first place is held by A. Kuenen, Over de mannen der groote Synagoge (Verslagen en Mededeelingen der Koninklijke Akademie van Wetenschappen, enz., Amsterdam, 1876); German translation, Ueber die Männer der grossen Synagoge (by Karl Budde) in Gesammelte Abhandlungen zur biblischen Wissenschaft von Dr. Abraham Kuenen, 1894, pp. 125–160. Kuenen finds the source of the whole legend in the narrative of the assembly in Neh. 8–10, a conclusion which has been adopted by many scholars. That the assembly described in those chapters had come to be called the Great Assembly, as the first, and an example and pattern for subsequent generations, had occurred to Krochmal (Moreh, ed. 1851, p. 102, cf. 52), as Kuenen notes (German translation, p. 144, n.), but the conception of this Assembly as a model for future generations make this suggestion essentially different from Kuenen's result.

D. Hoffmann, "Ueber die Männer der grossen Versammlung," in Berliner u. Hoffmanns Magazin für die Wissenschaft des Judenthums, X (1883), 45–63, discusses the accounts of the actions of the Great Synagogue in matters of the canon and the Eighteen Prayers. That the Assembly of Neh. 8–10 was the Great Assembly, and is so designated in rabbinical sources, he accepts (p. 49); but dissents from Kuenen's conclusion that "unter כנסת הגדולה nur die in Neh. 8–10 geschilderte grosse Volksversammlung verstanden sei" (p. 51, 54 f.). He thinks of the Sanhedrin as the successor to the Great Synagogue — there is no room for two such bodies at the same time — and calls attention to the use of כנישתא for the Sanhedrin in Megillat Ta'anit c. 10. — In regard to Simeon the Righteous, "one of the last survivors of the Great Synagogue," he asks the pertinent question whether this is historical, or the utterance of a later Tanna "auf Grund der späteren Chronologie." — See also H. Englander, "The Men of the Great Synagogue" in the Hebrew Union College Jubilee Volume (1925), pp. 145–169.

I, 31 l. 20f.

That the prophets prophesied by the holy spirit until the time of Alexander of Macedon, from which time the learned (חכמים) took their place, is said in Seder 'Olam c. 30 (ed. Ratner, f. 70b). In a Baraita in Sanhedrin 11a the departure of the holy spirit from Israel was with the death of the last prophets, Haggai, Zechariah, and Malachi; cf. Vol. I, p. 240. For other references, see Ratner's note 41. — That in Abot de-R. Nathan (ed. Schechter, f. 1b, both recensions)

Haggai, Zechariah, and Malachi transmit the tradition from the prophets to the men of the Great Synagogue is perhaps connected with the view that prophecy ceased with the destruction of the First Temple and that thenceforth the learned succeeded the prophets (Baba Batra 12a).

I, 32 l. 6 ff.

In one of the letters prefixed to 2 Macc. (2, 13) Nehemiah is said to have founded a library and collected in it *τὰ περὶ τῶν βασιλέων καὶ προφητῶν βιβλία, καὶ τὰ τοῦ Δαυείδ, καὶ ἐπιστολὰς βασιλέων περὶ ἀναθεμάτων.*

I, 32 n. 2

Jer. Megillah 70d: eighty-five elders (cf. Neh. 10, 2–29), among them about thirty prophets. Bacher (Jewish Encyclopedia, XI, 641) cites Krochmal's conjectural harmonization of this with the hundred and twenty elders of Megillah 17b (Moreh, 1851, p. 111 n.) See also Büchler, Der galiläische 'Am-ha 'Ares des zweiten Jahrhunderts, p. 7 n., who surmises that the 85 may come from the number of elders who sat under Rabban Gamaliel at Jamnia on one occasion (Tos. Kelim iii. 2, 4).

I, 32 n. 6

On the corrections of the Scribes see Lauterbach, Jewish Quarterly Review, V, 34f.

I. 33 l. 1–6.

The Christian parallel was early pointed out. It was remarked: Patres olim, quicquid auctoritatem habere voluerunt, atque usu diuturno observatum viderunt, cujus tamen primum auctorem ignorarunt, sub nomine Apostolicae traditionis commendasse; sic quoque, quae inter Judaeos vigebant incerti auctoris instituta, Viris Synagogae Magnae fuisse tributa. J. Alting, Opera, V, 382 (Epist. 69).

I. 33 l. 8

On the first precept cf. Sifrè Deut. § 16, where, in the example given, 'patient' would perhaps be a better equivalent than 'deliberate.' Cf. Sanhedrin 7b, below.

I. 34 N. 4 bis

See Vol. I, pp. 6, 158 f. The chronology of the post-exilic period operates with the 490 years of Daniel, taken as the interval between the first destruction of the Temple (Nebuchadnezzar) and the second (Titus). Seventy years being subtracted for the "exile," there remained 420 years for the second Temple. From the time when the Jews had the Seleucid era (312 B.C.) to reckon by, their chronology was not far out of the way. The Seder 'Olam gives to the Herods down to 70 A.D., 103 years (apparently including both Agrippas in a continuous succession of Herodian kings, disregarding the Roman procurators as an interim administration), and to the Asmonaeans 103 years. Counting back in our way from the destruction of the Temple (70 A.D.), we should get for the accession of Herod the Great 33 B.C. (instead of 37), for the Asmonaean era (1 Macc. 13,41 f.), 136 B.C. (instead of 142); and with 180 years for the rule of the Greeks should find Alexander the Great in Palestine in the year 316 B.C. (instead of 332). Before this, however, the schematic 420 years for the existence of the second Temple leaves but 34 years from the completion of the Temple (according to our Ptolemaic chronology 516 B.C.) and Alexander the Great (332 B.C.), instead of 184. In other words, the only large error is in the Persian period. The author may have known that the Persian king conquered by Alexander was Darius (in the Canon of Ptolemy the *third* of the name, 336–332 B.C.), and he finds in his biblical sources but two Persian kings (Cyrus and Darius — and even these two are identified), Artaḥshasta (Artaxerxes) in Nehemiah being taken as a title of both, like 'Pharaoh' in Egypt (cf. Rosh ha-Shanah 3b, below), and Ahasuerus in Esther being counted as a Median king.

I, 34 N. 5

See G. F. Moore, "Simeon the Righteous," in the Israel Abrahams Memorial Volume (1927), pp. 348–364; cf. also above (p. 10) Note 4.

I, 35 l. 1f.

For an account of these wars utilizing the scanty sources see E. Meyer, Ursprung und Anfänge des Christentums, II, 121–128: Antiochus overran all Coelesyria (including Palestine) in 201 B.C.; Gaza alone offered him obstinate resistance. In the winter of 201–200, Antiochus having withdrawn his army, a strong Egyptian force commanded by the Aetolian Skopas brought the Jews again into subjection to their former Egyptian master (Josephus, Antt. xii. 3, 3 § 135, from Polybius xvi.). After the defeat of Skopas at Panion (200 B.C., Niese), and his surrender at Sidon, Antiochus, in the years 199 and 198, annexed all Palestine (Josephus, xii. 3, 3 § 136, on the same authority), and the Jews living around the Temple in Jerusalem came over to him (ibid.). See the rescript addressed by Antiochus III to Ptolemaeus (probably the governor of the new province), Josephus, xii. 3, 3 § 138–144, from which it appears that the senate (γερουσία) of Jerusalem had received him with demonstrations of friendship. The battle of Panion is commonly dated in the year 198 (see Vol I, p 48, where this date is accepted), but Meyer's combination now seems to me preferable. From this time on Palestine was part of the Seleucid empire; for the proposal to give Coelesyria as a dowry to Cleopatra, daughter of Antiochus III, on her marriage with Ptolemy V, Epiphanes, which would have brought it back under Egyptian sovereignty, was never carried out. The marriage took place in the winter 194/193 (Meyer, p 124 f.), but Antiochus and his successors kept their hold on the conquered provinces.

I, 35 l. 18f.

The name Antigonos occurs repeatedly in the Asmonaean line, the first of whom we have record being a son of John Hyrcanus, brother of Aristobulus. It probably first became known to the Jews through the campaign of Antigonos (Monophthalmos) in which he made himself master of the seaboard of Phoenicia and Palestine (315 B.C.), ejecting Ptolemy, who had conquered this region in 320.

I, 35 l. 18–25

אל תהיו כעבדים השמשמשים את הרב על מנת לקבל פרס. The word פרס is often understood and translated "reward," as though equivalent to שכר, 'wages.' So, recently, Marti in his translation of Abot, and notes (p. 10), who finds it "betrübend" that Herford understands the word as "present," "unconditional gift." A good example of the difference may be found in the "comparisons" of Samuel the Little, Ta'anit 25b, below. Maimonides distinguishes correctly in his commentary on Abot: פרס is something that the master is under no obligation to pay, but may voluntarily offer to give, as, e.g., he may say to a slave, a minor son, or his wife, 'Do so and so for me, and I will give you a *dinar*' (as a present). The word is not a common one, and if the author had meant שכר it would have been natural to employ this usual word for 'wages.' In Abot de-R. Nathan, c. 5 (ed. Schechter, f. 13b), in the discussion of this saying in the schools of Zadok and Boethus, שכר is used, but it should be observed that the slave (who has no claim to 'wages' for personal services to his master) has here become a day-laborer (פועל) who works all day expecting to receive his wages at evening. In the second recension (ed. Schechter, ibid.) the reward (שכר) of the righteous, partly in this world, partly in the world to come, is discussed.

I. 38 l. 20

The common Stoic definition. See C. L. W. Grimm, on 4 Macc. 1, 16; von Arnim, Stoicorum Veterum Fragmenta, II, 15.

I. 39 l. 30

Another way of acquiring this knowledge would be by attendance on the courts and learning from the procedure and the decisions.

I. 42 l. 15ff.

Ezra, according to a recent Jewish historian, published what had been revealed to Moses at Sinai, and had been from that time on handed down in the keeping of the priests, so that it was made accessible to laymen. Jawitz, ספר תולדות ישראל, III, 132.

I, 43, l. 30f.–44, l. 1 f.

In earlier times Rabbi ('my master') was a respectful form of address or way of speaking of a man, as we find it in the Gospels; in the second century it was a title conferred on an officially recognized or ordained teacher. It is not used in speaking of Hillel and Shammai, for example, or in quoting them, nor of the preceding "Pairs," nor of Simeon the Righteous or Antigonos of Socho, e.g. "Hillel said" (Abot 1, 12), but "Rabbi Eliezer said," "Rabbi Joshua" (and the other disciples of Johanan ben Zakkai) "said" (Abot 2, 9), and so in the following generations. The five whom Judah ben Baba ordained in despite of Hadrian's edict ('Abodah Zarah 8b, below) are all called Rabbi — R. Meir, R. Judah (ben Ila'i), R. Jose, R. Simeon (ben Yoḥai), R. Eleazar ben Shammu'a, while Ben Azzai and Ben Zoma, although among the leading scholars of their generation, never receive that title. The connection of the title Rabbi with ordination is made in the "Second Letter" of Sherira Gaon (ed. Lewin, p. 125), where Sanhedrin 13b is quoted: "They ordain him by (pronouncing his) name, and address him as 'Rabbi', and confer on him authority to give judgment in cases in which a (monetary) penalty is imposed" (fine or amends). The דיני קנסות are distinguished from דיני ממונות, actions about rights of property, but the system is so different from ours that no single word can be found to translate it; דיני נפשות are capital cases, and fall within the cognizance of the regularly constituted courts, not of individual rabbi. — The varieties of specific authorizations in ordination are numerous; see Maimonides, Hilkot Sanhedrin 4, 8. Cf. also the case of Rab, Vol. I, p. 105 and Note on that place. The response of Sherira is printed in the Aruk, s.v. אבי״ (see Aruch Completum, with Kohut's supplements and notes), and in Juḥasin, ed. Filipowski, p. 83 f. See Lewin's Introduction, p. 123, and "Ordination" in the Jewish Encyclopedia, IX, 428 f.

An older name which never went completely out of use was זקן, 'elder,' which is perpetuated in the Christian communities (*πρεσβύτερος*), with a rite of ordination (Acts 14, 23), but with functions different from the Jewish Elders.

Rab is Babylonian in distinction from the Palestinian, Rabbi.

A higher dignity than Rabbi is intended by the title Rabban ('our master'), perhaps better, 'great master.' According to the so-called Second Letter of Sherira Gaon (ed. Lewin, p. 125) it was given only to the Nasi, beginning with Gamaliel the Elder and his son Simeon ben Gamaliel "who lost his life at the destruction of the second temple," and Rabban Johanan ben Zakkai, "all of them were patriarchs" (נשיאים). "Rabbi" began to be used as a title from the ordinations of that time, e.g., R. Zadok and R. Eliezer bar Jacob, and from the disciples of Rabban Johanan ben Zakkai onward. "Rabbi is greater than Rab; Rabban is greater than Rabbi; and greater than Rabban is the man's bare name" (without any title, as in the case of Hillel, above).

There seems to be no reason why the honorific Rabban should be confined to those who held the office of Nasi. Rabban is used of Johanan ben Zakkai, to whom the title Nasi is not ascribed, and on the other hand the Patriarch Judah ha-Nasi is Rabbenu ha-Ḳadosh, or simply Rabbi by way of eminence, but never Rabban. His son, however, is "Rabban Gamaliel, son of Rabbi Judah ha-Nasi" (Abot 2, 2).

One might conjecture that Nasi was the native title (ultimately from Ezekiel?) of the Ethnarch, or Patriarch, whom the Romans recognized as the head of the Jewish nation (*ἔθνος*), and that in this sense it is not likely to have been borne by any one before Simeon ben Gamaliel II (under Antoninus Pius), whether or not it was earlier used of the president of a rabbinical assembly or academy. Rabban Gamaliel (II) is said, however, to have gone to Syria to the Hegemon (Legate?) "to get authority" (ליטול רשות), which is interpreted by Derenbourg and others of investiture with patriarchal authority (M. Eduyot 7, 7); see Juster, I, p. 393, n. 3 (against Derenbourg, cf. p. 394, n. 6).

The use of Mar ('my Lord') as a title is Babylonian. It is given to the Exilarch (ריש גלותא) "the presidents who are designated to the presidency of the house of David," e.g. Mar Uḳba, though they were not necessarily scholars; it was also borne as a proper name and is sometimes appended to a name (e.g., Huna Mar). His disciples gave it to Mar Samuel, the head of the school at Nehardea.

Abba. In Matt. 23, 9 Jesus forbids his disciples to let themselves be called Rabbi, as the Pharisees want to be saluted (vs. 7); or to call any man "father," i.e., to address any one with the word Abba (Aram. 'my father,' as a title). As a mode of address to scholars Abba is said to be unusal (Strack-Billerbeck, Kommentar zum Neuen Testament aus Talmud und Midrasch, I, 919, 3); but it is regularly prefixed to the personal name of many Tannaim and Amoraim, e.g., Abba Saul ben Baṭnit (before the destruction of Jerusalem, business partner of R. Eleazar ben Zadok), and the better known Tanna, Abba Saul, in the middle of the second century; also Abba Ḥanin, who in Mekilta and Sifrè transmits many traditions of R. Eliezer (ben Hyrcanus).

The title Rabbi is not prefixed to the names which begin with Abba (e.g., not R. Abba Saul, or the like), though the same man is occasionally called in one source Abba, in another Rabbi. In such cases copyists may be responsible for the substitution. On the possible local (Galilean) usage of Abba as a (courtesy) title, and other questions connected with it, see A. Büchler, Die Priester und der Cultus im letzten Jahrzehnt des jerusalemischen Tempels, 1895, pp. 31–35; Der galiläische 'Am-ha 'Areṣ des zweiten Jahrhunderts, 1906, pp. 332 ff.

I. 44 l. 17–21

Here and elsewhere I have emphasized the continuity in the moral and religious teachings of normative Judaism and illustrated it from the extraneous literature including the Synoptic Gospels. This continuity of development is, however, not undisputed; it is maintained that Judaism after the fall of Jerusalem was essentially different from what it had been before. Some believe that the rise of Christianity made the difference; others think that the supremacy which "Pharisaic Judaism" attained after the War, with the resulting unification and, so to speak, standardization of Judaism, made an epoch which sharply divides what came after from what went before.

These opinions are reflected in the selection and evaluation of the sources, and it will make the matter plainer if I summarize and discuss here some recent presentations of these views which may be considered typical, premising that, as I have said in the Preface to this volume (p. vii), an inquiry — even incidental — into the religion in which Jesus and his immediate disciples were brought up, or of the origin of Christianity, lies wholly outside my plan and purpose.

R. H. Charles (The Apocrypha and Pseudepigrapha of the Old Testament, 1913, Vol. II, Introduction, pp. vi–xi) insists on a sharp distinction between "Apocalyptic Judaism" and "legalistic Judaism." He recognizes that "in pre-Christian times they were not fundamentally antagonistic"; both unreservedly acknowledged the primacy of the Law, so that they may be called "apocalyptic and legalistic Pharisaism" respectively. "To all Jewish apocalyptic Law was of eternal validity, but they also clung fast to the validity of the prophetic teaching as a source of new truth and the right of apocalyptic as its successor in this respect." The difference was that legalistic Pharisaism in time "drove out almost wholly the apocalyptic element as an active factor . . . whereas apocalyptic Judaism developed more and more the apocalyptic, i. e., prophetic, element." When the latter "passed over into Christianity, and therein naturally abandoned this view of the Law [*sc.* of its perpetual validity], it [*sc.* Apocalyptic Judaism] became in a measure anti-legalistic." "From this it follows that the Judaism that survived the destruction of the Temple, being almost bereft of the apocalyptic wing which had passed over into Christianity, was not the same as the Judaism of an earlier date. Before A.D. 70 Judaism was a Church with many parties: after A.D. 70 the legalistic party succeeded in suppressing its rivals, and so Judaism became in its essentials a Sect."

The author confuses a literary form or a conventional fiction with a kind of religion, which he calls "prophetico-ethical," in contrast to "legalistic Judaism" and eventually in conscious opposition to it. The characteristic form of revelation in the apocalypse is vision, frequently demanding and receiving a supernatural interpretation; the content may be anything to which the writer chooses to give this form and the authentication which attaches to it. Primarily and most naturally this form is chosen for things which are beyond the scope of sense and intelligence, the heavens and what is in them or goes on in them, or the future beyond human ken or conjecture in the course of universal history and after its end. That there is a sense in which apocalyptic is the successor of prophecy had never been questioned; but that it was the sole, or even the principal, heir of the religious and moral teaching of the great prophets of Israel and as such the opposite of "legalistic Judaism" is far from the truth.

Ezekiel 40–48 is a typical apocalypse which is wholly devoted to the reconstruction of the Temple, and the plan of the city of Jerusalem, and its environs as it is to be in the restoration, and to particulars of the reformed cultus. The Book of Jubilees, which is described by Charles himself as the "most triumphant manifesto of legalism," and "the narrowest book that ever emanated from legalistic Judaism," is in form an apocalypse of Moses. The Testaments of the XII Patriarchs contain incidentally some apocalyptic elements (e. g. Levi 5 and 8), but in the main they are moral precepts and exhortations enforced by examples. The great religious and moral book in what Protestants call the Apocrypha, Ecclesiasticus, has nothing of apocalypse about it; its author was a professional student and teacher of the Law (Scribe). The two great apocalypses after the fall of Jerusalem, 4 Esdras and the Syriac Baruch, were written by men who had the learning of the schools, and of an "antilegalistic" tendency there is in them no trace. Their affinity to the teaching of the Tannaim of the second century, on the contrary, is extensive and obvious. That apocalyptic is "essentially ethical" is as far from the truth as it would be to ignore the large "ethical" element in "legalistic Judaism," as exhibited in the Tannaite Midrash, often side by side with the development of laws of very different character, as, e.g., in Sifra on Lev. 19. The reader will find in this juristic midrash much casuistry, but a casuistry which, unlike that satirized by Pascal in the "Lettres Provinciales," is directed not to minimizing the demands of the law by "probable opinions," but to giving them the widest application and the deepest significance.

In his Religion des Judentums im neutestamentlichen Zeitalter (1903, 2 ed. 1906) Bousset drew his material chiefly from the apocryphal and the pseudepigraphic writings, including the apocalypses (4 Esdras, Syriac Baruch) from the end of the first century of the Christian era, with only incidental — it would not be unfair to say accidental — reference, through translations, to the rabbinical sources. He recognizes in the latter "eine unerschöpfliche Fundgrube älteren Materials, das leider noch nicht systematisch bearbeitet ist, wohl auch in absehbarer Zeit nicht bearbeitet werden wird" (2 ed. p. 45). "Eine systematische Behandlung dieser späteren Literatur würde ungemein viel wertvolles Material auch für die Erkenntnis des früheren Judentums zu Tage fördern" (2 ed. p. 48).

Hugo Gressmann, who edited the third edition (1926) under the new title, Die Religion des Judentums im späthellenistischen Zeitalter," without change in the scope and plan of the book, justifies the exclusion of the rabbinical sources on the ground that the political collapse of the Jewish state (about the year 100 A.D.) and the separation from Christianity made a fundamental change in the Jewish religion — at least, in view of the extraordinary mutability of the Israelitish-Jewish religion, this must be assumed until the contrary is proved (3 ed. pp. 40 f.)

What Gressmann had in mind (ed. 3, p. 41) I surmise to be similar to what Bousset had said about the consequences of this catastrophe: "Wenn es vorher oft den Anschein hatte, als könnte das Judentum sich zu einer völkerumspannenden Universalreligion entwickeln, zieht es sich nun ganz auf sich selbst zurück und erstarrt völlig in seiner Eigenart, während das junge Christentum sein Erbe in der Welt antritt" (cf. ed. 3, pp. 2 ff.). That is, as I understand it, after the destruction of Jerusalem in 70 A.D. and the cessation (in Jewish apprehension at the time, suspension) of the national worship in the Temple, and after the disastrous outcome of the rising of the Jews in the Mediterranean region and Mesopotamia under Trajan and of the rebellion in Palestine under Hadrian, the national (racial) exclusiveness of Judaism gained the complete supremacy; it lost faith in its destiny, as the one true religion, to become the universal religion, and in the mission of Israel to promulgate it and win the world over to it, in both which tasks Christianity succeeded it.

That the expansion of Judaism in the Diaspora, by conversion suffered a severe check, not solely by edicts like Hadrian's, but through the dislike of the Jews, who were regarded by the Gentile population as the aggressors in all these disturbances, is only what would be expected (see Vol. I, p. 108), but whether this had on Judaism itself the effect which is attributed to it, may, I think, reasonably be doubted in the light of later evidence, both Jewish and Christian (see Vol. II, pp. 346 ff.)

An opinion which might be described as the antipodes of that of Charles and of Gressmann is expressed by Burkitt (The Gospel History and its Transmission, pp. 169–174). Raising the pertinent question, "how far the Rabbinical religion is the immediate descendant of the main current of the Judaism of the first century A.D.," he argues that the catastrophe of Jewish nationalism in the wars of 66–72 and of 132–135 taught the Remnant of the Jews "that the Kingdom of God was not of this world; there was now no inducement to serve the God of Israel left for those who did not still love Him and trust His promises. Can we wonder that Judaism tended to become a more spiritual religion, narrow indeed in its outward aspect, but animated within by humility and grace, even by mysticism? But in so far as the Rabbinical religion is all this, it has been metamorphosed from the prevailing Judaism of the 1st century. I do not think we need deny the real spirituality of the Rabbinical religion because we believe what the Gospels say about the Scribes, or that we need disbelieve what the Gospels say about the Scribes in the 1st century because we recognize the real spirituality of the Rabbinical religion. We have a right to believe that the spiritual descendants of the Scribes whom Jesus denounced perished in the two Revolts during the century after the Crucifixion, while the spiritual ancestor both of the Jews who became Christians and the Jews who developed and maintained the Rabbinical religion is represented by the Scribe who was 'not far from the Kingdom of God.'" (pp. 171–173). — See Montefiore, The Synoptic Gospels (2 ed., 1927), I., pp. 197–200 (cf. I., pp. 147–152, and II, pp. 224–227); Strack-Billerbeck, I, pp. 711 ff. (on the Corban).

It is hardly worth while to revert to a notion of Franz Delitzsch which G. Kittel has exhumed, nor to stretch it beyond the author's intention. The resemblance of the story about the birth of the Messiah in Bethlehem on the night in which the Temple was destroyed in Jer. Berakot f. 5a and parallels (Vol. II, 348 n.) to the Gospels led Delitzsch to ask how such features in the Haggadah can be accounted for. He dwells upon the large numbers of Nazarenes (Jewish believers in Jesus), and continues: Als diese grosse judenchristliche Partei, welche der Kirche nicht minder als der Synagoge häretisch erscheinen musste, dem im Hebräerbriefe gedrohten Gottesgerichte verfiel und sich in die christusfeindliche Synagoge zurückverlor, da wurde die synagogale Haggada mit mancherlei Bestandteilen versetzt, welche, wie die obige Erzählung, immer noch das evangelische Urbild verraten, dessen Verzerrungen sie sind. Die Talmude und Midraschim enthalten in vielen unverkennbaren Resten den letzten Niederschlag der untergegangenen judenchristlichen Evangelien. — That this "Niederschlag" included reports of the religious and moral teaching of Jesus as well as stories like the one he quotes, Delitzsch does not say, and it should not be inferred.

The war of 66–72, as Josephus describes it, eliminated classes or parties among the Jews which had previously been important factors. The sacerdotal and lay aristocracy, and the rich, to which classes the Sadducees chiefly belonged, had been the especial object of the fury of the Zealots and their allies. Many of them perished during the siege of Jerusalem; their political power was completely broken, and with it their resistance to the Unwritten Law. The Zealots — fanatical nationalists — had destroyed one another, and the remnants had been exterminated by the Romans. Individual Essenes appear here and there in the pages of Josephus as combatants, prophets, or martyrs, but of the Essene Order, from that time on, nothing is heard. The recovery of Judaism from the catastrophe of the Jews was the work of men whom we are accustomed to call Pharisees — whether they commonly called themselves so or not — with whom were associated many priests as well as biblical scholars and men learned in tradition. Judaism, which had previously been diversified, and on important points contentious, attained in the following generation or two a homogeneity and an authoritativeness which have been its character to modern times.

It was natural that one consequence of the wars with Rome should have been wide-spread demoralization among the people, showing itself in negligent observance of the distinctive institutions of Judaism or even in gross infractions of its moral obligations; and the first task of the religious leaders was to bring the people back to an orderly way of life in conformity with the law of God as contained in the Scriptures and in the ordinances and restrictions of the Unwritten Law. That they found it necessary in many cases to define the rules more precisely and in some particulars more strictly and that there was a great development of the Halakah in the schools of the second century is plain. But there is, I think, no indication that the development was on new lines or on different principles from that which preceded it.

Nor is there any evidence that in the fundamentals of religion or of morals there was any corresponding development after the fall of Jerusalem. On the contrary, these principles and doctrines were long established; they lay on the surface of the Scriptures, and no new promulgations were needed to define them. Men might ignore them; it might be necessary to emphasize them in the demoralization of the times, and press them home on the conscience, but they did not have to be discovered.

As to the facts, in the foot notes to the two volumes of "Judaism," I have given many references to places in the extra-canonical Jewish literature which anticipate in time the teaching of the Tannaim and of the homilists of the third and fourth centuries of our era, and to the passages in the Scriptures from which both are drawn, thus illustrating at once the continuity and the progress.

I. 45 n. 3

See Notes on Vol. I, p. 85 (below, p. 32 f.) and on pp. 255, 260 f. (below, pp. 75, 80.)

I. 45 n. 4.

See S. Krauss, Griechische und Lateinische Lehnwörter, s.vv. אסכולי (σχολή) and אשכולות, II, 87, 135. — Soṭaḥ 47 b, bottom: מאי אשכולות . . . איש שהכל בו (popular etymology, in the name of Mar Samuel); cf. Jer. Soṭaḥ 24a: No אשכול — no such universally learned man — arose before R. ʻAkiba, וכל הזוגות לא היו אשכולות. See the sequel.

I. 46 l. 5f. and n. 3

Shabbat 14b, also (verbatim) 15a. In 15a another date is given for a decree (גזרה) that foreign lands are unclean, viz. eighty years before the destruction of the temple. Repetition of such a decree on more than one occasion is not improbable; Zeitlin, Jewish Quarterly Review, N. S. XVI (1926), 386 f.

I. 48 l. 4f.

The battle at Panion (the modern Banias) is commonly dated in 198; but see Note on Vol. I, p. 35 ff. (above, p. 13 f.), for a different construction (Ed. Meyer).

I. 49 l. 19–21

In 1 Macc. 1, 11 most manuscripts and versions (Latin, Syriac) have the plural, ἐξῆλθον ἐξ Ἰσραὴλ υἱοὶ παράνομοι,, but Cod. Alex. and a Venetian manuscript collated for Swete (V = 23 of Holmes and Parsons) have ἐξῆλθεν . . . υἱὸς παράνομος, presumably having in mind Jason (whom 1 Macc. does not name). So E. Meyer, Ursprung und Anfänge des Christentums, II, 144. — The following verbs, however, in the same codices are plural (καὶ ἀνέπεισαν πολλοὺς λέγοντες . . .), and a different explanation is possible.

I. 50 n. 3

The variation (or confusion) of Benjamin and Minyamin (as personal names) occurs in rabbinical texts; thus in Tos. Ḳiddushin 5, 4 (ed. Zuckermandel, p. 342, lines 6 and 9) the Vienna codex, like the current printed editions has בנימין, while the Erfurt codex and the parallel in Yebamot 78a have מנימין [L. G.]. Eleazar ben Zadok, who according to some modern scholars was a priest, describes himself as מבני סנאב בן בנימין (ʻErubin 41a, cf. Tosafot in loc.; cf. Taʻanit 12a).

In M. Ta'anit 4, 5 the בני סנאה בן בנימין bring their wood offering to the Temple on the tenth of the month Ab. R. Eleazar ben Zadok relates what they did on one occasion when the 9th of Ab happened to fall on a Sabbath. The priests and levites bring their wood offering with a Judaean clan on the 15th of Ab (ibid.).

I. 51 l. 13f.

In 143 Seleucid = 170/169 B.C.; The campaign fell in the summer of 169 B.C. (E. Meyer, op. cit. II. 151 n.).

I. 51 l. 25–27.

Polybius xxix. 27; Diodorus Siculus xxxi. 2; Appian, Syriaca, 66; Livy xlv. 11 f. The ultimatum rudely delivered by Popilius Laenas is a familiar story (*ἐνταῦθα βουλεύου*, Appian).

I. 52 n. 3

A contrary inference is drawn by E. Meyer (Ursprung und Anfänge des Christentums, II, 163, top) from Diodorus xxxiv. 1 (Poseidonios), where the measures taken against the Jews by Antiochus Epiphanes are recounted to Antiochus Sidetes as an example: *τῶν τε κρεῶν* (swine's flesh) *ἀναγκάσαι προσενέγκασθαι τὸν ἀρχιερέα καὶ τοὺς ἄλλους Ἰουδαίους.*

I. 53 n. 1

This reconsecration is commemorated by the festival called Ḥanukkah (Vol. II, p. 49 f.). The date of the desecration is put on the same day and month, just three years earlier, though 1 Macc. 1, 54, at variance with 4, 52–54, names the *fifteenth* of Kisleu. Daniel's scheme calls for three and a half years or more (1290 days) between the cessation of the daily burnt offering and its restoration.

I. 55 l. 14f.

Καὶ ἤρξατο ὁ λαὸς Ἰσραὴλ γράφειν ἐν ταῖς συγγραφαῖς καὶ συναλλάγμασιν Ἔτους πρώτου ἐπὶ Σίμωνος ἀρχιερέως μεγάλου καὶ στρατηγοῦ καὶ ἡγουμένου Ἰουδαίων. — For some outside judgments on Jews especially in this period (Tacitus, Strabo) the ultimate source of which is probably Poseidonios, see E. Meyer, Ursprung und Anfänge des Christentums, II, 277 f.

I, 57 ff.

The literature on the Pharisees and Sadducees is enormous; I shall content myself here with giving the titles of some of the more recent contributions to its swelling volume, beginning with J. T. Lauterbach, "The Sadducees and Pharisees. A Study of their Respective Attitudes towards the Law," in Studies in Jewish Literature in Honor of Professor Kaufmann Kohler (1913), pp. 176–198; Eerdmans, "Farizeen en Sadduceen," Theologisch Tijdschrift, XLVIII (1914), pp. 1–26; I. Elbogen, "Einige neuere Theorien über den Ursprung der Pharisäer und Sadduzäer," in Jewish Studies in Memory of Israel Abrahams (1927), pp. 135–148 [E. Meyer, Herford, 1924, Simon Dubnow]; Leo Baeck, "Die Pharisäer," in Jahresbericht der Hochschule, Berlin 1927; Strack-Billerbeck, "Die Pharisäer u. Sadduzäer in der altjüdischen Literatur" (Excursus 14, Kommentar zum Neuen Testament aus Talmud und Midrasch, IV (1928), 334–352 (the differences and controversies enumerated, p. 344 ff.); L. Finkelstein, "The Pharisees: Their Origin and their Philosophy," Harvard Theological Review, XXII (1929), 185–261. See also V. Aptowitzer, Parteipolitik der Hasmonäerzeit, 1927.

I. 60 l. 7 ff. and n. 3

This interpretation would correspond to the account of the observance of the first Passover after the rebuilding of the temple: ויאכלו בני ישראל השבים מהגולה וכל הנבדל מטמאת גויי הארץ אלהם לדרש ליהוה אלהי ישראל (Ezra 6, 21).

The name "Pharisees" has often been connected with these *nibdalim*, who "separated themselves from the uncleanness of the peoples of the land to seek the Lord, the God of Israel." In Ezra 9, 1 f.; 10, 11; Neh. 10, 29 ff., however, where the same verb is used, the separation is expressly from intermarriage with "the peoples of the land," or with "foreign women" (Ezra 10,11). Cf. particularly Ezra 6, 21 with 10, 11.

I. 60, l. 25f. and n. 7 (2d impression)

On פרש in the Targums see Buxtorf, Lexicon Chaldaicum Talmudicum et Rabbinicum, 1639, cols. 1846–1851 (for Hebr. הבדיל, נבדל, and other verbs meaning 'separate, be separated,' etc.). — Buxtorf assumes the priority of the Targums to the Talmudic literature. — The name is common in Josephus (and his sources, including Nicolaus of Damascus, in the time of Herod) and in the Gospels, Acts 5, 34; 15, 5; 23, 6–9; 26, 5; Phil. 3, 6, frequently in contrast with the Sadducees. Similarly in M. Yadaim 4, 6 f., in an interchange of carping between Sadducees and Pharisees, beginning with a Sadducean jibe at the absurdity of the Pharisaean rule that sacred books make the hands unclean while the books of המירם (Homer, example of profane literature — so commonly; Bertinoro takes it as ספרי המינים, with an etymological explanation) do not. Reply on this point is there made by Johanan ben Zakkai.

The פרושים who multiplied after the destruction of the Temple (Tos. Soṭah 15, 11), not eating flesh or drinking wine, and are reproved by R. Joshua (ben Hananiah; see Vol. II, p. 262) are probably not the sect or party so named, but individuals — perhaps particularly priests — who in this respect separated themselves from the commonalty (Büchler, Priester und Cultus, p. 22 n.). See also M. Ḥagigah 2, 7.

When Jews scrupulously observant are contrasted with the ignorant and negligent *vulgus* (עמי הארץ), the former are generally designated by the name חברים, "associates" (Vol. II, p. 159 f.); the same scrupulous observance and avoidance is naturally expected of scholars (תלמידי חכמים), and in the second century sources these names are usual. Cf., however, M. Ḥagigah 2, 7: בגדי עם הארץ מדרס לפרושים, i.e., is a primary cause of contagious uncleanness in the highest degree. In the sequel there is perhaps a lacuna in the text: but the conjunction of *'am ha-'areṣ* and *perushhi* is the point with which we are here concerned (cf. Niddah 33b), whether the *perushim* are what we should call Pharisees or not. The common outright identification of the Pharisees with the "associates" is without warrant in our sources. See A. Büchler, Der galiläische 'Am-ha'Areṣ des zweiten Jahrhunderts (1906); Israel Abrahams, "'Am ha-'Areç," Excursus in Montefiore, The Synoptic Gospels, 2 ed. II, 647–669 (especially p. 665 ff.).

That the name פרושים continued in use among the people for such as seemed to them extravagantly pious is shown by the survival of the nicknames for the varieties of extravagance preserved in both Talmuds (see Vol. II, p. 193 f.).

I. 61–62 l. 1–2 and n. 1

For another surmise about the origin of the name, viz. that it was used in a derogatory sense of the lay teachers (חכמי ישראל, in contrast to the חכמי כהנים) who drew apart and were not loyal supporters of John Hyrcanus, or who were put out of the Sanhedrin by him (Ḳiddushin 66a), see Lauterbach, "Sadducees and Pharisees," in Studies . . . in honor of K. Kohler, pp. 195 f., note.

I. 62 l. 3–12 and n. 3

This explanation of the name suggested itself to the author of the (mediaeval) Josippon ("Joseph ben Gorion"), who, upon his first mention of the Pharisees (under John Hyrcanus), writes: חכמי ישראל והמה הפרושים המפרשים את התורה (Bk. iv, § 29, ed. Venet. 1544. f. 48a; cf. f. 48b; ed. Breithaupt, p. 272, cf. 274). This explanation may have been suggested to the author by places in Josephus (e.g. Bell. Jud. i. 5, 23) where the Pharisees are said to interpret the laws more precisely than others.

I. 64 l. 18

Queen Alexandra, wife of King Aristobulus and after his death (104 B.C.) of Alexander Jannaeus. Her Jewish name was Σαλώμη (Josephus, Antt. xiii. 12, 1 § 320 — Niese, Σαλίνα). Salome is itself probably an abridgment of the name borne by one of Herod's daughters, Σαλαμψιώ (Josephus, Antt. xviii. 5, 4 § 130), שלמציון. (See Schürer, Geschichte des jüdischen Volkes, u. s. w., I, 407).— In Lev. R. 35, 8 the name of this queen is written שלמצה, perhaps a caritative form.

I. 67 n. 3

From the Megillat Ta'anit it is commonly gathered that the Sadducees had a written criminal code. The text notes: "On the fourteenth of Tammuz passed away the book of decrees (עדא ספר גזירתא); mourning prohibited." The Hebrew glossator explains that the Sadducees had a law-book in which were prescribed the specific penalties of various crimes — stoning, burning, decapitation, strangulation. The Boethusians applied the law of talio literally, "an eye for an eye, a tooth for a tooth," etc. The subject is one on which the conflicting principles of the Sadducees and the Pharisees are well attested; but it is intrinsically more probable that the decrees are those of some foreign government, and the glossator has a penchant for commemorating successes of the Pharisees over their rivals. Zeitlin, Megillat Ta'anit, p. 83, following Cassel, thinks of the annulment of the decrees of the Greeks by Alexander Balas and Demetrius (1 Macc. 10); but this is only one possibility. And, after all, is it likely that the edicts of the Seleucid Kings aimed at the religion of the Jews would be called ספר גזירתא?

I. 68 l. 23–25

That there were "bad" Jews (פושעי ישראל) who denied that the Prophets and the Ketubim are "Torah," see Tanḥuma, ed. Buber, Re'eh § 1 (f. 10a; quoted below on Vol. I, p. 263, N. 28).

I. 68 l. 27f.

These words should not be understood as implying that the Pharisees admitted legal deductions from these books, independently of the Pentateuch. — On this point one may compare the arguments of Rabina and R. Ashi about an inference from Ezekiel, Ta'anit 17b.

I. 69 l. 23 ff.

On the origin of these sects there is a dissertation by E. Baneth, Ursprung der Saddokäer und Boethusäer, 1882, which contributes nothing substantial to the solution of the problem. The story in Abot de R. Nathan is the only one we have; the author seems to think that it must for that reason be taken as having at least an historical kernel. See also Jewish Encyclopedia s.v. Boethusians (III, 284 f.), and the literature on the Sadducees. The passage in Abot de-R. Nathan is found in both recensions (ed. Schechter, f. 13b), with differences and variants in the manuscripts of both, and other sources recorded and discussed by Schechter in his notes. The heresy is apparently not ascribed to Zadok and Boethos themselves; it arose among their disciples in a succeeding generation. They are said to have drawn the consequences for this life also: "They used vessels of silver and gold every day, *not* [the negative lacking in some copies] from pride; but the Sadducees said, The Pharisees have a tradition that they make themselves miserable in this world (in anticipation of a reward hereafter), and in the world to come they get nothing at all." We should perhaps read with this the words appended in some manuscripts and editions of the Abot de-R. Nathan to the saying of Antigonos in Abot ("Be like slaves who serve their master without expectation of a gratuity; and let the fear of Heaven be upon you"), "that your reward (שכרכם) may be double in the future" (לעתיד לבא).

I. 71 n. 4

The refinements of the so-called "dietary laws" belong to a later stage in the development of the Halakah, but it is not improbable that the obvious difference between such natural products and the concoctions of culinary art in the royal kitchens was early observed. — Cf. Josephus, Vita c. 3 § 14. The priests in whose behalf he went to Rome, although in evil plight, were not forgetful of their religion, but lived on figs and nuts.

I. 71 n. 5

The belief that the unburied dead suffer from the lack of burial is widespread; it is sufficient to recall the appeal of Palinurus to Aeneas

(Virgil, vi. 337 ff.) or the motive of the Antigone of Sophocles (especially Antigone's defence, verses 450 ff.). — On the scrupulousness of the Jews in this matter see Josephus, Bell. Jud. iv. 5, 2 § 317. In his account of the siege of Jerusalem Josephus repeatedly notes as a peculiar atrocity the refusal of burial to those who were murdered by the factions in the city or the failure of kinsmen to bury their murdered relatives through fear of the Zealots and their allies, though a few handfuls of dust surreptitiously thrown on the body sufficed as a (symbolical) interment. Cf., beside the passage cited above, Bell. Jud. iv. 5, 3 § 326 ff.; iv. 6, 3 § 380 ff.

I, 71 n. 6

Priests, Sifra Emor, at the beginning (on Lev. 21, 1, ed. Weiss, f. 93c); nazirites, Sifrè Num. § 26; high priest, nazirite, M. Nazir 7, 1 (Nazir 48a; Jer. Nazir 55d). — Josephus, c. Apion. ii. 29 § 211, recites among the good deeds which the law enjoins Israelites to do to aliens in need of them, ἄταφον μὴ περιορᾶν.

I. 73 l. 1–3

The illegitimacy of a dynasty of other than Davidic lineage is expressly affirmed in the Psalms of Solomon (17, 5 ff.; Vol. II, p. 328). See also L. Ginzberg, Unbekannte jüdische Sekte, p. 355–357; cf. Jer. Horaiyot 47c below, אין מושחין מלכים כהנים (with the sequel). [L. G.] See also Aptowitzer, Parteipolitik, pp. 49 ff.

I. 75 n. 4

There was a Babylon in Egypt near Memphis (Old Cairo), Strabo xvii. 30, p. 807; cf. c. 40, p. 812). According to Diodorus Siculus i. 56 (cf. Strabo, p. 807) it got its name from some Babylonians, prisoners of war in Egypt in remote antiquity whom the king Σεσωσις, after the suppression of a revolt, allowed to occupy the place. According to Josephus (Antt. ii. 15, 1 § 315) it was founded by Cambyses, which has a less mythical sound. It has been guessed that the "Babylonians" (בבליים, according to R. Judah ben Ila'i they were really "Alexandrians") who plucked out the hair of the scapegoat (M. Yoma 6, 4, with Yoma 66b) were Jews from this Egyptian Babylon.

I. 77 n. 3

On Hillel's studies in his native country and his brother Shebna who was engaged in gainful pursuits, and on the mysterious voice (*bat ḳol*) which quoted Cant. 8, 7b, see Soṭah 21a. [L. G.]

I, 78 n. 2

The note refers solely to the conventional transliteration of בתירא, "Bathyra," which comes eventually from the Latin version of Josephus, xvii. 2, 2 § 26. Herod's military colony in Batanaea is, of course, later than the meeting of Hillel with the Bene Bathyra, and an historical connection is not assumed. The spelling of the name is not constant either in Hebrew or in the manuscripts of Josephus. (On the former see Krauss in Jewish Encyclopedia, II, 599).

I, 79 n. 2

Mention should perhaps be made here of the statement of Isaac Halévy (Dorot ha-Rishonim, II, 95b) that after the death of Shemaiah and Abṭalion, under the rule of Hyrcanus (II) and Antipater the father of Herod, when Gabinius dissolved the general Sanhedrin [57 B.C.], the people of Jerusalem had such confidence in this family that they entrusted the leadership for the time being to the Elders of the Benè Bathyra. As soon as Hillel came up from Babylon and they recognized his greatness, these Elders of their own accord made over to him the presidency. They were thus chiefly instrumental in establishing Hillel and his descendants in that office, and from that time on loyally adhered to the presidents and were their right-hand men. — For this ingenious combination no testimony is adduced; apparently there is none.

The Benè Bathyra turn up again in the time of Johanan ben Zakkai, and are treated by him as high authorities in the law (Rosh ha-Shanah 29b, below). Several rabbis bear the patronymic "ben Bathyra," the best known being Judah ben Bathyra (two of the name, see Vol. I, p. 105 f.); others are Joshua ben Bathyra and Simeon ben Bathyra. R. Judah Bathyra (without *ben*) in the Jerusalem Talmud (Frankel, Darkè ha-Mishnah, 2 ed. p. 99) seems to be an abridgement.

I. 80 l. 8

On the Prosbul see Note **25** on Vol. I, p. 260 f. (below, p. 80).

I. 80 l. 24 ff.

Of differences between the two masters Hillel and Shammai but few are recorded as such; M. 'Eduyot 1, 1 and Shabbat 15a report three (in none of which, it should be observed, did the ultimate decision of the doctors (חכמים) agree with either of them); Jer. Ḥagigah 77d counts four, including the old controversy of the Pairs about the

סמיכה. The differences between the Bet Shammai and Bet Hillel amount, according to Weiss' enumeration (Dor, I, 168 f.), to 316, classified as follows: Halakot 221; Midrash 29; Seyagim 66. Discrepancies between Hillel and his school, and between Shammai and his school, are also reported (Dor, I, 185). The causes and consequences of this multiplication of differences are set forth in Jer. Ḥagigah 77d (see Vol. I, p. 46); the same statement, less fully, in Sanhedrin 88b and elsewhere. It is commonly thought that some of the differences attributed to the schools originated with Hillel and Shammai themselves and were perpetuated in the school tradition.

Other scholars are of the opinion that Shammai and Hillel, far from being the founders of the rival schools that bear their names, were really the last representatives of two tendencies, respectively rigorist and liberal, or, as we might say, conservative and progressive, which had existed in Pharisaism from the beginning. (See L. Ginzberg, in Hebrew Union College Annual, 1924, pp. 307 ff.) — The two tendencies are no doubt older than these two great teachers; and they were certainly not the last representatives of them, as the controversies between R. Eliezer ben Hyrcanus and other disciples of Johanan ben Zakkai prove.

I. 82 l. 1 ff., n. 4.

See Juster, Les juifs dans l'empire Romain, I, 400 f. On the composition of the Sanhedrin, and the presidency in it, see Note on Vol. I, p. 85 (below, pp. 32ff).

I. 82 l. 14f.

See Note on Vol. II, p. 115 n. 4 (below, p. 182).

I. 83 ff.

At Lydda R. Eliezer ben Hyrcanus, regularly named first among the disciples of R. Johanan ben Zakkai, lived; R. Tarfon, who was of priestly lineage and had boyhood memories of the service in the Temple, taught there. R. Ishmael (ben Elisha) had his home at Kefar 'Aziz on the Idumaean border. After the war under Hadrian and the removal of Rabban Simeon ben Gamaliel II and his Bet Din to Usha in Galilee, the schools of the South (Darom) continued to be held in high esteem, though sometimes a feeling of rivalry may be discerned.

Büchler (Priester und Cultus, pp. 23 ff.) endeavors to show that the traditions about the temple and the priesthood in Jerusalem come ultimately from the schools at Lydda, where priests who had served in the Temple before its destruction settled, while Johanan ben

Zakkai was little interested in matters which to scrupulous priests seemed of the greatest concern, so that on these points there was a different attitude, if not a fundamental discord, between the two schools. His argument does not admit of condensation, and the reader must be referred to the volume cited. What is certain is that Lydda and the region about it had its part, besides Jamnia, in the preservation and perpetuation of tradition. — Lydda is on the way from Jerusalem to Joppa (distant about a dozen miles) and about a dozen miles by road northeast of Jabneh.

I. 85 l. 5 ff.

On the composition and organization of the Great Sanhedrin before the destruction of Jerusalem and especially on the presidency of that body, there is an extensive literature for which the reader may be referred to Schürer, Geschichte des Volkes Israel, u.s.w., II, 188–214 (bibliography 188 f.), to be supplemented by Kuenen, Over de samenstelling van het Sanhedrin (1866); in Budde's translation, Ueber die Zusammensetzung des Sanhedrin, pp. 49–81 (see above, p. 11). The latest monograph which I have seen is entitled הנשיא בסנהדרין הגדולה, by Ṣebi (Hirsch) Taubes, Vienna, 1925 (Bettelheim Memorial Foundation). The author gives a summary and criticism of his predecessors, Jelski (and incidentally D. Hoffmann), Büchler, Chwolson, and others, discusses at length the rabbinical sources for different periods, and develops an opinion of his own.

The problem lies in the sources. From the New Testament and from Josephus we should gather that in the first century of our era the Great Sanhedrin in Jerusalem was a senate and at the same time a supreme court, constituted of the chief priests, elders, and scholars (scribes), and presided over by the high priest, as I have described it in the text. In the rabbinical sources, on the other hand, which purport to give us an insight into the matter beginning a century or two further back, it appears as a body of men learned in the law, at the head of which were the Nasi (which, to avoid discussion, I have rendered "President"), and the Ab Bet Din (commonly understood as Vice-President, see Vol. I, p. 45, n.). In these sources the membership of this body in the later years of John Hyrcanus and under Alexander Jannaeus is represented as prevailingly Sadducean; in the reign of Queen Alexandra it became chiefly, if not exclusively, Pharisaean.

Especial attention should be called to Adolf Büchler, Das Synedrion in Jerusalem und das grosse Beth-Din in der Quaderkammer des jerusalemischen Tempels, 1902. Büchler, as the title indicates, would distinguish in the rabbinical sources themselves two bodies, one of which was made up chiefly of the members of the great priestly families, presided over by the high priest, while the other, called from its place of meeting the Bet Din which sat in the Marble Hall (לשכת הגזית), was composed of experts in the law (*jurisperiti*), and as such, mainly Pharisees, with a president and vice-president of its own. The article "Sanhedrin" in the Jewish Encyclopedia, by Lauterbach, substantially represents Büchler's theory, distinguishing the "Political" from the "Religious" Sanhedrin. The latter has therefore frequently been thought of as the continuation or successor of the Great Synagogue. The president of the religious Sanhedrin, or Bet Din, was always a great authority in the Law, from the days of Jose ben Joezer (M. Ḥagigah 2, 2) down to Hillel and his descendants in hereditary succession: "Hillel and Simeon, Gamaliel and Simeon, filled the presidency for a century while the Temple was standing" (Shabbat 15a). After the destruction of Jerusalem came successively Gamaliel (of Jabneh), Simeon ben Gamaliel, and his son Judah the Patriarch (ha-Nasi).

Others have supposed that the Nasi of the rabbinical sources, for instance Gamaliel I or Simeon ben Gamaliel, was the chairman of what we might call a judicial committee or commission of the Sanhedrin to which questions of law may have been referred. D. Chwolson, Das letzte Passamahl Christi, u. s. w. (1892), p. 30; see also Joseph Klausner, היסטוריה ישראלית, Part 3 (1925), p. 104, of Hillel.

Ordinances of Hillel and his successors (e.g. M. 'Arakin 9, 4; M. Giṭṭin 4, 2–3; M. Keritot 1, 7) indicate that "long before the establishment of the Academy at Jabneh, the Pharisees must have stood at the head of some authoritative body which had the power to regulate civil and domestic laws. The rabbinic tradition about the old Sanhedrin seems to contain a good historical kernel. . . . The matter is not as simple as Kuenen and Wellhausen thought it." [L. G.]

The matter is certainly not simple; but the passages cited from the Mishnah are deliverances of Hillel, Gamaliel the elder, and Simeon ben Gamaliel, which do not purport to be decisions of an organized body (Sanhedrin) having authority to lay down the law.

On the whole subject see the article "Sanhedrin" (by Bacher) in Hasting's Dictionary of the Bible, IV (1902), 397–402 (literature p. 402).

For the subject and period of these volumes, the question is of minor importance.

The word 'Sanhedrin' is found, of course, in later sources, but not in reference to a contemporary institution. For example in Sifrè Deut. § 41, ed. Friedmann, f. 79b, l. 20 ff. (= Midrash Tannaim, p. 34): "If a man hears a word from the mouth of a little one (קטן) in Israel he should be in his eyes as if he heard if from the mouth of a great one, . . . and not only so, but as if he heard it from the mouth of a learned man (חכם, Eccles. 12, 11), . . . and not only so, but as if he heard it from the mouth of a sanhedrin (deduced from Eccles. l. c. בעלי אסופות, taken with Num. 11, 16, אספה לי שבעים איש מזקני ישראל), . . . and not only so, but as if he heard it from the mouth of Moses (ibid., the shepherd), . . . and not only so, but as if he heard it from the mouth of the Holy One, blessed is He, as it is said (Eccles, ibid), מרועה אחד (אחד, One, v. Eccles. R., *in loc.*) When in Seder 'Olam Zuṭa (ed. Neubauer, Mediaeval Jewish Chronicles, II (1895), 76 below; cf. Yuḥasin, ed. Filipowski, p. 93) Mar Zuṭra is called ראש לסנהדרין the term seems to be purely antiquarian (cf. shortly before לריש פירקין — i.e., probably, *ἀχριφερεκίτης*, on which Juster I, 399 and ibid. n. 7. — Mar Zuṭra (bar Mar Zuṭra) was of the family of the exilarchs in Babylonia, and would have succeeded to that dignity. After the execution of his father, he migrated to Palestine, and was apparently raised to the highest position which the Palestinian Jews had to bestow after the extinction of the hereditary Patriarchate of the house of Hillel.

I. 86 l. 10 f.
See Note on Vol. II, p. 388 (below, p. 206).

I. 86 l. 25 ff.
See Note on Vol. I, p. 242 f. (below, p. 65f.).

I. 86 (last line), 87, top.
See G. F. Moore, "The Definition of the Jewish Canon and the Repudiation of Christian Scriptures," in Essays in Modern Theology and Related Subjects, a Testimonial to Charles Augustus Briggs, New York, 1911, pp. 99–125.

For a learned and searching criticism of this contribution see Louis Ginzberg, "Some Observations on the Attitude of the Synagogue towards the Apocalyptic-Eschatological Writings," Journal of Biblical Literature, XLI (1922), pp. 115–136 (Presidential Address at the meeting of the Society of Biblical Literature and Exegesis). See also below, Note on Vol. I, p. 243.

Various points in my contribution to the Briggs volume I should no longer maintain, especially the adventures in the critical emendation and interpretation of Jer. Sanhedrin 28a, and the identification of ספרים החיצונים (Extraneous Books) with heretical books (ספרי המינים), though the Babylonian academies so understood the phrase (Ginzberg, l.c., p. 129). For the present purpose it is unnecessary to make these retractations more specific.

I. 87 l. 4
See also Vol. I, p. 243 f.

I. 93 l. 10–12.
According to tradition the offence of R. Akiba was gathering a congregation and teaching the law publicly, despite the edict of the government (Berakot 61b). Similarly, in almost the same words, R. Ḥanina ben Teradion ('Abodah Zarah 18a). "It is very unlikely that private study was forbidden" [L. G.]. For the statement in the text that the possession of a copy of the Law was made a capital crime, there seems to be no evidence; it was probably an erroneous reminiscence of 1 Macc. 1, 57 (see Vol. I, p. 53).

I. 94 l. 6–9.
'Ulla quotes an utterance of R. Johanan ben Zakkai, provoked by the neglect of the Galileans to profit by his presence and teaching in 'Arab: "O Galilee, Galilee, thou hatest the Law; thine end will be to have to deal with robbers" (Jer. Shabbat 15d, end). See, however, Büchler, Der galiläische 'Am ha-'Areṣ, p. 274 ff. and elsewhere, who maintains that there were flourishing schools in Galilee before 136 C. E., and many rabbis of Galilean extraction and education.

I. 95 n. 4
Legend (Giṭṭin 56a), which tells of the conversion of Nero to Judaism, makes R. Meir a descendant of his. As has been observed, the association is probably by way of popular etymology which saw in Nero's name the Hebrew *ner*, 'lamp.' — The significance of the name Meir ("Illuminator") has given rise to the question what his real name was. On Nehorai (Aramaic equivalent in meaning 'Erubin 13b), see Bacher, Tannaiten, II, 6; the better attested reading there is מיישא or מיאשא. The name Μηϊρός occurs in Josephus, Bell. Jud. vi 5, 1 § 280 (son of Belga, who, with another distinguished man, plunged to his death into the fire of the burning Temple). It has been noted

that, unlike the other great disciples of Akiba, Meir's father's name is nowhere mentioned.

I. 97 f.

A collection of the opinions of mediaeval Jewish authors on this question (texts and translations), and of modern scholars down to Graetz, will be found in A. Sammter's edition of Baba Meṣi'a (1876), pp. 121–124. Other literature, including the more recent, is cited in Strack, Einleitung in Talmud and Midrasch, § 2, "Verbot des Schreibens" (pp. 9 ff.).

I. 98 l. 7f.

For some of Rashi's exegetical grounds see L. Löw, Graphische Requisiten bei den Juden, II (1871), 113, with n. 524.

I. 98 n. 2

See Goldziher, Muhammedanische Studien, II, 194 ff. (Die schriftliche Aufzeichnung des Hadit; see also Zahiriten p. 95). It appears that the antipathy to committing the traditions to writing increased in later generations, and was perpetuated into a period when large and critical collections of tradition were in circulation. The enemies of writing fortified themselves by a fictitious utterance of the Prophet: "Do not write down anything as from me except the Koran, and if anyone has written down anything, let him obliterate it." (See Goldziher, *op. cit.* II, 398 ff.

I. 101 l. 10f.

To secure uniformity of pronunciation, and thus, in a measure, of interpretation, by an apparatus external to the text, the vowel-points were introduced, and the cantillation was similarly regulated by the so-called accents. The cadences of the recitative served to separate clauses and sentences as by a kind of audible punctuation, and the corresponding signs served as a visible one. This innovation did not make its way, however, into the Rolls of the Law; the lessons from the Pentateuch are still read from manuscripts written in the ancient mode, with only the bare text. When this is called "the consonant text" this must not be understood — as it sometimes is — to mean that only consonants in the definition of our English grammars were written.

The entire apparatus of vowel-points and accents is post-Talmudic, though there is no doubt that it embodies a traditional pronunciation and interpretation. It is known that two or three different systems of indicating the vowels were tried; the one with which we are familiar probably owes its general use to the fact that it was employed by the Massoretic school of Tiberias, who became the great authorities on the text of the Scriptures, and was probably preferred by them because it was capable of distinguishing more minutely between vowel sounds. It is fundamentally a phonetic notation; not concerned with etymology and only accidentally with quantity. Before the adoption of some such system a man could pronounce only what he had learned to pronounce and understand from the lips of a living teacher.

I. 101 l. 21–23

On the version of Symmachus see Field, Origenis Hexaplorum quae supersunt, Prolegomena, c. iii; Swete, Introduction to the Old Testament in Greek (1900), pp. 49–53. Theodotion, Field, Prolegomena, c. iv; Swete, *op. cit.*, pp. 42–49. Theodotion is said by Irenaeus to have been an Ephesian, and, like Aquila, a proselyte to Judaism; Symmachus was, according to Eusebius (Hist. Eccles. vi. 17), an Ebionite, and there is a presumption that he was by birth a Jew.

Aquila the proselyte is frequently mentioned in the rabbinical sources; Theodotion would probably be in Hebrew "Jonathan," if there were any reference to him; the name Symmachus (סומכוס) is borne by a disciple of R. Meir, but Geiger's proposed identification of this scholar with the translator has not been accepted.

I. 101 l. 23f.

Into the history of these recensions it is unnecessary to digress here. The best known, and even in its fragmentary and indirect transmission the most tangible of the survivals is the Hexapla of Origen.

I. 101 n. 1

Aquila (Onkelos the proselyte) is brought into association with Gamaliel himself, Tos. Shabbat 7, 18, where Gamaliel הזקן is named; Tos. Ḥagigah 3, 2 f.; Tos. Kelim iii. 2, 4; Tos. Miḳwa'ot 6, 3. [L. G.] How Aquila became a proselyte, and on his study of the Law, see also Tanḥuma ed. Buber, Mishpaṭim 3, where he is said to have been a nephew of Hadrian (sister's son), and conversations with Hadrian before and after his conversion are related. The story, like the connection of R. Meir with Nero (above, p. 35), illustrates the inclination to give a distinguished ancestry to converts. See also Vol. I, p. 347.

I. 102 l. 22–24

The version of Aquila was made primarily for Greek-speaking Jews in the dispersion, as a more exact rendering of the Hebrew original than the translations in use which we designate collectively by the inappropriate name "Septuagint." The latter, moreover, had already been taken over by Gentile Christians and employed by them, not only as an instrument of propaganda but in their controversies with Jews. The need of a standard Aramaic translation as a measure of restraint on the liberty of midrashic paraphrase in the oral rendering of the lessons in the synagogue (Vol. I, pp. 302 f.) was different, but perhaps not less real. The Targums (Vol. I, pp. 174–176) presuppose a traditional interpretation and to some extent, at least, a conventional expression.

The statement in the text (Vol. I, 102, lines 22–24) is the impression made by continuous reading of the Targum of Onkelos and the Targum of the Prophets; whatever the authors inherited from tradition, they wrought out of it a literary unity which I can only ascribe to redaction, and I doubt whether, on internal grounds, any critic would come to a different judgment. In support of the opinion entertained by many scholars that written translations of the Scriptures in Aramaic were condemned and on occasion suppressed by those in authority is specifically alleged the example of Rabban Gamaliel and the translation of Job which he was shown on the temple mount, Shabbat 115a. With Shabbat 115a cf. Tos. Shabbat 13 (14), 2; Jer. Shabbat 15c, above.

I. 104 l. 16 ff.

Nathan seems to have been a young man when he migrated to Palestine; he was nearer the age of Simeon ben Gamaliel's son Judah (afterwards, Judah ha-Nasi), whose opponent in controversy on legal points he frequently was. See, e.g., Baba Batra 131a.

I. 105 l. 2f.

Ordination by the Patriarch conferred authority to decide questions of religious law (licit or illicit) submitted to him; to give judgement in certain classes of cases; and to inspect firstlings and pronounce them free from blemishes that would make them unfit for sacrifice; see Note on I, p. 43 (above, p. 15f.). Rabbi conferred on Abba Arika (Rab) the first two, but withheld the third, and thus left the authorisation conspicuously incomplete. The motive for this slight is discussed by Weiss, Dor, cited in n. 1.

I. 106 l. 1 ff., and n. 1

On Sifrè Deut. § 80, see Bacher, Tannaiten, I, 374; II, 275.

I. 106 l. 10

On the Jews in Rome, see Philo, Leg. ad Gaium c. 23, § 155 ff., and on the emancipation of Jewish slaves who would not abandon their own laws and customs, ibid. (ed. Mangey, II, 568). Inscriptions in Jewish cemeteries have disclosed the existence of numerous synagogues; see G. La Piana, Harvard Theological Review, XX (1927); Hugo Gressmann, "Jewish Life in Ancient Rome," in the Abrahams Memorial Volume, 1927, pp. 170–191.

I. 107 l. 22–25

The "Alexandrian scholars" here referred to are those of the time of Philo, and so far as their attitude can be inferred from the writings of Philo. The case investigated by Hillel (Baba Meṣi'a 104a) arose out of customs and doings of "men of Alexandria," but the scholars who were disposed to declare the sons of this marriage ממזרים may have been Palestinian authorities.

That students of the Law went from Egypt to study under Palestinian masters is well-known, but the attested instances are apparently all later than the destruction of Jerusalem. So also the visits of Palestinian rabbis to Alexandria. Tos. Nega'im 9, 9, end; Alexandrians propound a question to R. Joshua, but not necessarily in Egypt.

I. 108–109

See Juster, Les Juifs dans l'empire Romain, I, 391–399. With the extinction of the family of Hillel, in which line the patriarchate had been hereditary, the latter also came to an end. The "archipherecites" (ראש פרקים) of the following period did not succeed to the prerogatives and privileges of the Patriarch in Roman law. See also L. Ginzberg, Geonica I, 2.

I. 109 n. 1

"The Talmud (Sanhedrin 5a) confuses the later conditions with the earlier; from the data given there I am convinced that down to Sassanid times the Patriarch had the authority in civil matters also, as it was he who ordained the judges." [L. G.]

I. 109 n. 2

On the relation of the Christian "apostles" to the Jewish, see La Piana, "Foreign Groups in Rome," Harvard Theological Review, XX (1927), p. 373 n. (with references to the literature).

I. 120 l. 26

The words מן התורה are not found in the best texts of M. Sanhedrin 10 (11), 1. [L.G.] — See Note on Vol. II, p. 381 (below, p. 205).

I. 125 l. 10 ff.

Critical study of the vast and varied literature which, for want of a better name, we are accustomed to call "rabbinical" is an enterprise to which Jewish scholars first seriously addressed themselves in the 19th century. For an important part of it, especially for the Midrashim, Leopold Zunz (b. 1794, d. 1886) was a pioneer. (Die gottesdienstlichen Vorträge der Juden historisch entwickelt, 1832; 2 ed., 1892.) Other critics who took part in different ways in the work were Krochmal (b. 1785, d. 1840: Moreh Nebukim ha-Zeman, 1851, in Hebrew, edited by Zunz), Rappoport (b. 1790, d. 1867), and A. Geiger, Urschrift und Uebersetzungen der Bibel in ihrer Abhängigkeit von der innern Entwickelung des Judenthums, 1857. The historians (Jost, Herzfeld, Graetz, and others) made incidental but not insignificant contributions. Comprehensive works on the history of tradition are Isaac H. Weiss, Dor Dor we-Doreshau, 5 vols. (in Hebrew), 1871–1891, and in later editions;[1] and Isaac Halevy, Dorot ha-Rishonim. Die Geschichte und Literatur Israels, 4 vols. (in Hebrew, 1898–1918). Intended to be an antidote to Krochmal, Frankel, Weiss, and the critical school generally. Sharply polemic and sometimes extremely ingenious, but very learned.

I. 127 l. 13–16.

See Vol. II, Part vii. A few passages in the Talmuds are sometimes noted as of apocalyptic character, but "apocalyptic" is such a vague word and so loosely used that the designation has little significance.

I. 128 n. 1

See Vol. II, pp. 334 f., 337.

I. 130 l. 1–10

A. Hilgenfeld, Die jüdische Apokalyptik in ihrer geschichtlichen Entwickelung. Ein Beitrag zur Vorgeschichte des Christenthums, 1857. Messias Judaeorum libris eorum paulo ante et paulo post Christum natum conscriptis illustratus, edidit A. Hilgenfeld, 1869. — The literature of the controversy of that decade (Bruno Bauer, and especially Volkmar — the Jewish apocalyptic secondary and post-Christian) is registered in Hilgenfeld's Prolegomena.

[1] In the present volumes Weiss is quoted by the pages of the 4 ed. (Wilna, 1904).

For the literature on the several books, reference may be made to Schürer, Vol. III, to Charles, Apocrypha and Pseudepigrapha, and to Bousset's Religion des Judentums (3 ed., edited by Gressmann, 1926).

I. 135 n. 1

The name Sifrè was applied to what is usually called Mekilta as late as the 12th century, the word covering all the Tannaitic Midrashim except Sifra; see Ginzberg, Geonica, II, 307, n. 2. [L. G.]

I. 136 l. 9 f.

There is a Tannaite Midrash on the plans of the tabernacle, the so-called מלאכת המשכן (edited by Friedmann); which may possibly be one of the missing parts of the Mekilta. [L. G.]

I. 138 n. 3

Ginzberg discusses the grounds on which Israel Lewy, the only scholar who had dealt specifically with the attribution (1889), came to the conclusion that this Midrash has nothing to do with R. Simeon ben Yoḥai or his school; and sets forth (pp. 414 ff.) reasons for holding that the (mediaeval) ascription to R. Simeon ben Yoḥai is correct. That it represents the school of Akiba, Lewy had no doubt.

Against the attribution, see S. Horovitz, Beiträge zur Erklärung und Textkritik der Mekilta des R. Simon (Jahresbericht des jüdisch-theologischen Seminars, Breslau 1919.

I. 142 l. 14–19

The best edition of the Sifra is that of Warsaw, 1866, with the commentary of R. Samson of Sens and very valuable notes by R. Jacob David of Vishgrad. [L. G.]

This edition of the Sifra, which at the time the text was written I had not seen, should be mentioned here. It was published at Warsaw in 1866 with the commentary of R. Samson of Sens (d. ca. 1230), one of the most eminent Tosafists, and very useful notes by the editor, R. Jacob David of Vishegrad. In the commentary as printed, apparently from a unique manuscript, there are considerable gaps which need not here be further defined and discussed.

It may be added that for the scope and method of juristic exegesis (including the ritual and ceremonial laws) in the schools of the second century, and the application of what we should call moral principles to matters of civil and criminal law, the Sifra is an especially instructive introduction. For an illustration of such an extension of the law see Sifra on Lev. 19, 11, 'Ye shall not steal' (take by stealth any thing that belongs to another) "for the purpose of causing vexation (we might say, as a practical joke)"; "ye shall not steal, with the expectation of making double restitution or of restoring four or five fold (see the law in Exod. 21, 36 ff. — E.V. 22, 1 ff.). "Ben Bag Bag (an early Tanna) says, Thou shalt not steal after the thief what belongs to thyself (that is reclaim your own stolen property by stealth from another's house or court-yard), lest thou seem to be a thief." See also Tos. Baba Ḳamma 10, 38, where ben Bag Bag, in a second saying, allows recovery by force. Baba Ḳamma 27b, end: "Do not enter the court-yard of thy fellow to take what belongs to thee without permission, lest thou appear to him as a thief." This is perpetuated in the codes, e.g., Maimonides, Hilkot Genibah 1, 2: it is forbidden to steal in fun, or with expectation of making restitution; Shulḥan 'Aruk, Ḥoshen Mishpaṭ, Genibah, beginning. Children who steal are whipped — with due regard to what they can endure — "that they may not form the habit."

The immediate sequel in Leviticus is, 'and do not (falsely) deny, and do not lie to one another, and do not swear by my name to a falsehood.' The Sifra (Ḳedoshim Parashah 2, 5) connects closely: "If thou hast stolen, thou wilt end by denying, lying, swearing by my name to a falsehood." — 'By my name,' means not only the proper name יהוה, but covers all the names, titles, and appropriated epithets of God (כינויים). 'And profane the name of thy God. I am Jehovah,' teaching that a vain (false) oath is the profanation of the Name (Vol. II, p. 108 f., an unpardonable sin). — Another far-fetched etymological) interpretation is added.

I. 144 l. 19

An English translation of selections from the Sifrè on Numbers has been published by Paul P. Levertoff, under the title Midrash Sifre on Numbers, London, 1926.

I. 146 l. 14

Kahan, who was associated with G. Kittel in the translation of Sifrè, died in 1924.

I. 147 n. 1

An additional fragment was published by Schechter in the Lewy-Festschrift (Breslau, 1911), Hebrew Part, pp. 189–192. — Two much defaced leaves (not continuous) from a quire containing remains of a Midrash on the first verses of Deut. 12.

I. 147 l. 24–29

For a significant exception See Midrash Tannaim, p. 62 n. 9.

I. 152 l. 24 f.

In the older authorities and in manuscripts of the Babylonian Talmud, also, the paragraph is indicated by the word "Halakah," not by "Mishnah," as in our editions. In the current separate editions of the Mishnah the paragraphs are merely numbered.

I. 154 l. 22–28

Mention should also be made of the edition, with punctuation, German translation, and notes, published by H. Itzkowski, Berlin, (from 1887 on; unfinished). The several Parts (Orders) of the Mishnah, by different scholars, are of different value. Of conspicuous worth are Neziḳin (by David Hoffmann) and Ṭoharoth (by the same, unfinished). — The paper, at least in my copy, is so bad that the earlier Lieferungen went to pieces of their own brittleness before the first volume was completed, and could not be bound.

I. 156 l. 15

It should be added that in some cases the Tosefta preserves an older stage in the development of the Halakah than that which is represented in our Mishnah.

I. 156 l. 19 f.

Zuckermandel's Erfurt manuscript, the older and better of the two, extends only over the first four orders of the Tosefta and three chapters of Zebaḥim; the Vienna codex covers all six orders, but lacks sixteen leaves in different places; see the Preface to his edition (1881), p. 4, referring to fuller descriptions published by him elsewhere.

I. 156 l. 31 f.

Between Antigonus of Socho and the two Jose's a link seems to have fallen out (קבלו מהם); ממנו, "from him," sc. Antigonus, is a facilitating emendation of the copyists. For a conjecture that at this point the names of Zadok and Boethus, in whose schools the Sadducean heresy (denial of retribution) originated (Vol. I, pp. 69 f.), have been cut out, see G. F. Moore, "Simeon the Righteous," in the Israel Abrahams Memorial Volume (1927), p. 356.

I. 157 l. 2–4

It is pertinent to compare the apophthegms of the Fathers in the first chapter of Abot with the traditional maxims of the Seven Sages of Greece, and the succession of teachers with the *διάδοχαι* of Greek philosophers, but the analogy is not to be pressed. See Clement of Alexandria, Stromata, i. 14 f. (pp. 350 ff. Potter), and especially Diogenes Laertius, i. 13 ff.

I. 157 l. 25–27.

More recent editions: R. T. Herford, פרקי אבות (Text, Introduction, Translation, Commentary), New York, 1925; translation and notes by the same author also in Charles' Apocrypha and Pseudepigrapha, II, 686–714; Marti und Beer, 'Abot (Väter); Text, Übersetzung, Erklärung, nebst einem textkritischen Anhang, 1927.

I. 158 n. 2

On Tannaite elements in the Derek 'Ereṣ see L. Ginzberg, in Jewish Encyclopedia, IV, 526–529.

I. 158 l. 17–20

Schechter revised the current text of the Abot de-R. Nathan as printed in the editions of the Talmud by the aid of two manuscripts, one an Oxford codex, and a second which he designates as Codex Epstein, and of quotations. The "second recension" is found in its entirety, so far as was known to him, only in a Vatican manuscript, (Assemani's catalogue, No. 303). See Schechter's introduction, cc. 8 and 9; and on the relative age and value of the two recensions and their relation to each other, c. 5. He shows that the attempt to identify one of these recensions with a copy brought from Palestine (following a hint in the commentary ascribed to Rashi on Abot 1, 5) leads to no certain result, and that the conjecture of R. Zebi Hirsch Chaies (חיות) in his *Imre Binah* that recension B is that which is referred to by "Rashi" as current in France (צרפת), is not sustained. Recension A is that generally quoted not only by the scholars of France and Provence but by Spanish scholars. The references to the Abot de-R. Nathan in my "Judaism" are accordingly made in the customary form to this recension, which is conveniently found in the printed editions of the Talmud. Where readings of Schechter's second recension are referred to, it is cited as such, and by the pages of his edition, which is the only way to find anything in it.

I. 159 l. 5 f.

According to the rabbinical chronology, the second temple stood for 420 years (Yoma 9a, Johanan). This is the sum of the numbers in Seder 'Olam, c. 30 (34 years from the completion of the Temple to Alexander;[1] 180 for the Greek kings; 103 for the Asmonaean kingdom; 103 for Herod and his house). — On the schematic chronology of Seder 'Olam see I. Loeb in Revue des Études Juives, XIX, 202–205. — Compare the chronological data in Josephus, Bell. Jud. vi. 10, 1 (cf. vi. 4, 8 § 269 f.). In the place last cited Josephus gives the second temple, from the rebuilding by Haggai (in the second year of the reign of Cyrus) to its destruction by Titus, a duration of 639 years and 45 days. On the chronology of Josephus the monograph by Peter Brinch (1699), reprinted in Havercamp's edition, may be consulted for a collection of the scattered data, especially in the Antiquities, and a criticism of Voss.

I, 160 l. 28–30

Of editions of the Megillat Ta'anit it may be sufficient here to name Johann Meyer, מגלת תענית. Volumen de Jejunio, Amsterdam, 1724, with Latin translation, notes, and indices. — Meyer mentions in his preface two preceding editions of the work; his own text is taken from the Amsterdam edition of 1659 with extensive commentary by R. Abraham Levita. — Adolf Neubauer, in Mediaeval Jewish Chronicles, II (Anecdota Oxoniensia, 1895), pp. 3–25. For the sources from which the text is edited see the editor's preface, pp. vii–viii. — The Aramaic text (without the Hebrew glosses), based chiefly on Neubauer, is printed in G. Dalman, Aramäische Dialektproben, 1896. Brief notes are appended (pp. 32–34). — Other editions, and literature, Strack, Einleitung in Talmud und Midrasch, 5 ed., p. 12. — Moïse Schwab: La Meghillath Taanith ou Anniversaires Historiques. Actes du Onzième Congrès International des Orientalistes, Paris, 1897 (1898), pp. 199–259. Editions, p. 201 note. — Tammuz 14 (p. 234), suppression of the Sadducean penal code. Schwab refers this to the supremacy which the Pharisees had acquired through the sympathy of Queen Salome Alexandra, which made it possible for them to abrogate the Sadducean code and substitute their own rules. He suggests that the Pharisees after their victory rejected the Sadducean code for the simple reason that "traditional laws must not be written down," but notes also the possibility that the objection of

[1] So far the prophets prophesied by the holy spirit (ed. Ratner, p. 70b); from that time on, הט אזנך ושמע דברי חכמים.

the Pharisees was not to the mere writing down of the laws, but to the great severity of the Sadducees in the administration of justice. For the translation of ספר גזירתא by "le livre de *l'ordre*," he quotes P. Cassel, who understands this of the edict of Antiochus IV, repealed by "his son" Alexander (Balas) at a time when he and Demetrius were rival bidders for the support of the Jews (1 Macc. 10), an interpretation which is adopted by Zeitlin (p. 83).

On the age of the Hebrew commentary or glosses on Megillat Ta'anit the opinions of Jewish scholars differ widely, Graetz making it contemporary with the redaction of the Talmud or shortly after, while Rappoport (Erech Millin, pp. 189, 278) makes it as late as the ninth century (see Schwab, p. 255 f.), on the ground that the writer has confounded (23 Iyyar) the inhabitants of the Acra in Jerusalem with the Karaites — an interpretation which is more than doubtful, though the error may be an old one. Even if the earlier date is accepted, the question what the author of the commentary knew about the circumstances, or from what sources he derived what he professes to know, remains to be answered. The uncritical confidence with which scholars have erected imposing historical constructions on this foundation of sand, for want of anything better, has had consequences which the author of this commentary on the Megillat Ta'anit could not foresee and should not be held responsible for.

I. 161 n. 4

See Lauterbach, Jewish Quarterly Review, I, 29 ff., 503 ff.; Neumark, Maybaum Festschrift (1914), pp. 179 ff [L. G.]

I. 163 l. 8–10

The Tanḥuma (i.e. the Tanḥuma of the current editions) in its present form is a Babylonian compilation. [L. G.] See below, Note on I, 170.

I, 164 n. 3

Raimund Martini writes simply, "in Bereschit Rabba, id est in Expositione Geneseos" (f. 222, Voisin); on which the editor, Voisin, (f. 243) remarks: Non in eo libro, qui vulgo Bereschit Rabbah inscribitur, editus cum aliis Pentateuchi Midraschot; sed in alio ejusdem nominis, cujus Auctor est R. Moses Hadarsan. On f. 235 Raimund writes: "in Bereschit Rabba" (quoting from it in Hebrew), on which Voisin (f. 249): Majoricanum Manuscriptum addit in Bereschit Rabba Ketana, sive minori: Commentarius est in Genesin, qui vulgo edi solet cum aliis Pentateuchi Medraschot. Sic vocatur ad distinctionem alterius commentarii, R. Moses Hadarsan, qui a Raymundo saepe nominatur vel Bereschit Rabba simpliciter, vel Bereschit Rabba major, vel Bereschit Rabba R. Moses Hadarsan.

The name "Bereshit Rabba Rabbati" is perhaps only Raimund's *major* done back into supposed Hebrew, in reminiscence of Ekah Rabbati, Pesikta Rabbati. So far as I see Raimund never uses Rabbathi (or Rabba Rabbathi), and his "major, minor," are not employed as titles, but descriptively, the 'larger' being R. Moses ha-Darshan; his *Ketana* being what we know as Bereshit Rabbah.

See Zunz, Die gottesdienstlichen Vorträge der Juden, 2 ed. (1892), pp. 300–306; and especially A. Epstein, in several writings to which references will be found in Winter and Wünsche, Jüdische Literatur, II, 335 (Bacher).

I. 164 n. 5

Zunz, Die gottesdienstlichen Vorträge, 2 ed., p. 189, n. e: רבתי twice in Lam. 1, 1; רבתי בגוים, רבתי עם. The contradictory opinion is expressed by Buber in the Introduction to his edition (f. 2a, n. 1) — רבתי meant to distinguish it from a smaller Midrash, איכה זוטא). In the first editions of the Midrash on the Five Megillot (Pesaro, 1519) the Midrash on Canticles is headed שיר השירים רבתי , and before the proems to the Midrash on Lamentations, מדרש איכה רבתי (similarly the colophon). Otherwise neither רבה nor רבתי occurs in the titles or colophons of this edition. Older writers (e.g., the author of the 'Aruk) find it sufficient to cite the Midrash as מדרש קינות, מגלת איכה, אגדת איכה (see Buber, f. 2a, n.).

I. 165 l. 25–27

So Zunz, Gottesdienstliche Vorträge, 2 ed., p. 267. In view of the existence of manuscripts of the last Parashahs and extracts in the Midrash ha-Gadol exhibiting a different type of text from that of the printed editions and one consonant with the preceding parts of Genesis R., it is a more probable supposition that a remote ancestor of the current text had suffered considerable mutilation toward the end and that the missing sections were replaced from other sources, chiefly of the Tanḥuma species. A Midrash on the Blessing of Jacob (Gen. 49) differing from that in the editions was printed as שיטה חדשה at Venice in 1602 and a second time at Hamburg, 1782. About half of it (beginning and end) is derived from Tanḥuma homilies on the Sedarim Gen. 49, 1 and 49, 27 (see Theodor cited below, pp. 153 f.).

In 1915 Theodor printed in "Festschrift zum siebzigsten Geburtstage Jakob Guttmanns" (pp. 156–171; Drei unbekannte Paraschas aus Bereschit Rabba — critical introduction, pp. 148–155), from a manuscript of Bereshit Rabbah in Rome (Cod. Vat. Ebr. 30) three Parashahs (95–97) previously unknown in manuscripts or through quotations in the Yalkuṭ and 'Aruk, but from which many extracts are found in the Midrash ha-Gadol. They have the characteristics of Bereshit Rabbah, and, as Theodor showed, strong presumption of genuineness in contrast to the texts of the current editions.

In the edition of Theodor–Albeck, now completed (1929), both the שיטה חדשה (pp. 1199–1230) and the new sections (pp. 1231–1244) published in the Guttmann Festschrift are edited, the latter with the use of a second manuscript (Yemenite) in the Elkan Adler collection now in the library of the Jewish Theological Seminary in New York. See the editor's notes on pp. 1185, 1199, 1231, 1245.

I. 167 l. 5 ff.

The Babylonian Talmud is used in the first part of Shemot Rabbah [in the form in which we have it], which is consequently younger than the second part. [L. G.]

I. 167 l. 19

The numeration of the proems found in current editions is the work of editors, who set off in this way 34. Buber has shown that there should be 36 (the numerical value of איכה), and has divided them accordingly. The number 33 (my note 3) was taken from Zunz, the source for whose error is shown by Buber (f. 2b, n. 1).

I. 168 l. 11

Here should have been mentioned the edition, "Midrasch Echa Rabbati," by S. Buber, with an extended introduction, and commentary on the text (Wilna, 1899). The text of the two manuscripts on which this edition is based is said to be of a type on the whole inferior to that of the editio princeps and its successors, but the editor's introduction and notes are of great value.

I. 169–171.

For the literature on the vexed and perplexed problems of Yelammedenu and Tanḥuma, in addition to the bibliography appended to Lauterbach's article Tanḥuma in the Jewish Encyclopedia, Vol. XII, pp. 45 f. (1906), see L. Ginzberg, Genizah Studies in Memory of Doctor Solomon Schechter, I, 1928, p. 32. Among the authors there named A. Epstein perhaps contributed most to the definition and elucidation of the problems of the Tanḥuma. (For an outline of Epstein's opinions on the evolution of the Midrash, see Bacher, Agada der palästinensischen Amoräer, III, 512–514.)

New light has been thrown upon the question by fragments found by Schechter in the Cairo Genizah in 1896–1897 and now deposited in the library of the University at Cambridge, England. One of these fragments, from a "lost Midrash" which "may possibly be the Yelamdenu," [1] was printed by Schechter in "Studies in Jewish Literature, issued in Honor of Professor Kaufmann Kohler" (1913) pp. 260–265, and others of greater extent and more distinctive character are for the first time published by Ginzberg in the Genizah Studies cited above, pp. 37 ff., with an Introduction (pp. 23–37) and an Essay discussing the whole problem in its various aspects (pp. 449–513) including the relation of the Yelammedenu to the Tanḥuma in the common editions with the supplementary matter introduced in the Mantua edition of 1563; to the recension edited by Buber in 1885; to the quotations in the name of the Yelammedenu in the 'Aruk and in the Yalḳuṭ; to the Yelammedenu homilies in Deuteronomy (Rabbah and Zuṭa), and to those in the Pesiḳta of R. Kahana and the Pesikta Rabbati. An enumeration and detailed examination of all these Yelammedenu exordiums is given in the Essay cited, pp. 454 ff.

Ginzberg's general conclusion is that the question of the priority of the (original) Tanḥuma and the original Yelammedenu cannot be decided on the evidence of the fragments now in hand, but that in any case the Yelammedenu was a distinct work, independent of the original Tanḥuma, not a compilation of excerpts from that work, although in the 'Aruk and in the Yalḳuṭ the name Yelammedenu was probably used for a particular form or recension of the Tanḥuma known to those compilers (p. 35). — "The Yelammedenu is distinguished from the Tanhuma by its diction and even more by its special form of composition. Each chapter of the Yelammedenu consisted apparently of three parts: the exordium, which was of an halakic nature; the exposition of the question raised in the exordium; and the conclusion, in which the halakic discussion was connected with the verse to which the particular paragraph was attached." [L. G.]

I. 170 l. 17–19

By an error, which was corrected in the second printing of this volume, it was said that the current editions of the Tanḥuma repro-

[1] Compare now p. 263, l. 3 ff. with Ginzberg, op. cit., p. 37, l. 4 ff.

duce the text of the Constantinople edition (1520–1522), whereas in fact they follow that of the Mantua edition of 1563, in which the editor (Ezra of Fano) introduced many additions. Of the recension which Buber edited from manuscripts he says (Introduction, f. 15a) that all the answers to halakic questions in it are in conformity with the explanations in the Mishnah or the Tosefta, while in the recension previously in print (frequently cited as "the old Tanḥuma") many correspond to the Babylonian Talmud, and that it introduces many things from that Talmud. Buber gives (f. 15b–19b) a list of sixty-one such questions and answers in his edition, with notes on the sources and parallels. Compare Ginzberg, Genizah Studies, I, pp. 482–487.

I. 170 n. 2 and n. 4

The compiler of the Midrash ha-Gadol had three recensions, as the author of the Yalḳuṭ also apparently had. [L. G.]

I. 171 n. 1

The exchange of Halakah for Yelammedenu in the exordium may be due to the predilection of copyists. In the Paris manuscript of Bemidbar Rabbah the formula is ילמדנו רבינו, not הלכה. See A. Epstein קדמות התנחומא, 11. In the fragments of the Yelammedenu in Ginzberg's Genizah Studies, I, 23 ff., הלכה is used throughout (ibid. p. 36).

I. 171 l. 10–12

The first part of Naso (c. 6) differs in character from the Midrash, being a running commentary of a literal kind.

I. 171 l. 15

A word should have been said about the Midrash Tehillim (on the Psalms, also cited as Shoḥer Ṭob), which is occasionally quoted in "Judaism," generally in parallel to other sources. It is a relatively late and apparently gradual compilation, but often preserves excerpts from older sources. For particulars see Buber's Introduction, f. 2b–3a; Strack, Einleitung in Talmud und Midrasch, 5 ed., p. 217. The first edition (Constantinople, 1512) has the printer's colophon at the close of Psalm 118, and at this point the manuscripts examined by Buber also end. The Midrash on the rest of the Psalms (from Ps. 119–150) — first printed by itself in 1515, at Saloniki as is recognized from the typography — is supplied from other sources, among which the Yalḳuṭ, for a considerable stretch (Psalms 122 to 137 inclusive, except Pss. 123 and 131) reproduced verbatim, is the largest contributor. The compilation is not the work of one editorial hand. Aside from the appendix, Pss. 119 ff., it contains both old Haggadah and matter lacking early attestation. The parallels are chiefly Palestinian.

An edition of the whole, based on a Parma manuscript compared with several others, was published by Solomon Buber (Wilna, 1891), with a comprehensive introduction and a commentary.

I. 173 ll. 8–11

See above, p. 22, also (on Sirach) Vol. I, p. 44.

I. 173 ll. 17–20

The folios and columns (though not the lines) in the Krotoschin edition correspond to those of the Venice edition (1523–1524), of which there is a recent anastatic reproduction. — More recent editions (Zitomir, Piotrokow) with commentaries have a different pagination, and — what is more confusing — frequently a different division of the chapters (Perakim) and numeration of the Halakot. — Since Bomberg's first edition (Venice, 1520–1523) in twelve folio volumes, complete editions of the Babylonian Talmud have usually been printed with identical folios, whatever the number of volumes in which it is bound up, and notwithstanding the addition of many commentaries.

I. 177 l. 5

Writing down prayers was disallowed in Talmudic times; see Shabbat 115b, above; מכאן אמרו כותבי ברכות כשורפי תורה (for the point of מכאן see the preceding context), enforced by an anecdote of Rabbi Ishmael's investigation of the case of a man in צידן (Sidon?) who was reported to him as writing prayers. He found him with a volume (טומוס) of prayers; which the owner plunged in a basin of water, whereupon R. Ishmael said: "The last offence is greater than the first." See further L. Ginzberg, Geonica, I, 119 f.

I. 177 l. 27

A commentary on the Prayers composed by R. David ben R. Joseph Abudarham (or Abudrahim) in Seville about 1340 was found very useful, and has been repeatedly printed. He drew, as he tells us, upon the Talmuds, the words of the Geonim, and earlier and later commentators, being led to undertake the task by the prevailing ignorance of the prayers and the proper modes of reciting them, and by the variations of custom (מנהגים) and disputes about them. He is concerned, however, not only with matters of form and order but even more that the worshippers should apprehend the meaning of the petitions and benedictions and of their place in the liturgy, and he brings to the task not only ample learning — he is said to have been a disciple of Jacob ben Asher, Baal ha-Turim — but a genuinely religious spirit. See Kohler in Jewish Encyclopedia, I, 139.

I. 177 l. 31

For the study of the early liturgy the considerable fragments of the Palestinian prayers published by Schechter, Elbogen, and Mann are important.

On the customs (*minhagim*) of the several countries in this field, their history and their diversity, see Zunz, Ritus des synagogalen Gottesdienstes (1859); Elbogen, Der jüdische Gottesdienst § 43, and notes; L Ginzberg, Geonica, I, 119 ff.

I 177 n. 3

The North-French forms of the liturgy stand between the Sephardic and the Askenazic rites; but are not identical with the latter.

I. 180 l. 21

In Box and Oesterley the attempt to reconstruct the original by an eclectic procedure in translation is carried out with great pains to a result that may well be a warning to critics of a divinatory turn.

I. 182 n. 3

For Ryssel *read* R. Kittel.

I. 183 l. 11

In the second edition of Swete (1899), III, 765–787, the apparatus has been revised in some particulars by fresh recourse to collations (cf. p. xvi. f.). On these Psalms it is still profitable to read Hilgenfeld, Prolegomena to Messias Judaeorum libris eorum paulo ante et paulo post Christum natum conscriptis illustratus (1869), pp. xi–xviii (previously in Zeitschrift für wissenschaftliche Theologie, 1868, pp. 140 ff.), especially for the older controversies about their age and their original language. The Psalms are printed ibid. (pp. 3–25), with critical notes to the text and appended "adnotationes" (pp. 25–33). They are edited also in O. F. Fritzsche, Libri Apocryphi Veteris Testamenti Graeci (1871), pp. 569–589 (cf. Praefatio, xxv)

In Beihefte zur Zeitschrift für die alttestamentliche Wissenschaft, Giessen, 1896, W. Frankenberg has written on Die Datierung der Psalmen Salomos, ein Beitrag zur jüdischen Geschichte, in which, against the prevailing opinion of the day (Wellhausen, Die Pharisäer und die Sadducäer, 1874), he reverts to the earlier view (Ewald, al.) that the situation represented in the Psalms of Solomon is that of the Syrian conflict, and offers a retroversion into biblical Hebrew (pp. 66 ff.).

I. 183 l. 12

Another English translation, by G. Buchanan Gray, in Charles, Apocrypha and Pseudepigrapha of the Old Testament (1913), II, 625–652, with an Introduction to which the reader may be referred for an account of the recently recovered Syriac version (from Greek), edited by Rendel Harris, The Odes and Psalms of Solomon, 1909 (2 ed. 1911). A German translation by R. Kittel in Kautzsch, Apokryphen und Pseudepigraphen des Alten Testaments, II, 127–148.

I. 184 l. 9–18

This summary description of the "Two Document Hypothesis" on which a majority of the critics have in recent years been working is a simplification, which may, however, be regarded as sufficient for the present purpose. For readers who wish to acquaint themselves more fully with the present state of what is known as the "Synoptic Problem," the titles of two or three recent books in which the question is treated in different ways may be mentioned here: B. H. Streeter, The Four Gospels; a Study of Origins, etc. (1925), especially, to begin with, chapters vii and viii; B. W. Bacon, The Story of Jesus, 1927; Henry J. Cadbury, The Making of Luke-Acts, 1927.

I. 184 l. 19 and n. 2

See G. Kittel, Die Probleme des palästinischen Spätjudentums und das Urchristentum (1926). Das sprachliche Problem, pp. 34 ff. (literature, p. 34 n.). That in cities like Tiberias, or, if you will, in places like Capernaum, many people spoke more or less Greek is not improbable; that the Galileans in general were bilingual is an assertion for which no evidence exists, and which, in the nature of the case, there is no evidence to disprove. What I would insist upon is that whether they knew more Greek or less, when Jesus and his Galilean disciples talked on religious subjects they spoke their mother tongue. The words and phrases in which they could express themselves on such subjects were learned in the home and in the synagogue, especially from the homilies. To have a corresponding vocabulary in Greek they would have had to be familiar with the language of the Greek Bible, in which the translators had found or invented equivalents or at least conventional counterparts for the words and ideas of the Jewish religion. That the upper classes in Jerusalem spoke Greek from Ptolemaic times on (Vol. I, p. 48 f.), as the upper classes in Rome did in the centuries before our era, is not in question. That many Greek-speaking Jews settled there and many more came with the pilgrimage is also well known.

I. 184 l. 26–28 (cf. Vol. I, p. 186).

Jerome says (De viris illustribus, c. 3) that of the Hebrew Gospel (of which he makes Matthew the author — Hebraicis literis verbisque composuit), there was to his day a copy in the library which Pamphilus had collected in Caesarea. Years before, he had himself had the opportunity of transcribing this Gospel, which was in use among the Nazarenes in Beroea (Aleppo); and remarks especially that whereever the Evangelist, either in his own discourse or in the words of Jesus, quoted the Old Testament, he did not follow the authority of the Septuagint, but of the Hebrew, of which Jerome cites two instances. — How much Hebrew Jerome knew when he was in the region of Beroea may be uncertain; he probably communicated with members of the Nazarene community there in Greek, for they had a Greek version of the Old Testament which may have been that of Symmachus. It may be admitted that he or his informants were mistaken in the opinion that their Gospel was the original of Matthew, subsequently translated into Greek by some unknown hand. But that what they showed him in Beroea, or what he afterwards saw in Caesarea, was an "Aramaic" Gospel, based on the Greek Matthew, as is confidently asserted by some modern critics, and that Jerome did not know the difference or misrepresented the facts, is improbable.

I. 185 l. 2 ff., and n. 1

In his "Jesus–Jeschua" (1922) Dalman has rendered the words of Jesus in an Aramaic such as he probably spoke and in a transcription which brings out the Galilean pronunciation, discussing alternative suggestions or possibilities. For this task Dalman possessed exceptional qualifications through his grammatical and lexical studies of Palestinian Aramaic and of the Gospels. The principles of this retroversion, both in the controverted question of dialect and in the method of retroversion from the Greek text, seem to me to be sound. How many uncertainties remain Dalman shows at length in the discussion which leads up to his restoration or comments upon it. They are perhaps greatest in matters of expression which do not profoundly affect the sense. Students of the Gospels will find this volume — the contents and significance of which are concealed rather than revealed by its title — suggestive and helpful in many ways.

I. 186 l. 21

Δευτερώσεις. Mishnah (שנה, repeat, learn by repetition). — In the Novel (146) of Justinian it is likely that the whole oral tradition, including Haggadah, was meant; the object being to clip the wings of the homilists. An unforeseen result was a great development of the synagogue poetry (the didactic Piyut). See Israel Davidson, Maḥzor Yannai (1919), Introduction, pp. xiv ff.

I. 186 l. 28 ff.

Cf. Eusebius, Hist. Eccles. iii, 27, on two classes of "Ebionites," so called, according to Eusebius, because of their poor and mean opinions about Christ or "the poverty of their intelligence." The two species of Ebionites in Eusebius agreed in insisting on the observance of the Jewish law; but differed in their opinions about Christ, one kind holding him to be a mere man, conceived and born in the natural way, while the other kind believed that he was born of a virgin and a holy spirit, but denied his previous divine existence as Logos and Wisdom. One of these subdenominations rejected the Epistles of Paul, calling him in disparagement an apostate from the Law. — On the attitude of the Nazarenes in Beroea, see Vol. I, p. 186 f. Indubitable Jews like Maimonides have recognized in the spread of Christianity and of Islam a preparation of the world for the Messianic times through the knowledge and worship of the one true God. (See Kohler, Jewish Encyclopedia, IV, 56 f.)

The etymological witticism about the poverty of the Ebionites' intelligence is at least as old as Origen (De Principiis, iv. 1, 22); it is more likely, however, that the name originated in the time when collections were being made in the Pauline churches for "the poor of the saints in Jerusalem (Romans, 15, 26; cf. Gal. 2, 10, "the poor"). 'Poor in intelligence' can be expressed in Hebrew in various ways, but of the seven or eight words for "poor" enumerated and explained in Lev. R. 34, 6 and parallels אביון is the least likely to be employed in such a phrase, if indeed it could be so used at all. — It may be noted by the curious that in Baba Ḳamma 117a R. Huna bar R. Judah arrived at בי אביוני (which might be understood as a settlement of Ebionites), where he met Raba (d. 352) and consulted with him about a point of law. See also Kohut, Aruch Completum, II, 46 f. (s.v. בי אבידן), who discusses the surmise that אבידן in the Talmud is everywhere a cryptic reading for אביון and נצרפי for נוצרי (Nazarene). — In no other place in the Talmuds or Midrashim is there any mention of "Ebionites," and a settlement of "Ebionites" in Babylonia in the fourth century (or a place preserving in its name the memory of an earlier settlement) is improbable.

I. 186 n. 3

The etymological interpretation of the names may be Jerome's own wisdom; it is less likely that his Nazarenes would have derived the name הלל (Hillel) from the root חלל, a confusion which suggests an ear unaccustomed to the sounds of a Semitic language.

I. 187 l. 23–26

James, the brother of Jesus, became the head of the community in Jerusalem. Eusebius, from the point of view of the church organization and theory of a later time, says that the episcopal throne had been committed to him by the Apostles (Hist. Eccles. ii. 23, 1). How it actually came about we do not know; but inasmuch as the successor of James was Simeon son of Clopas, according to Hegesippus a cousin of Jesus (Euseb. Hist. Eccles. iii. 11, cf. the list of bishops "of the circumcision" down to Hadrian's time in Hist. Eccles. iv. 5), it seems probable that, although James had not been a believer in Jesus' life-time, not to say one of the apostles, it was felt that, until the expected coming of Christ, the headship of the community should be in the family of Jesus. Cf. also Eusebius, Hist. Eccles. iii. 20; iii. 32.

James was according to Hegesippus (Euseb. Hist. Eccles. ii. 23, 4 ff.) distinguished for what we should call strict Jewish piety and observance, by which he secured the title, the Righteous. In the Clementina he appears as the head of the church in Jerusalem, to whom Peter reports on his missionary activities (Hom. i, 20).

That a considerable number of priests early "became obedient to the faith" (i.e. that Jesus was the Messiah) is reported in Acts 6, 7, and is in no wise improbable. The commonalty of the priesthood, in distinction from part of the priestly aristocracy, was pious and observant, especially in the rules of sacerdotal purity which particularly concerned them. In Acts 15, 5 the adhesion of some of the sect of the Pharisees, also, to the new faith is recorded, and we are told that at the beginning of the controversy in Jerusalem over the reception of Gentile converts these took the consistent Jewish ground that such converts must be circumcised and bound to observe the law of Moses — in other words, they must become proselytes to Judaism to have any claim to the promises. The attitude of James subsequently, in the matter of commensality with Gentile believers (Gal. 2, 12 ff.), is that of the Ebionites of Eusebius (supra, p. 55), and of the Nazarenes at Beroea according to Jerome. It is the attitude ascribed to Jesus himself as reported in Matt. 5, 17–20; where v. 19 (ὃς ἐὰν οὖν λύσῃ μίαν τῶν ἐντολῶν τούτων τῶν ἐλαχίστων καὶ διδάξῃ οὕτως τοὺς ἀνθρώπους, ἐλάχιστος κληθήσεται ἐν τῇ βασιλείᾳ τῶν οὐρανῶν) might be imagined to be in this form a Nazarene protest, given its particular point by the career of Paul.

I. 188.

Taylor, Charles, The Teaching of the Twelve Apostles, with illustrations from the Talmud, 1886. On the Theology of the Didache, 1889. Klein, G., Der älteste Christliche Katechismus und die jüdische Propaganda–Literatur, 1909. In Klein's opinion, the tract belonged to the Derek-Ereṣ literature, and whatever may be thought of this thesis his parallels and illustrations are very instructive.

I. 189 n. 1

Cf. Euseb. Hist. Eccles. iii. 5, 2, who quotes Matt. 28, 19: πορευθέντες μαθητεύσατε πάντα τὰ ἔθνη ἐν τῷ ὀνόματί μου without any reference to baptism.

I. 190 n. 2

On these wars of Jacob and his sons in Midrash see L. Ginzberg, Legends of the Jews, Vol. V, p. 315 f. (note 292; cf. also notes 297 and 317).

I. 192 n. 2

Test. Levi 16, 1 — not in all manuscripts; see Charles's apparatus.

I. 193 l. 19

Charles's translation, with introduction and commentary, is also to be found in his Apocrypha and Pseudepigrapha of the Old Testament, etc., II (1913), 282–367.

I. 193 l. 30 ff. — 195, line 8.

The questions presented by the calendar of Jubilees are perplexing, but fortunately do not involve what we may call the author's reformed calendar as described in Vol. I, p. 194, top. It may not be superfluous to add that the calendar now in general use among the Jews was not definitively fixed until the age of the Gaonim. See Poznanski, in Encyclopaedia of Religion and Ethics, III, 117–124. For investigations of the older calendars, cf. J. Morgenstern, The Three Calendars of Ancient Israel, Hebrew Union College Annual, 1924; W. A. Heidel, The Calendar of Ancient Israel, Proceedings of the American Academy of Arts and Sciences, LXI, No. 2, December 1925. No historical trace has been found of a year such as the author of Jubilees measures and lays out. Changes in the calendar, even demonstrable improvements, are seldom favorably received. They make so much trouble for the generation that has first to use them that this quite outweighs in their mind the saving of trouble to future generations. The chorus in Aristophanes' Clouds, which voices the grievances of the Moon and the complaints of the gods about the dislocation of their festivals, has been thought to allude to the improvement in the calendar introduced by the astronomer Meton about 432 B.C., with his nineteen year cycle of intercalation in place of the old octaeteris: "She (the Moon) says that she does well by you, but that you (Athenians) do not rightly keep the days, but turn everything topsy-turvy. (Nubes 615 f., — see the sequel, which may well be compared with Jubilees.) As a matter of fact the Metonic cycle and its further refinement by Kallippos does not seem to have been generally adopted outside of Attica.

I. 198 n. 3

See L. Ginzberg, Legends of the Jews, V, 268, and his criticism of Charles's note on Jubilees 15, 14, in connection with M. Shabbat 19, 5.

I. 204 n. 1

Widely at variance with the opinions summarized in the text, others hold that the fragments published by Schechter are the product of a schismatic movement dating from about the tenth century of our era. See Büchler, Jewish Quarterly Review, III, Levi, Revue des Études Juives, LXI, LXV. [L. G.]

To the literature may be added G. F. Moore, "The Covenanters of Damascus," Harvard Theological Review, IV (1911), 330–377; Charles, Apocrypha and Pseudepigrapha of the Old Testament, II

(1913), 785–834. There is an edition, with a commentary in Hebrew, by M. H. Segal, in Ha-Shiloah, XXVI, 390–406; 483–506.

I. 206 l. 13f

On the division between these two letters, their original language, and their historical significance, see C. C. Torrey, Zeitschrift für die alttestamentliche Wissenschaft, XX (1900), 225–242; Encyclopaedia Biblica, III, cols. 2875–2878; Herkenne, "Die Briefe zu Beginn des Zweiten Makkabäerbuches" in (Bardenhewer's) Biblische Studien, 1904. Others make out three letters (Laqueur, p. 52 f.). See, for the whole question, Moffatt in Charles, Apocrypha and Pseudepigrapha, I. 129 f.

I. 206 n. 1

See note on Vol. I, p. 49, l. 19–21 (*υἱὸς παράνομος*).

I. 208 l. 24–26.

Laqueur, Richard, Der jüdische Historiker Flavius Josephus. Ein biographischer Versuch auf neuer quellenkritischer Grundlage, 1920; Thackeray, H. St. John, Josephus. The Man and the Historian, 1929.

I. 210 l. 23–27, and n. 3

Synagogues (meeting-houses) are mentioned also, as Professor J. E. Frame reminds me, in Bell. Jud. ii. 14, 5 § 289 (Caesarea) and Antt. xix. 6, 3 § 300, 305 (Dora).

I. 211–214.

See Bousset–Gressmann, Die Religion des Judentums im späthellenistischen Zeitalter (1926), pp. 438 ff. To the literature there noted (p. 438) may be added, Windisch, Hans, Die Frömmigkeit Philons, 1909.

I. 212 l. 10–13

Bousset, Jüdisch-Christlicher Schulbetrieb in Alexandria und Rom, 1915, seems to me to go much beyond the evidence.

I. 212 l. 18–22

The contrary opinion, viz. that the "theosophy" of Philo was much older than Philo and had long been current among Alexandrian Jews, and that, transplanted to Palestine by such sects as the Therapeutae and the Essenes, it took root and flourished there, being the theology of philosophically-minded thinkers among the rabbis, though not of the juristically inclined nor of the common man, is the theory of August Friedrich Gfroerer, in his Geschichte des Urchristenthums (1831–1838), on which see "Christian Writers on Judaism," in Harvard Theological Review, XIV (1921), 222–228.

I. 216 l. 30 f.

It should be observed that Codex B never contained the Books of the Maccabees, and that in places where it is defective another manuscript has to take its place in Swete's "Old Testament in Greek" (in Gen. 1, 1–46, 28, cod. A: in Psalms 105 (106), 27–137 (138), 6, cod. א. Cod. A furnishes him the text for 1–4 Maccabees.

I. 217 ff.

Christianity inherited from Judaism the idea of revealed religion and appropriated its Scriptures. In that age, indeed, men, grown weary of the contentions of philosophic schools, and having lost confidence in the ability of reason to attain certainty in the spheres in which certainty is of the utmost importance, were seeking assurance in the authority of revelation, and confirmation of it in mystical experience. The claim to the possession of such an authoritative revelation in its Scriptures may have attracted converts to Judaism, as it did afterwards to Christianity.

Christianity added to the Jewish Scriptures, which it called the Old Testament, its Gospels and Epistles, Scriptures of the New Testament. In them it had a distinctive doctrine of the divine nature of Christ and his relation to the Father (Paul, Hebrews, John), and began the corresponding development of a sacramental liturgy. These doctrines and practices it held to be a new revelation, which it interpreted in terms of Greek philosophy and theosophic mysticism, and, after much controversy, defined in dogmas upon the acceptance of which membership in the Catholic Church and the salvation of the individual depended. The subtleties of the Rabbis were mainly in the sphere of observance, those of the theologians of the Church in that of correct beliefs, or to express it more accurately of intellectual apprehension. The one is called "legalism," we might name the other "creedalism"; both Rabbis and Church Fathers were convinced that they were showing men exactly how to conform to the revelation of God.

It is unnecessary to pursue the parallel farther. Both results, in their different ways, were the logical consequence of the idea of revealed religion embodied in divinely inspired Scriptures. The conception of historical development is equally foreign to both, and as irreconcilable with the finality of the Mosaic Law as with the finality of the "faith once for all delivered to the saints" (Jude vs. 3). The idea of development is the germ of dissolution for legalism and creedalism alike. The Protestant Reformation was in its own conception and intention a return to the revelation in the New Testament — that in this it deceived itself, as every attempt to turn time backward deceives itself, is here irrelevant. Rationalism — the word taken in a wide sense — did not effect the emancipation even of the minds that embraced it; it substituted a universal revelation in human reason, and turned to it for authority. The evolutionary conception of religion was as unknown to the English Deists as to their opponents. The conflict between "Fundamentalism" and "Modernism" which is waging in Christianity and Judaism is not the conflict of religion with science, but the irreconcilable conflict between the finality of revelation and the process of history.

I. 219 N 1

The discovery (or invention) of "Jehovah" has been commonly attributed to Petrus Galatinus, in his *De arcanis catholicae veritatis*, 1518, and this pronunciation of the consonants of the Tetragrammaton with the vowels of the Jewish substitute, אדני, has sometimes been held up as evidence of peculiar ignorance on his part. I have shown elsewhere that this ascribes to him more originality than he is really guilty of. The pronunciation was evidently current in his time, and he defends it against those who would say and write *Jova*. On this point, and on the controversies of the 16th and 17th centuries see "Notes on the Name יהוה," in Old Testament and Semitic Studies in Memory of William Rainey Harper, 1908, Vol. I, pp. 145–163 (also in American Journal of Theology, XII (1908), 34–52); and on other questions connected with the history of the name, American Journal of Semitic Languages and Literatures, XXV (1909), 312–318, XXVIII (1911), 56–62. On the ancient pronunciation see Judaism, Vol. I, p. 427.

I. 226 l. 18f.

It gratified the national vanity of the Jewish author who writes under the pseudonym "Artapanus" to make Moses, whom he identifies with Μουσαῖος, the author of the whole Egyptian civilization, including the religion of the thirty-six districts, with their several gods (ἑκάστῳ τῶν νομῶν ἀποτάξαι τὸν θεὸν σεφθήσεσθαι), but this is hardly a reminiscence of the Deuteronomic notion.

I. 227 **N 2**

The "seventy nations" are a standing feature of Jewish ethnology, in distinction from the unique nation, Israel. Thus the seventy bullocks offered in the week of the Feast of Tabernacles correspond to the seventy heathen nations; the one bullock on the eighth day (Num. 29, 36) to the unique nation, Sukkah 55b (R. Eleazar). Cf. Pesikta, ed. Buber f. 193b–194a, with the parallels adduced in the editor's notes there. See S. Krauss, "Die Zahl der biblischen Völkerschaften," Zeitschrift für die alttestamentliche Wissenschaft, XIX (1899), 1–14, XX (1900), 38–43; S. Poznanski, "Zur Zahl der biblischen Völker," ibid. XXIV (1904), 301–308; Jewish Encyclopedia, IX, 188–190. In Sifrè on Deut. 32, 8 (§ 311) R. Eliezer son of Jose the Galilean figures from Cant. 6, 8 that the nations received among them one hundred and forty portions of territory, twice the number of the fathers who went down to Egypt (i.e., each received two portions). In the Midrash ha-Gadol on the same verse: He fixed the boundary of the nations that they should not come into the land of Israel (so far also in Sifrè). How many nations are there? Seventy. And how many Israelites went down to Egypt? Seventy, as it is said, 'With seventy persons thy fathers went down to Egypt' (Deut. 10, 22). Therefore it is said, According to the number of the children of Israel. See D. Hoffmann, Midrash Tannaim, p. 190.

The Palestinian Targum on Deut. 32, 8 (cf. on Deut. 11, 8) reads as follows: "When the Most High gave the world in possession to the nations which sprang from the sons of Noah, when he gave mankind different ways of writing and different languages in the generation of the dispersion (after the Tower of Babel), at that time He cast lots with the seventy angels, princes of the nations, with whom he appeared to see the city (Gen. 11, 5), and at that time He established the boundaries of the peoples corresponding to the number of the persons of Israel who went down into Egypt. And when the holy people fell to the lot of the Lord of the world, Michael lifted up his voice and said, A good portion, for the name of the word of the Lord is with him! (i.e., the name of God, ישר־אל), and Gabriel said, For the house of Jacob is the lot of His possession. Cf. Pirkè de-R. Eliezer, c. 24. God assigned an angel to each several people, but Israel fell to his own portion and possession; therefore it is written (vs. 9), 'For the portion of the Lord is His people.'

L. Geiger, Urschrift und Uebersetzungen der Bibel, p. 294, sees in the Targum evidence of the antiquity of the variant in the Greek version, but does not affirm its priority.

I. 229 N. 3

The Jewish interpretation which takes Isa. 53 as a whole of the mission and martyrdom of the Jewish people is first attested in Origen, Contra Celsum, i. 35, and seems to have been evolved in contradiction to the early Christian apologetic which found in the chapter minute predictions of the rejection, suffering, death, and exaltation of Christ. For the whole history of the Jewish exegesis of the chapter see A. Neubauer and S. R. Driver, The Fifty-third Chapter of Isaiah according to the Jewish Interpreters, 1876–1877, 2 volumes (texts and translations).

I. 233 N. 4

Dio Cassius, xxxvii. 16, 5–17, 4. (The whole country along the Mediterranean from Phoenicia to Egypt was anciently called Palestine.) "They have another name later acquired; for the country is called Judaea and the people Jews. I do not know how this designation originated; but it is applied also to all other men who, though of different race, take up with their customs (νόμιμα). This class of men is found even among the Romans, and though often repressed has increased enormously, to such a point that they have won the right to practice their customs openly."

I. 234 n. 4

See Israel Lévi, "De l'origine davidique de Hillel," Revue des Études Juives, XXXI (1895), 202–211; XXXIII (1896), 143 f.

It is doubtful (notwithstanding Shabbat 15a, below) whether the title Nasi was borne by anyone before Gamaliel II (Gamaliel of Jabneh), toward the close of the first century, to whom it may have been given in reminiscence of Ezekiel as an appropriate designation for the head of the nation. The office became hereditary in his family, down to Gamaliel VI, with whose death in the fifth century (ca. 425) the patriarchate became extinct. See W. Bacher, Jewish Encyclopedia V, 560, 563; Juster, Les Juifs dans l'empire Romain, I, 390, n. 1, 395, 397.

I. 234 N. 6

It has been inferred from M. 'Eduyot 7, 7 that the patriarch had to be confirmed in his office by the Roman authorities. It is said there that Rabban Gamaliel (II) went to get authority from the legate in Syria, *sc.* to perform the functions of his office. See above, Note on Vol. I, pp. 43f. The language is not altogether explicit, but apart from any direct testimony the necessity of such recognition would be assumed as in conformity with Roman practice. See Juster, Les Juifs dans l'empire Romain, I, 394 f.

I. 237 l. 22

Ezra is sometimes identified with Malachi (Vol. I, p. 31, n. 2). On Daniel see Megillah 3a, where it is said that he was not a prophet. He is, however, included in the catalogue, Seder 'Olam c. 20 (ed. Ratner f. 44a; see Ratner's note 51). See A. Marx, Revue des Études Juives, LXXV (1922), 93 f. Clement of Alexandria (Stromata i. 21; ed. Potter, p. 400) counts thirty-five prophets, beginning with Adam, and including Daniel, besides five prophetesses.

I. 239 n. 1

Christian Fathers entertained the same conception of inspiration, comparing the prophet to a musical instrument (lyre or flute) played upon by the spirit, while his own faculties were in complete abeyance; his words are not his own, but those of the divine Logos speaking through him. See e.g. Justin Martyr, Apol. c. 36; cf. Cohort. ad Graecos c. 8.

I. 239 n. 5

An example of Kabbalah in the sense of 'tradition' is found in Abot de-R. Nathan (ed. Schechter, 2d recension § 42, f. 59a), עליו היה ר' מאיר אומר בקבלה in a sentence which makes the impression of being genuinely Tannaitic. [L. G.] — R. Meir quotes Lev. 26, 6b; see also Schechter's note 19.

I. 240 N. 7

הכתוב, הכתובים ;כתבי הקדש, Bacher, Terminologie, I, 90–93. On these and other names of the Bible and the several groups of books in it see Blau, Zur Einleitung in die heilige Schrift, pp. 1–31. In כתבי הקדש the genitive is not to be taken as a metonymy for God (Blau), but as attributive, 'holy Scriptures' (Bacher, *l.c.* p. 169 f.). Note the contrast כתבי הקדש, כתבי הדיוט 'the holy Scriptures' . . . 'private (secular) writings, Tos. Yom Tob 4, 4. With the article, Ketubim designates the Scriptures as a whole, and is equivalent to הכתוב (Bacher, *l. s. c.* p. 92; without the article (כתובים), it became the usual name for the third group of books in the collection — Torah, Nebi'im, Ketubim. It is probable that they were once called, 'the rest of the books' (שאר הכתובים). Blau, *l.c.* p. 29; cf. the translator's preface to Sirach: ὁ νόμος καὶ αἱ προφητεῖαι καὶ τὰ λοιπὰ τῶν βιβλίων. A parallel to this abbreviation would be found in the use of Sifrè for

(בי רב) ספרי (שאר), of the Tannaite Midrash on Exodus, Numbers, and Deuteronomy (our Mekilta and Sifrè), in distinction from Sifra, i.e., the Midrash on Leviticus (תורת כהנים).

I. 240, lines 24–26.

Jer. Soṭah 24b: משמתו נביאים האחרונים חגי זכריה ומלאכי פסקה מהם רוח הקדוש אע"פ כן משתמשין היו בבת קול. See Vol. I, p. 421 with n. 4, and p. 422. In Seder ʿOlam c. 30 (ed. Ratner f. 70b) the prophets prophesied by the holy spirit until the time of Alexander. This limit is in accord with the chronology of the book; see Vol. I, p. 6.

I. 241 N. 8

כתובים, originally a name for the Scriptures as a whole (e.g. Sifrè Deut. § 99), is used specifically of the books not comprised in the Law and the Prophets, e.g. by Akiba in M. Yadaim 3, 5: שכל הכתובים קדוש ושיר השירים קדוש קדשים. So in a Baraita on the order and authorship of the Biblical books, Baba Batra 14a: סדרן של כתובים רות וספר תהילים וג'ו, "The order of the Ketubim is Ruth, Psalms," etc. The appropriation of the general title כתבי הקדש to the Ketubim is later, appearing first in the Amoraim, unless Tos. Shabbat 13, 1 is to be understood in this sense. See the authors cited in the N 7.

The translator's preface to Ecclesiasticus shows that in his time there was no recognized title for these books; he can only say "the rest of the books," or *τῶν ἄλλων πατρίων βιβλίων*. The name *τὰ ἁγιό-γραφα sc. βιβλία* in Epiphanius; Hagiographa in Jerome, e.g. Prol. Galeatus: Tertius ordo Hagiographa possidet.

I. 241 l. 20 ff.

The use of select Psalms in the ordinary service of the synagogue, and especially in the festivals, which has so large a place in the liturgy as we know it, is probably very old. The statement in the text that the Psalms furnished no lessons for the synagogue is not meant to call in question this liturgical use. See Vol. I, p. 296.

I. 242 N. 9

The passages in rabbinical sources which bear on the Jewish canon are collected and discussed in books and articles on the Canon of the Old Testament.

I. 243 N. 9

M. Yadaim 3, 5: "All holy Scriptures make the hands unclean. The Song of Songs and Ecclesiastes make the hands unclean. R.

Judah (ben Ila'i) says: The Song of Songs makes the hands unclean, and about Ecclesiastes opinions are divided. R. Jose says: Ecclesiastes does not make the hands unclean and about the Song of Songs opinions are divided. R. Simeon says: Ecclesiastes is one of the things on which the school of Shammai took the laxer view and the school of Hillel the stricter (i.e. the former recognized the book as sacred, while the latter denied it that character).

Simeon ben Azzai says: I received it by tradition on the authority of the seventy-two elders on the day on which they installed Rabbi Eleazar ben Azariah in the presidency, that the Song of Songs and Ecclesiastes (both) make the hands unclean. R. Akiba says: *Absit omen*! No man in Israel was ever of a different opinion about the Song of Songs, holding that it does not make the hands unclean For the whole age altogether is not equal to the day on which the Song of Songs was given to Israel; for all the hagiographa (*Ketubim*) are holy, but the Song of Songs is the most holy of all (holy of holies). If there was a division of opinion, it was only about Ecclesiastes. R. Johanan ben Joshua, son of Akiba's father-in-law, says: It is as ben Azzai says; so they were divided, and so they decided. Cf. Tos. Yadaim 2, 14.

Sacred Scriptures are distinguished from all other books by the fact that contact with them makes the hands unclean, so that to say of a book that it makes the hands unclean is equivalent to declaring it sacred, or in our phrase 'canonical.' The origin and significance of the rule itself are obscure (see Shabbat 14a; Maimonides, Abot ha-Tuma'ot 9, 5); it was probably meant to prevent careless and irreverent handling of sacred books particularly by priests, who by such uncleanness would be prevented from eating their Terumah. The Sadducees scoffed at the absurdity of teaching that sacred Scriptures defile the hands and that profane — perhaps heathen — books do not (M. Yadaim 4, 6), and the answer of Johanan ben Zakkai, that the reason is the greater affection in which sacred books are held, does not sound very convincing. Somewhat more definite, but hardly more plausible, are his words in Tos. Yadaim 2, 19. In fact, all that Johanan does in either place is to give the Sadducees an *ad hominem* good enough for them.

I. 243 N. 10

Finis sermonis verbi universi auditu perfacilis est: Deum time, et mandata ejus custodi. Hoc est enim omnis homo, quia omne factum Deus adducet in judicium de omni abscondito, sive bonum, sive malum sit. Ajunt Hebraei quum inter caetera scripta Salomonis quae antiquata sunt, nec in memoria duraverunt, et hic liber obliterandus videretur, eo quod vanas Dei assereret creaturas, et totum putaret esse pro nihilo, et cibum, et potum, et delicias transeuntes praeferret omnibus, ex hoc uno capitulo meruisse auctoritatem, ut in divinorum voluminum numero poneretur, quod totam disputationem suam, et omnem catalogum hac quasi ἀνακεφαλαιώσει coarctaverit, et dixerit finem sermonum suorum auditu esse promptissimum, nec aliquid in se habere difficile, ut scilicet Deum timeamus, et ejus praecepta faciamus. Ad hoc enim natum esse hominem, ut creatorem suum intelligens, veneretur eum metu, et honore, et opere mandatorum.

I. 243 l. 15 ff.

See Note on Vol. I, p. 86–87 (above, p. 34). Professor Ginzberg is still of the opinion, expressed in his Presidential Address cited there, "that the question of the canonicity of the Gospels could never have suggested itself to people who, like R. Tarfon, would rather enter a pagan temple than a Christian house of worship."

I. 243 N. 11

הגיליוים וספרי המינים אינן מטמאות את הידים ספרי בן סירא וכל ספרים שנכתבו מכאן ואילך אינן מטמאין את הידים.

I. 244 n. 1

עון גיליון, און גיליון, Shabbat 116a. Other instances, see S. Krauss, Griechische und Lateinische Lehnwörter im Talmud, u. s. w., II, 21. גיליון itself is a blank leaf or margin, before, after, or on the sides of a volume (roll); as in M. Yadaim 3, 4. The Gospels are sometimes called simply גליונים, as in Tos. Yadaim 2, 13, where the juxtaposition with ספרי המינים and the rule that (unlike the blank margins or outside leaves of biblical books, M. Yadaim 3, 4) they do not defile the hands shows that the Gospels are meant.

The book of the Nazarenes (the disciples of Jesus the Nazarene) seems to have been called by them from the beginning εὐαγγέλιον (Tidings, News); the foreign word being a kind of proper name, as "Gospel" is in English, of the Anglosaxon etymology and meaning of which we are not conscious. The Jews know no other appellation for it, though they are acquainted with "other writings of the sectaries" (ספרי המינים); of a Hebrew (or Aramaic) title for it there is no trace. In the title of our Greek Gospels it is therefore not the translation of a Semitic word but the perpetuation of the original name. In modern Hebrew translations of the New Testament it is rendered by בשׂורה. (Biblical Hebrew for 'tidings).

I. 244 N. 11

Eliezer ben Hyrcanus is said to have been brought before a Roman magistrate on such an accusation; the magistrate dismissed the charge, but Eliezer was very much troubled that he should have been suspected of such a thing. He remembered, however, that he had heard from one Jacob of Kefar Sekanya an utterance of Jesus (on an halakic question) which he thought very good, and admitted that he had deserved the disgrace that had befallen him. ('Abodah Zarah, 16b–17a.) The same disciple of Jesus the Nazarene is said to have proposed to cure R. Eleazar ben Dama, a nephew of R. Ishmael, of a snake bite by using the name of Jesus ('Abodah Zarah 27b). R. Eleazar ben Dama would apparently have allowed the procedure in spite of the protests of R. Ishmael, but died in time to save him from thus "breaking through the ordinance of the sages." Hananiah, nephew of R. Joshua ben Hananiah, is said to have been bewitched by some sectaries in Capernaum so that he rode on an ass on a Sabbath. His uncle appeared on the scene, and said to him, Since that bad man's ass has brayed at you, you cannot remain in the land of Israel. So he went thence to Babylon, and died there in peace (Eccles. R. on Eccles. 1, 8, cf. on 7, 26). Bacher (Tannaiten, I, 385 n.) is doubtless right in seeing in this story an intention to discredit Hananiah, who made himself troublesome by his attempt to fix the calendar in Babylonia (Vol. I, p. 104). The interesting thing is that his fall is attributed to sectaries in *Capernaum*. In the same context in Eccles. Rabbah (on Eccles. 7, 26) a certain Judah ben Naḳosa is commended for his behavior in some experience with the Minim, but of the circumstances nothing is told.

That by the Minim who are so often named in the Talmuds and Midrashim, Nazarenes or Christians are always intended is going much beyond the evidence and sometimes contrary to it. The word means 'species,' 'kinds,' especially applied to peculiar kinds of people (a neutral word for party or sect is כת, while מינים implies disapproval) who differed from the majority in opinion or practice. The difficulty of dating the utterances is very great, and the substitutions of the censors, or of editors anticipating censorship — Sadducees, Philosophers, Epicureans, the wicked, and the like — have made the question all the more perplexing. Those who held that there were "two authorities" (Vol. I, p. 364 ff.), whatever variety of dualism they were addicted to, are called Minim, and have therefore sometimes been labelled "Jewish Gnostics." Of other proposed etymologies it is sufficient here to note that which finds in *minim* a contraction of

מאמינים, 'believers' (*sc.* in Jesus, *πιστεύοντες τῷ κυρίῳ*, Acts 5, 14). — When the rabbinical controversy is with (catholic) Christians in the third and fourth centuries, the turn of the argument often makes this plain. On the whole, an analysis of the very numerous testimonies yields little more than the fact that the disciples of Jesus are sometimes included under this comprehensive term.

The only distinctive name which occurs in our sources is "disciples of Jesus the Nazarene," or, more briefly, Nazarenes (נוצרים). The former is the name by which they called themselves, "the Disciples (sc. of Jesus) first got the name Christians in Antioch" (Acts 11, 26), probably given them by outsiders who took Christos for a proper name. The Jews had no corresponding expression; משיחי, which is found in modern Hebrew dictionaries for 'Christian', is unknown to talmudic and midrashic literature (it is apparently imitated from other Semitic languages, especially from Syriac, in which it was invented to render *χριστιανός* (the Peshitto takes over the Greek word); and if it had occurred to anyone to coin the word he would perhaps have been stopped by the obvious reflection that "Messiah" is not a proper name, and that "Messianist" could not be appropriated to a sect which had a Messiah of its own not acknowledged by the Jews, while the great body of Jews were themselves "messianists" in faith and expectation. Even now the proper way to say 'Christianity' in Hebrew in one word is נַצְרוּת, "Nazareneness."

I. 244 N. **12**

The words of Samuel imply the existence of manuscripts of Esther, but the book is not sacred scripture ("does not defile the hands"). The Talmud harmonizes the saying with the prevailing opinion about the inspiration of the book and saves Samuel's orthodoxy by distinguishing. In Sanhedrin 100a we read that Levi bar Samuel and Rab Huna bar Ḥiyya were once arranging the wrappers of the books in Rab's school; when they came to the roll of Esther they said, "This does not require a wrapper" (implying, it is not sacred scripture). It is possible, therefore, that Melito's informants (Vol. I, p. 246) may have entertained a similar opinion, which can hardly have been confined to the Babylonian schools.

I. 245 l. 10f.

See Note on I, 32, n. 2, above, p. 12.

I. 245 N. 13

On the victory over Nicanor and the appointment of an annual festival on the 13 of Adar, see 1 Macc. 7, 43, 49; 2 Macc. 15, 28, 36; Josephus, Antt. xii. 10, 5 § 409, § 412. It was given peculiar significance by the threats of Nicanor to destroy the Temple (1 Macc. 7, 33–35), which God thus signally delivered. Cf. Megillat Ta'anit, Adar 13; Jer. Megillah 70c; Jer. Ta'anit 66a, above (a passage utilized by the glossator in Meg. Ta'anit).

I. 247 l. 4

On the reading of Ezek. 1 in the synagogue, and on Ezek. 16, see note on Vol. I, p. 300 (below, p. 100). That, even after the labors of Hananiah ben Hezekiah in harmonizing it with the Pentateuch, Ezekiel was not regarded as a safe book for immature minds to meddle with is evident from the words of Jerome, who says that the third of the great prophets [Ezekiel], principia et finem tantis habet obscuritatibus involuta, ut apud Hebraeos istae partes cum exordio Geneseos ante annos triginta non legantur. — Epist. 53, ad Paulinum, Vallarsi I, 277.

I. 247 n. 1

By an inexact translation of Bacher's words "Ein Haupt der Schule Schammais" it was said in this note that Hananiah ben Hezekiah ben Garon "was the head of the school of Shammai in the generation before the fall of Jerusalem." More correctly (as in the second impression), he "was of the school of Shammai, and prominent in the generation before the fall of Jerusalem."

I. 247 N. 13 *bis*

A good example of the use of the verb for laying up treasures is the story of king Monobazos of Adiabene (Tos. Peah 4, 18, translated Vol. II, p. 91 f.). A particularly instructive illustration of laying aside things sacred to make them secure from profanation is M. Sanhedrin 10, 6 (Sifrè Deut. § 95) in the procedure for the execution of the ban on a city that has apostatized from the true religion (Deut. 13 13 ff.). The law prescribes that all the spoil of the city shall be collected in the public square and burned up; but "its spoil" does not include "the spoil of Heaven," i.e., things to which in any manner or degree sacredness attaches; hence the הקדשות that are in the city are to be redeemed, תרומות to be let decay, second tithe and sacred scriptures (כתבי הקדש) to be laid away (יגנזו; cf. Sanhedrin 112b, end).

The fact that the whole discussion is purely "academic" (Tos. Sanhedrin 14, 1; Sanhedrin 71a, עיר הנדחת לא היתה ולא עתידא ליהיות) does not make the example the less relevant. The book of cures which Hezekiah "laid away" (M. Pesahim 4, 9 *et alibi*) contained, we may suppose, not medicinal prescriptions, but formulas of incantation over the sick (perhaps to be employed with remedies), probably containing divine names, like that which Akiba denounces (Vol. II, p. 388). Reverence for the names of God is a probable reason for Rabban Gamaliel's ordering the masons who were making repairs on the temple-mount to wall up a Targum of Job which was shown him, and for his grandson's ordering such a Targum to be laid away (אף הוא צוה עליו וגנזו), Shabbat 115a. The identification of these two Gamaliels is a point of some uncertainty; the former incident falls at a time when the Temple was still standing; the younger Gamaliel is supposed to be living in Tiberias. For the present purpose the matter is not essential.

In Tos. Shabbat 13 (14), 5, where the question is about rescuing copies of sectarian books (הגליונים וספרי המינים) from a burning house, R. Jose the Galilean held that on a week day a man should tear out the mentions of God (האזכרות) and lay them by (וגונז), and burn the rest; while R. Tarfon would let them burn up, names of God and all, on week-day or Sabbath.

Modern writers of Hebrew "up to date" use גנוזים (ספרים) to express "Apocrypha" (in Protestant definition) and חיצונים for those books (e.g. Enoch) which have recently been labelled "Pseudepigrapha," ignoring the fact that the Rabbis were neither modern Protestants nor modern Jews, and had no corresponding categories.

The solitary instance that is adduced in support of the opinion that גנוזים was used of books excluded from the canon of Scripture is Abot de-R. Nathan, c. 1 (in both recensions printed by Schechter). The books named are Proverbs, the Song of Songs, and Ecclesiastes, from each of which quotations are made that sound questionable enough morally (Prov. 7, 7 ff., Cant. 7, 11–13, Eccles. 11, 9). According to the common text (Schechter's first recension) it is said that at the first these books were withdrawn as being (merely) proverbs and not belonging to the Scriptures, until the Men of the Great Synagogue came and explained them; while in the second recension this rehabilitation is attributed to Hezekiah's men (Prov. 25, 1): 'These also are Proverbs of Solomon which the men of Hezekiah, king of Judah, transcribed.' Inasmuch as the midrash turns on the word here translated 'transcribed' (העתיקו), it is probable that this ascription (in support of which Midrash Mishlè on the verse may be cited) is original, and that the author took העתיקו in the sense of 'consider deliberately, take time to it' (cf. Sifrè Num. § 78, ed. Friedmann, f. 20b), כל אחד ואחד מפורש במקומו (1 Chron. 4, 23) והדברים עתיקים; Sifrè Zuṭa on Num. 10, 29, בפני עצמו. According, to Abba Saul, לא שהמתינו אלא שפירשו, "they interpreted" — the whole passage is a play of midrashic ingenuity on the precept of the Men of the Great Synagogue היו מתונים בדין. Since the passage is apparently more frequently cited than read, it may not be amiss to quote the relevant part here: בראשונה היו אומרים משלי ושיר השירים וקהלת גנוזים היו שהם היו אומרים משלות ואינן מן הכתובים ועמדו וגנזו אותם עד שבאו אנשי כנסת הגדולה ופירשו אותם [Rec. B: למה נאמר אלא שאני אומר במשלות ושיר השירים וקהלת גנוזים היו עד שהן בכתובים]. Cf. Shabbat 30b.

It is evident that we are not dealing here with tradition, but with exegetical invention. The difficulties which the rabbis found in these books must, they thought, have been felt from the beginning, and therefore the men of old times "arose and withdrew them, until they should be explained." — An example of such an explanatory gloss which has made its way into the text are the last verses of Ecclesiastes (12, 13 f.).

In many cases this storing away involved withdrawing from circulation or use, for example, Bible manuscripts which had become imperfect, or were not copied according to rule, and other writings or inscriptions in which names of God (אזכרות) occurred. See Bacher as cited in Vol. I, p. 247, n. 3.

The Protestant use of "Apocrypha" is ultimately derived from Jerome, who after enumerating the twenty-two books of the Hebrew Bible, writes: Hic prologus . . . omnibus libris quos de Hebraeo vertimus in Latinum convenire potest, ut scire valeamus, quidquid extra hos est, inter apocrypha esse ponendum (Prologus Galeatus, prefixed to his translation of Samuel and Kings), and owes its currency to Luther's segregation of these books. No corresponding category existed among the Jews, and the use of the word in the Greek Fathers is different.

I. 248 l. 20 ff.

A description and a very unfavorable estimate of Jewish exegesis, both rabbinical and Alexandrian (Philo) is given in Bousset-Gressmann, pp. 160 f., with the recognition, however, that such methods are the inevitable consequence of the doctrine of inspired Scriptures, and that the Christian church has done the same kind of thing from the beginning. Modern philological exegesis and historical criticism are very new things.

I. 248, top.

Ginzberg, Eine unbekannte jüdische Sekte, p. 246, n. 2.

I. 249 N. 14

The seven rules of Hillel are enumerated in Tos. Sanhedrin 7, 11, and in the Introduction to Sifra (ed. Weiss f. 3a); the thirteen of R. Ishmael, Sifra, l.c. (f. 1a ff.); cf. Mekilta de-R. Simeon ben Yoḥai on Exod. 21, 1 (ed. Hoffmann, p. 117) — "delivered to Moses at Sinai." The Thirteen Rules were taken up into the morning prayer, where they have a place already in the Siddur of Rab Amram (Baer, p. 53 f.; Singer, p. 13 f.; Abudarham gives examples of their employment). The thirty-two rules ascribed to R. Eliezer son of R. Jose the Galilean are not mentioned in the Talmud, though some of them are undoubtedly old. In the current editions of the Babylonian Talmud these rules are enumerated and illustrated in the supplementary matter at the end of Berakot, from the Sefer Keritut of Samson of Chinon (13/14 century). On all these rules and their application see Strack, Einleitung in Talmud und Midrasch, 5 ed. pp. 95–109, with the literature there cited; Mielziner, Introduction to the Talmud, 2 ed. (1903), pp. 115 ff ("Legal Hermeneutics of the Talmud"). That a good book on Talmudic hermeneutics and methodology should not be forgotten, let me add A. G. Waehner, Antiquitates Ebraeorum (Göttingen, 1743), I. 396 ff. (the Thirty-two Rules, chiefly following the Halikot 'Olam of Jeshua b. Joseph Halevi — 15th century); pp. 422 ff. (the Thirteen Rules). On the technical terms in the latter, Bacher's Terminologie I. may profitably be consulted.

I. 249 N 15

On Philo's premises and method it is sufficient to refer the reader to James Drummond, Philo Judaeus (1888), Vol. I, pp. 16–23, with examples *passim*.

I. 251 N. 16

For the phrase תורה שבעל פה ("the Torah transmitted by word of mouth") and its first occurrence in our sources (Shabbat 31a — Shammai and Hillel) see Bacher, Tannaiten I², 76, n. 5 (against Weiss, Dor. I, 1 n.); Bacher, in Jewish Quarterly Review, XX, 595; Tradition und Tradenten, p. 22. Cf. Sifrè Deut. § 351 — Rabban Gamaliel

— two תורות given to Israel, אחת בכתב ואחת בעל פה. On the question why Mishna, Talmud, and Haggadah were transmitted only orally see on Vol. I, p. 254, Note 17, below.

I. 252 n. 1

Inasmuch as the high priest might be unacquainted with the complicated ritual, he was instructed in preparation for it, and put under the direction of an expert Master of Ceremonies.

I. 254 N. 17

Inasmuch as the revelation to Moses was complete, the question arose why only part of it was written down and the rest — the larger part — transmitted orally. Substantially the same answer is given in several places. The fundamental text for the *two* Torot is Exod. 34, 27: 'And the Lord said unto Moses, Write thou these words, for after the tenor of (על פי) these words I have made a covenant with thee and with Israel,' [1] and with them the words of Hosea (8, 12) are usually quoted: 'Should I write for him most of my law, they (the precepts) would be esteemed as a foreigners'. "When God (the Holy One, blessed is He) came to give the Law, he recited it to Moses successively — the Bible (מקרא), and the Mishnah, and the Agada, and the Talmud, as it is said, 'And God spoke all these words' (Exod. 20 1) — even what an attentive pupil will ask his teacher. . . . When Moses had learned it, God said to him, Go and teach it to my sons [Israel]. Moses said to Him, Lord of the World, write it for Thy sons! He answered, I should like to give it to them in writing, but that I foresee that the Gentiles are going to rule over them, and take it from them, and (then) my sons would be like the Gentiles. But give them the Bible in writing, and the Mishnah and the Agada and the Talmud by word of mouth . . . for these will make a difference between Israel and the Gentiles" (Tanḥuma ed. Buber, Ki tissa § 17). It is a breach of the covenant either to read (recite) the Scripture from memory or to commit the traditional law to writing (ibid. § 18, Temurah 14b). Compare also Tanḥuma ed. Buber, Wayyera § 6 (with reference to Targum). The passage in Ki tissa is reproduced with small variations in Exod. R. c. 47 (at the beginning).

In Pesiḳta Rabbati God declined to give the Mishnah in writing as Moses desired, because he foresaw that the Gentiles would translate the Torah and be in the habit of reading it (publicly) in Greek, and say, They (the Jews) are not Israel. God said to him, O Moses,

[1] Translation of the Jewish Publication Society.

The Gentiles will be saying, *We* are Israel,[1] we are the children of God, and it will be an even thing. Then God will say to the Gentiles, How can you say that you are my sons? I do not recognize any except him in whose possession my secret is (*μυστήριον* equivalent to סוד, cf. סוד י"י ליראיו, Psalm 25, 14); *he* is my son. They (the Gentiles) say to Him, What is this secret of Thine? He replies, It is the Mishnah. See also Jer. Peah ii. (6, f.17a). "What would be the difference between us and the Gentiles? One party would bring in their books, and the other their books; one party would bring in their parchments and the other their parchments." Pesikta Rabbati, Perek 5, ed. Friedmann, p. 14b.

In this midrash — most explicitly in its later forms — there is plain reference to the Christian empire, and echoes of controversy with Christians who made the Old Testament their own and claimed to be the true Israel, the children of God. It should be needless to say that the reasons why tradition was an unwritten law lie in the nature of tradition itself, not in such considerations as are presented in the midrash; but it is true that when Gentile Christians appropriated the Scriptures, interpreted them as *Christian* Scriptures from the beginning, read them in Greek in their churches, based on them their pretensions, and sometimes (as in the Epistle of Barnabas) denied that the Jews had ever had any rights in them, Mishnah and Talmud remained the exclusive possession of the Jews, and this unwritten tradition was the specific difference of Judaism.

I. 254 l. 8–10

See below, Note **20** (on Vol. I, p. 256).

I. 255 N. **18**

See on Vol. I, p. 31 f. (above, p. 11 f). In the letter of Sherira Gaon (ed. Lewin, p. 73) we read: When Ezra went up (and Zerubbabel) from Babylonia, and the Golah with them, and they built the temple, and there were there the heads of the Sanhedrin such as Simeon the Righteous and Antigonus of Socho and the rest of those Pairs (זוגות), etc. — French recension "those generations" (דורות).

As an example of the use of this chain of tradition reference may be made to Jer. Peah 17a (in the Mishnah, 2, 6). In a question in which R. Simeon of Mizpah and Rabban Gamaliel were concerned, "Nuhum the scrivener (הליבלר) averred, I received it from Rabbi Measha (my teacher), who received it from his father, who received it from

[1] Tanhuma ed. Buber, Wayyera § 6, "We also are Israel."

the Pairs, who received it from the Prophets, an Halakah (given) to Moses from Sinai (God)." The case is of especial interest because this testimony is from a time when the temple was still standing. See further on Vol. I, p. 256, Note **19**.

I. 256 N. **19**

See W. Bacher, "Satzung von Sinai," in Studies in Jewish Literature issued in honor of Professor Kaufmann Kohler (1913), pp. 56–70, where all the known occurrences of this phrase are collected and discussed.

I. 256 N. **20**

The legend about Moses and Akiba is attributed to Rab (early third century, a frequent reporter of Palestinian tradition): In the hour when Moses ascended to high heaven he found the Holy One — blessed is He — sitting and weaving crowns for the letters (putting on them the ornamental Tagin). He said, Lord of the World, who hinders Thee (from giving the Law without these)? He (God) replied, There is a man who will live ever so many generations hence, named Akiba ben Joseph, who will derive from every single stroke (literally 'thorn') heaps and heaps [playing on the words of Canticles, 5, 11, cf. 'Erubin 21b end] of legal norms (Halakahs). Moses said, Lord of the World, let me see him! God said, Turn and go back He went and took a seat eight rows back (where Akiba and his future disciples were sitting), but he did not understand what they were saying, and he became faint. When he (Akiba) came to one point, his disciples said to him, Rabbi, where did you get that? He answered, (It is) an Halakah to Moses from Sinai, whereat Moses was reassured. He turned and went to the Holy One, blessed is He, and said, Lord of the World, Thou hast a man like that, and Thou givest the Law by me"! Then he asked to be shown Akiba's reward. He was told to look behind him, and saw how the executioners were carding Akiba's flesh with (iron) claws. (Cf. the account of Akiba's martyrdom in Berakot 61b, below.) Whereupon he exclaimed, "Such learning and such a reward!"

A variant of this story in the Alphabet of R. Akiba (Jellinek, Bet ha-Midrasch, III, 44), tells how the angel who presides over all learning and insight showed Moses myriads of scholars, sanhedrins, and scribes sitting and interpreting the meaning of Torah, Bible, Mishnah, Midrash, Halakahs and Agadas, etc., and saying, "An Halakah to Moses from Sinai."

I. 257 N. 21

The branches of a complete education were: the Bible (Miḳra, "Reading," where we say Scripture, "Writing"); Midrash, exegesis; Halakot, concisely formulated rules for every sphere of life; Haggadot, edifying applications of Scripture illustrated from biography or legend (*exempla*) and by parables (invented comparisons). See Vol. I, p. 319 ff., and for a fuller exposition, Bacher, Terminologie I, under the several terms (pp. 103–105; 43 f.; 33–37; cf. Tannaiten I², 475–485). The first included the learning of Biblical Hebrew, a language widely different in vocabulary and syntax from the Aramaic mother-tongue, and even from the contemporary Hebrew "language of the learned." This ancient language could be learned only from a living teacher: dictionaries, grammars, commentaries — the whole apparatus which with us supplements the instruction of the teacher or is substituted for it — did not exist. As the Bible was written then, no one could even pronounce intelligently a passage which he did not rightly understand, and the traditional pronunciation was itself an interpretation. The learned man might read and interpret differently, sometimes taking liberties even with the letter of the text (אל תקרי, and the like), but the learner had first to learn the tradition to know enough even to depart from it. — Midrash is what we call exegesis, especially the exegesis which tries to penetrate beneath the literal sense (פשט) to discover a profounder meaning or lesson, comparing scripture with scripture according to its own hermeneutic rules. This exegesis may be either juristic, applied to the laws in the Pentateuch for the purpose of deriving from them the definite rule to go by (Halakic Midrash), or educational and homiletic, drawing from the Scripture religious and moral lessons and enforcing them by religious motives (Haggadic Midrash). — The succinct rules (Halakot) were memorized, and it was expected that they should be reproduced with verbal accuracy. — The Haggadot were chiefly sermonic material out of which the synagogue homilists brought forth in their discourses things old and new, including their own contributions.

It is perhaps worth while to correct here a common misapprehension of the word 'midrash' and of the nature of the thing. Some Christian writers use the word midrash as equivalent to legend, and even define it thus, having especially in mind the fictional element in legend. The origin of this error is probably the use of the word מדרש in 2 Chron. 24, 27 (cf. 13, 22), the legendary character of the source (or sources) cited under this title in the judgment of critics, and the assumption that the rabbinical use of the term was similar. See Budde, "Vermutungen zum Midrasch des Buches der Könige," Zeitschrift für die alttestamentliche Wissenschaft, XII (1892), 37–51; cf. Driver, Introduction to the Literature of the Old Testament, 1891, p. 397. Driver, op. cit. 529, says, "Hagadah is a synonym of Midrash." When these scholars call Tobit and Susanna "Midrashim" they mean only that they are fictions, which would be as intelligible to most of their readers in English or in German as in imaginary Hebrew. As a matter of fact, the oldest rabbinical use of the name Midrash is for the juristic exegesis of the legislative parts of the Pentateuch, which belongs with the Halakah in distinction from Haggadah. Bacher, Terminologie I, p. 43. — On the *midrash sefer hammelakim* in 2 Chron. 24, 27 reference should be made also to Kuenen, Onderzoek[2] (1887), I, 493.

In the passage from which I set out (Sifrè § 48, ed. Friedmann f. 84b), no one familiar with this literature will be likely to doubt that halakic Midrash, such as is found in Sifra and Sifrè, is meant. See D. Hoffmann, Zur Einleitung in die halachischen Midraschim, 1887. In the Tannaite (Halakic) Midrash, the word *midrashot* is a common equivalent for the biblical *ḥuḳḳim*; for instances see Bacher *op. cit.* p. 103 f. A good example is Sifra on Lev. 26, 46 (ed. Weiss f. 112c). The Haggadot are also derived from the Bible, or connected with it by exegetical processes, and thus there is a Midrash Haggadah as well as a Midrash Halakah (Jewish Encyclopedia, VIII, 550–569, 569–572). All these belonged to the Jewish science of tradition (Mishnah) in distinction from Biblical learning (Miḳra), but the traditional exegesis (Midrash) connects the two fields.

In Sifrè Deut. § 48 and (with a text in some respects preferable) in Midrash Tannaim on Deut. 11, 22 (ed. Hoffmann, p. 41 f.) may be found interesting remarks on the subject of study (primarily biblical study), and sound paedagogic observations on the acquisition, cultivation, and retention of learning. Learning is as hard to get as gold and as easy to lose as a glass vessel (by breaking). That the loss is no trifling matter is illustrated by a parable: A king had snared a bird and gave it to his slave to keep for the young prince, warning him, If you let it get away, do not think you have lost a bird worth a few cents, but it is as if you had lost your life, as it is said, 'For it (the law) is no vain thing for you, for it is your life' (Deut. 32, 47).

Learning, like wealth, is accumulated little by little — a verse or two a day, a paragraph or two a week, a chapter or two a month, so in time a man becomes rich (in learning). It requires constant and laborious cultivation; the proverbs about the indolent and negligent husbandman (e.g. Prov. 24, 30 f.) are applied to the slothful scholar who by neglect of study lets his field and vineyard get overgrown with thistles. The utmost accuracy is required; a man may forget two or three words and get all astray in consequence, while if he forgets day by day as regularly as he learns he will have nothing at all. Learning is like a field or a vineyard. The acquisition of it is only a beginning; that it may yield anything and even that it may not go back to the wild, it must be assiduously cultivated. — There is much else in this passage, e.g., that the learning of the modest scholar (Vol. II, p. 245 f.) like wine grows better with maturity, which, being the result of experience, might with advantage be pondered in these days of educational theory, for instance, the native difference in capacity — the pupil of good ability is like a sponge which takes up all that is offered; another is like a bunch of tow whose absorbent capacity is limited. Nor was retentive and exact memory the only faculty cultivated; minute investigation and acute discrimination were necessary, especially in matters of licit and illicit, clean and unclean; otherwise a man might break through the bounds set by the authority of the learned, with disastrous consequences. Under these conditions independence of judgement is commended. In these pursuits the sons of great men or of scholarly elders have no precedence, much less prerogative; in the Law all men are on an equality, learning is a pure democracy.

I. 259 N. 22

On the authority of these enactments see Vol. I, p. 262, and Note 27 there.

I. 259 N. 23

On the powers of a rabbinical court and its limitations see the Jewish Encyclopedia, s.v. "Authority." In M. 'Eduyot, 1, 5, it is laid down that one such court cannot abrogate the enactment of a former court unless it is superior to the latter in learning and in numbers, and this principle is alleged in several other places (e.g. Giṭṭin 36b). The whole history of Judaism seems to show that, whatever may have been the theory, the authorities of every generation felt warranted in adapting the working of the law to the changing conditions of life. See Weiss, Dor (4 ed., 1904), II, 57; Solomon Zucrow, Adjustment of Law to Life in Rabbinic Literature (Boston, 1928), chapter iv.

I. 259 N. 24

For particular occasions in connection with which Psalm 119, 126 is thus quoted in the Mishnah see Vol. I, p. 427. On the transposition of the clauses, Jer. Berakot, 14c–d: רבי נתן מסרס קראי. A very drastic example of doing something for the Lord, with quotation of this verse, is found in Yoma 69a, end. Other occurrences, Tamid 27b, Giṭṭin 60a, Temurah 14b, *et alibi*.

I. 260 N 25

The prevailing spelling seems to be פרחבול, though פרוסבול is not infrequent. The word is obviously foreign, and etymological conjectures have been rife from the days of the Babylonian Amoraim (Giṭṭin 36b–37a) down; for a survey of those proposed in ancient and modern times see L. Blau in the monograph cited below. Formally it corresponds to προσβολή, but the difficulty has been to find any meaning of this not uncommon Greek word which would be applicable to a legal instrument such as the Jewish Prosbul (or Prosbol). Greek papyri from Egypt have, however, recently afforded several instances of the use of the word in a technical juridical sense. Preisigke (Wörterbuch der griechischen Papyrusurkunden, *s.v.*), on the basis of studies by Mitteis of the legal documents in which the word occurs, defines it: "Eigentumszuschlag des Pfandes im Vollstreckungsverfahren." In the light of this new material Ludwig Blau has re-examined the whole subject of the nature and legal effect of the instrument introduced by Hillel, and of other rabbinical remedies — such as the delivery of a pledge, which might be of minimal value; or the deposit of the obligation (note) with the court, which could collect the debt at any time — for the evil to meet which the Prosbol was devised: "Prosbol im Lichte der griechischen Papyri und der Rechtsgeschichte" (reprinted from Festschrift zum 50 Jährigen Bestehen des Franz-Josef Landesrabiner-Schule. Budapest, 1927. Blau thinks it possible that in Hillel's time (under Herod) the instrument may not only have had a Greek name derived from Hellenistic-Egyptian law, but have been written in Greek, for purposes of record. Earlier literature on the Prosbol is listed at the end of his study.

I. 261 n. 1

See Vol. I, p. 262, n. 1 and Note on Vol. I, p. 85 (above, pp. 32 ff).

I. 261 N 26

A striking instance of this kind is narrated of Johanan ben Zakkai and a Sadducean high priest about the burning of the red cow, Tos. Parah 3, 7f. (cf. the corresponding Mishnah).

I. 262 N **27**

Jer. Berakot 3b, below; Jer. Sanhedrin 30a (Bacher, Pal. Amoräer III, 638, n. 1). The man who 'despises the word of the Lord' (Num. 15, 31) and makes void his commandments, etc., is interpreted by R. Nathan of one who pays no attention to the Mishnah (tradition). Sanhedrin 99a, below. In the case of the "contumacious elder" (זקן ממרא) the Mishnah (Sanhedrin 11, 3) says: חומר בדברי סופרים מדברי תורה, "The matter is more serious concerning words of the Scribes than words of the Law." The illustrative example is: If he says, "No Tefillin!" he is let go; but if he says, "*Five* compartments," he is guilty. The former is contrary to the words of the law (Deut. 6, 8, etc.); the latter contrary to the words of the Scribes, who, from the four occurrences of the word טוטפות learned that there should be *four*; the offender thus violated the law לא תוסיף (Deut. 13, 1). The biblical authority for implicit obedience to the enactments of a rabbinical court is Deut. 17, 11. On the subject in general see Krochmal, "Moreh Nebuke ha-Zeman" (ed. Zunz, 1851), p. 167 f.

It should be understood that in such cases as are here contemplated the interpretation of the Scribes is implicitly contained in the words of the law from which they derive it, and therefore carries the obligation of the Law itself. There are many commandments in the Pentateuch for which neither mode nor measure is laid down; these were left for the Scribes and the learned to discover and define so that whatever was done should be done right, that is, according to the intention of the lawgiver. Large, even extravagant, assertions of rabbinical authority are natural, but the supremacy of the Biblical law is not challenged. [See the discussion, Yebamot 89b–90b. L. G.]

I. 263 N **28**

"Torah" is a generic term for instruction in religion (including morals) rather than commandment (מצוה) or statute (חק); both of which are indeed included in it, but as particular species or forms may be distinguished within it (not *from* it). In Tanḥuma ed. Buber, Re'eh 1 (on Deut. 11, 26) exception is taken to Asaph's appropriation of the name Torah for his own instruction (Psalm 78, 1, האזינו עמי תורתי), and Solomon's (Prov. 4, 2, כי לקח טוב נתתי לכם תורתי אל תעזבו. Israel is supposed to say to Asaph: "Is there then another Torah, that thou sayest 'Listen, my people, to *my* Torah'? We received it long ago from Sinai." Asaph replies: "The wicked of Israel (פושעי ישראל) say that the Prophets and the Ketubim are not Torah; but we do not believe them" (quoting Dan. 9, 10, to prove that the Prophets and the Ketubim, among which the Book of Daniel stands, are Torah).

I. 264 l. 5

Compare Ezra 7, 14 (בדת אלהך די בידך) with verse 25 (כחכמת אלהך די בידך).

I. 264 N **29**

See C. L. W. Grimm, Kurzgefasstes Exegetisches Handbuch zu den Apokryphen (1857), IV, 304 f.; Philo, De Congressu, c. 14 § 79 (Mangey I, 530); Cicero, De Officiis, ii. 2, 5; cf. Seneca, Ep. 89, 5. The expansion of this definition by the addition of the clause, "and of their causes," which Seneca thinks superfluous, perhaps comes from Poseidonios (see Karl Reinhardt, Poseidonios, 1921, p. 58).

I. 265 N **30**

See Ecclus. 24, 28–34, and the translator's preface.

I. 265 N **31**

See also Sifrè Deut. § 309 (ed. Friedmann f. 134a), § 317 (f. 135b), all quoting Prov. 8, 22. On the Law and Wisdom see Syriac Baruch 51, 3 f. (cf. Zech. 7, 12); 77, 16.

I. 265 N **32**

Tanḥuma ed. Buber, Noah § 2; ibid. Bereshit § 5 = Bereshit Rabbah 1, 1; 8, 2; Pesiḳta ed. Buber f. 44b.; Shabbat 63a, 89a. References to Prov. 8, 22 could be multiplied almost indefinitely.

I. 266 N **33**

See Vol. I, p. 526, and below, p. 161.

I. 266 N **34**

Thus the words עד דכה (Psalm 90, 3) are interpreted by R. Meir, Jer. Ḥagigah 77c, top; Eccles. R. on Eccles. 7, 8; cf. Pesaḥim 54a; Nedarim 39b. To this interpretation Jerome also is a witness in his Psalterium juxta Hebraeos, "Convertis hominem usque ad contritionem."

I. 267 l. 7

Instead of *Omen* read *Umman*.

I. 268 N **36**

The world created for the sake of the Torah. See Vol. I, p. 383; L. Ginzberg, Legends of the Jews, V, 67 f.

I. 268 N 37

In Jer. Ta'anit f. 68a with the addition: "and all three of them are contained in one verse (Isa. 51, 15), 'And I have put my words in thy mouth' — this is the Law — 'and in the shadow of my hand I have sheltered thee' — this is personal kindness — 'to plant the heavens and to found the earth' — this is the sacrifices," etc.

I. 268 N 38

The way in which Moses begins the Law with the creation of the world is most remarkable, *ὡς καὶ τοῦ κόσμου τῷ νόμῳ καὶ τοῦ νόμου τῷ κόσμῳ συνᾳδοντος καὶ τοῦ νομίμου ἀνδρὸς εὐθὺς ὄντος κοσμοπολίτου πρὸς τὸ βούλημα τῆς φύσεως τὰς πράξεις ἀπευθύνοντος, καθ' ἣν καὶ ὁ σύμπας κόσμος διοικεῖται.* Life in conformity with the law was therefore, in Stoic phrase, "life according to nature."

I. 269 l. 28

The 'jot' (*ἰῶτα*) of the familiar English version is the *yod*, the smallest letter in the alphabet used by the Jews in Jesus' time. The 'tittle' (*κεραία*) was one of the pen-strokes (*ḳeren*, 'horn,' or *ṣiyun*, 'dagger'), forming the 'crowns' (*tagin*) with which some letters of the alphabet were ornamented in Scrolls of the Law. In Menaḥot 29b (in the story of Akiba, above, p. 76; see also 'Erubin 21b, end) the word *ḳoṣ* ('thorn') is used. It seems probable that these names for the ornamental pen-strokes that made up the 'crowns' were used indiscriminately; but *ḳoṣ* came to be associated especially with the pen-stroke on the letter *yōd*, a single small stroke, or spur, pendent from the head of the letter (see Maḥzor Vitry, plate facing p. 800, from the Sefer ha-Tagin, see ibid. p. 674; or the edition of that book, Paris, 1860). In Jer. Sanhedrin 20c (cf. Lev. R. 19, 2) Solomon, who multiplied wives, horses, silver and gold, contrary to Deut. 17, 17, eradicated the letter *yōd* in לא ירבה; the *yōd* became his accuser, and the Book of Deuteronomy prosecuted the case before God. In the same connection in Lev. R., R. Zeira (playing on Cant. 5, 11) says: Even things which you regard as *ḳōṣīn* (insignificant strokes) in the Law are great hills on hills (*teltele teltalīm*), capable of destroying the whole world (and making it a perpetual ruin (תל עולם)." Compare also the parallel Exod. R. 6, 1: God says: Solomon and a thousand like him may be busy abrogating, but not one *ḳōṣ* of thee (*sc.* the *yōd*) shall be abrogated." (For some variety of readings in these passages, see Kohut, Aruch Completum, *s.v.*, VII, 171 f.).

I. 270 l. 1f.

Compare Tanḥuma ed. Buber, on Deut. 11, 26 (Re'eh § 1): כל המבטל דברי תורה כאלו כופר בהקב"ה. Matt. 5, 19 ('Whoever therefore shall abrogate one of these very least commandments,' etc.) represents the attitude of the strictly observant party among the disciples of Jesus, perhaps reinforced by some believing Pharisees. In direct contradiction to this attitude is Mark 7, 19, where Jesus is understood to do away with all the so-called dietary laws, 'making all foods clean.' This interpretation, however, is a palpable gloss which, whether we read *καθαρίζων* or *καθάριζον*, refuses to be construed with the sentence to which it is appended, and is, moreover, foreign to the matter in controversy. Into the further question whether the issue itself (נטילת ידים) can have been raised in the lifetime of Jesus for him and his disciples we have no occasion to enter here. Reference may be made to Büchler in the Expository Times, XXI (1909–1910), 34–40, and to the extended discussion of the whole passage in Montefiore, "The Synoptic Gospels" (2 ed. 1927), I, 129–166, where other recent writers are quoted.

I. 271 l. 3

עתיד לבוא is often merely the immediate future as opposed to the immediate past (שעבר), e.g. Tos. Nazirut 3, 11. Cf. Mekilta, Yitro 5 (ed. Friedmann p. 66b; ed. Weiss p. 74a).

I. 272 N 41

In the Hebrew edition (Jerusalem, 1927), p. 333 f.

I. 272 n. 4

Compare the Revelation of John 21, 2 ff.

I. 273 N 42

Laws prescribing personal duties (מצות הגוף), including what we call morals, are binding everywhere. Laws dependent on residence in the Land (תלויים בארץ), are for the most part expressly connected with the Land, and are chiefly concerned with the religious taxation (see Vol. II, pp. 71 ff.); the rules about the 'Orlah (Lev. 19, 23–25) and Kilaim (Lev. 19, 19; Deut. 22, 9–11) are to be observed everywhere, and R. Eliezer adds the prohibition of eating of the new crop of grain before the Feast of Unleavened Bread (Lev. 23, 14). Sifrè Deut. § 44; Sifra, 'Emor Pereḳ 11; M. Ḳiddushin 1, 9).

I. 273 n. 2

See L. Ginzberg, Legends of the Jews, V, 228 (n. 111).

I. 273 N **43**

God says: "In this world I have given to you the Law, and individuals work laboriously in it, but in the future (Tanḥuma, "in the world to come") I am going to teach it to all Israel, and they will learn it and will not forget it (Jer. 31, 33)." Pesiḳta ed. Buber, f. 107a; Tanḥuma ed. Buber, Yitro § 13 (f. 38b). And again God says to Abraham who observed even the minute deductions: "Thou hast taught thy sons Law (Torah) in this world, and in the world to come I, in my glory, will teach them the Law (Isa. 54, 13)." Tanḥuma ed. Buber, Wayyiggash § 12, end. Another notion is that God gives lessons to the (souls of the) righteous in heaven, to which even the ministering angels, who occupy an adjacent suite in heaven, are not admitted. Jer. Shabbat 8d.

God is not like an earthly ruler who issues edicts and commands others to obey them, but does not observe them himself unless he chooses. "God does a thing, and commands Israel to do and observe the same." Exod. R. 30, 6; cf. Lev. R. 35, 3. These are homiletic conceits rather than serious conceptions; in Lev. R., l.c., God (in Gen. 18) sets the example of showing the honor to the aged which he enjoins in Lev. 19, 32. The picture of God teaching the Law, like the head of a rabbinical academy, as it is said (see Baba Mesi'a 85b, 86a), has been the occasion of some rather witless pleasantries from Eisenmenger down. But instruction in religion is not the most unbecoming occupation that can be imagined for God in heaven or in the World to Come.

I. 274 l. 14f.

Commandments to Adam are mentioned (but not specified) in Sifrè Num. § 111.

I, 274 N **44**

Some of the chief difficulties of this kind, things to which the "evil impulse" and the Gentiles raised objections, were the prohibited "mixtures" (e.g. in stuffs, *sha'ṭnez*, linsey-woolsey, or in animal kinds such as breeding mules), the scapegoat of the Day of Atonement, and the red cow (*parah*) and the purification by its ashes in water (see Vol. II, p. 7). It is observed that it is precisely in these cases that the word "statute" is used. To Moses God says: I will reveal to thee the meanings of the law, but for others it is a statute. Then from Zech. 14, 6, it is deduced that things that are covered up from men in this world will in the future be made as transparent as a globe (of crystal). (Pesiḳta ed. Buber, f. 38b–40a).

I, 274 **N 45**

For the numerous parallels and the variations in them see Theodor's notes in his edition of Bereshit Rabbah 16, 6 (on Gen. 2, 16). An older tradition adduces these commandments (except "courts" or "judges" as examples of ordinances of God (Lev. 18, 4) the obligation of which is so evident that, if they were not written in the law, they would have to be written in it on rational grounds. Sifra, Aḥarè Perek̤ 13, ed. Weiss f. 86a. On the commandments given by Noah to his sons see also Jubilees 7, 20 ff.; on the prohibition of blood (Gen. 9, 4) ibid. 6, 7–10; 7, 29–33. See Jewish Encyclopedia, "Laws, Noachian" (VII, 648 ff.).

I, 275 n. 1

The meaning of the Mishnah is that the Law was made binding on the Israelites by the revelation at Sinai, but when Moses put the Torah in order, he wrote this prohibition only in connection with the occasion that gave rise to it (Bertinoro). Whatever commandments had been previously known and observed by the patriarchs were renewed at Sinai (Vol. I, p. 276).

I, 276 **N 46**

The '*erūb tabshīlīn* ("combination of cooked food") is as minute a point of the traditional law as could well be imagined. In case a holy day (יום טוב) is immediately followed by the weekly Sabbath, the cooking of a dish intended for the Sabbath is "combined," on the eve of the holy day, with the cooking for the meals of that day; the preparation for the Sabbath having thus been begun, it may be completed on the holy day (on which the prohibition of work is not so sweeping as on the Sabbath). (M. Beṣah 2.) On the '*erub ḥaserot* ("combination of domiciles") see Vol. II, p. 31, and note thereon, below, p. 172. On the sacrifices offered with correct ritual, and in general the observance of the law, by the righteous of ancient times (Adam, Psalm 69, 32; Noah, the Patriarchs), see Lev. R. 2, 10. That Abraham kept all the law before it was given (at Sinai) the rabbis found expressly affirmed in Gen. 26, 5, which indeed is comprehensive enough; (see Ḳiddushin 82a; cf. Yoma 28b; Lev. R. 2, 10). It was held that, in connection with the covenant sacrifice (Gen. 15, 9 f.), God showed Abraham all the piacula detailed in Lev. 4 f., except the sin-offering of the pauper (Lev. 5, 11); Simeon ben Yoḥai did not admit even this exception (Lev. R. 3, 3).

I, 278 N **48**

'The Lord came from Sinai' (Deut. 33, 2). When God (המקום) was revealed to give the Law to Israel, he was not revealed to Israel alone, but to all the peoples. Sifrè Deut. § 343; cf. Mekilta, Baḥodesh 5 (ed. Friedmann f. 67a; ed. Weiss f. 74a — the beginning of the story, in which Balaam figures, ibid. 1, Friedmann f. 57a; Weiss f. 65b). The (heathen) peoples were called that they might have no occasion of complaint against God (השכינה), saying, If we had been called, we would have taken it (the law) upon us. They were called, and did not take it upon them. . . . He was revealed to the children of Esau, the wicked, and said to them, Do you receive the law? They answered: What is written in it? He said to them: 'Thou shalt not kill.' They replied: This is our inheritance which our father left us, as it is said, 'By thy sword thou shalt live' (Gen. 27, 40). He was revealed to the children of Ammon and Moab, and said to them: Do you receive the law? They replied: What is written in it? He said to them: Thou shalt not commit adultery. They said to him: But we are all sprung from adultery, as it is written (Gen. 19, 36); and how can we accept it? He was revealed to the sons of Ishmael, and said to them: Do you receive the law? They said to him: What is written in it? He said to them: Thou shalt not steal. They replied: With this blessing our father was blessed, as it is written, 'He shall be a wild ass of a man, his hand against every man' (Gen. 16, 12), and it is written (Gen. 40, 15, where Joseph says, 'I was stolen,' viz. by the Ishmaelites.) And when he came to Israel, 'from his right hand proceeded a fiery law unto them' (Deut. 33, 2), they all opened their mouth and said: 'All that the Lord has said we will do and heed.' — See also Midrash Tannaim, ed. Hoffmann, p. 209 f.

I, 279 N **51**

This passage in Sifra (see Vol. I, p. 142) is presumably from the school of R. Ishmael. Bacher (Tannaiten II, 31, n. 2) thinks that the name "Jeremiah" is a mistake for "Meir." A Tanna Jeremiah is quoted in Mekilta Bo 2, and Beshallaḥ 1, as well as in the places cited by Bacher. On the attitude toward proselytes see Vol. I, pp. 341 ff.

I, 280 l. 12 ff.

It should be remembered that we posess no sources in which the Sadducees speak for themselves; all the testimonies about them come from unfriendly witnesses. In the current editions of the Talmud the matter is still further confused by the substitutions of the censorship or to forestall the censorship, which frequently put "Sadducee" in the place of names like *Mīn* that might be suspicious or obnoxious to Christians. An enumeration of the reported differences between the Sadducees and the Pharisees in the interpretation and application of the laws, with references, is given, e.g., by Weiss (Dor, 4 ed. I, 111–113) and by Klausner, ישו הנוצרי (ed. 1, 1922) pp. 224–227 (in Danby's translation, pp. 219 f.).

For a presentation of the historical and logical attitude of the Sadducees towards the law reference may be made to J. Z. Lauterbach, "The Sadduccees and Pharisees," in Studies in Jewish Literature issued in honor of Professor Kaufmann Kohler (1913), especially pp. 180–190.

It is also to be said that, if the Sadducees as a party among the Jews ceases to be significant after the fall of Jerusalem, their way of thinking did not become extinct; it was perpetuated, and had, if not a survival, at least a notable revival in the Karaites from the eighth century on.

I, 281 (Chapter v)

On the Synagogue see in general S. Krauss, Synagogale Altertümer, 1922. — The extensive literature is cited at the beginning of the main divisions of the volume and in the footnotes to the text. — For the worship of the Synagogue from the dawn of our knowledge to modern times, I. Elbogen, Der jüdische Gottesdienst in seiner geschichtlichen Entwickelung, 1913.

I, 283 N **52**

For opinions and discussions about the antiquity and origin of the Synagogue, see S. Krauss, *op. cit.*, pp. 52–102.

Note may be made here of the names given to it in Hebrew and Greek sources. The usual name in the former is כנסת, a word in itself applicable to any 'gathering,' or 'assembly,' of which the Greek equivalent is συναγωγή, from which the name "synagogue" in English and other modern languages is derived (through the Latin). The locality, or building where such a gathering was customarily held was בית כנסת ("meeting house"), but it was not always necessary to be so specific, and כנסת sufficed, or there are variations in the texts. In Greek the distinction could be expressed by the word συναγώγιον (Philo, De somniis, ii, c. 18 § 127; Leg. ad Gaium c. 40 § 311); but this does not seem ever to have become usual. Among Greek-speaking Jews the name προσευχή (place of) "prayer" seems to have been more common at Rome, "in qua te quaero proseucha?" (Juvenal, Sat. 3, 296); *συναγωγή*, which is very common in the New Testament, occurs but once in Philo (in a description of the Essenes): *εἰς ἱεροὺς ἀφικνούμενοι τόπους οἳ καλοῦνται συναγωγαί* (Quod omnis probus liber sit, c. 12 § 81, ed. Mangey II, 458), and in Josephus only in three places (always of a building).[1] Note should also be made of the name בית השתחוות in the use of the Damascene schismatics, "house of prostration," like *mesjed*, mosque.

The Proseuchè (Prayer-house) in Tiberias is described by Josephus (Vita c. 54 § 277) as a very large building, capable of holding a great crowd. What was going on there on the occasion which led Josephus to speak of it was a political meeting on a Sabbath morning convened at the instance of the commissioners who had been sent from Jerusalem to supersede Josephus. According to his account the meeting would have broken up in a riot, had not the noon hour come when everybody went home for sabbath dinner. Early on the following (Sunday) morning they were convened again, the most not knowing what it was all about. They were beginning the prayers when Jesus got up and began to accuse Josephus. The sequel need not be recited here. What is to our purpose is that the synagogue building — to use the more familiar name — was not used exclusively for what we should call religious purposes, but for popular assemblies and for meetings of the city council (§ 300). In fact, such buildings served various other communal interests, and were sometimes called by the common people בי עם, "people's house" (public hall), a disrespectful name which is censured by a Tanna (Ishmael ben Eleazar, Shabbat 32a, below).

Another word of similar meaning to *συναγωγή* is *ἐκκλησία*, in the sense of 'assembly.' Inasmuch as the name *συναγωγή* was in general use for the "assembly" of the Jews, the "assembly" of Christians was called for distinction *ἐκκλησία*. It is unnecessary to go back to the Greek translations of the Bible, in which both occur, or behind the versions to the Hebrew (עדה, קהל) which they render, for subtle distinctions of usage or of etymology. The Targum of Onkelos renders both Hebrew words by כנישא.

In the Epistle of James (2, 2) *συναγωγή* is used of a Christian assembly, or meeting, and occasionally elsewhere. Epiphanius (Haer. xxx. 18) in the 4th century writes of the "Ebionites": *συναγωγὴν δὲ οὗτοι καλοῦσι τὴν ἑαυτῶν ἐκκλησίαν, καὶ οὐχὶ ἐκκλησίαν.* In the Pales-

[1] B. J. ii. 14, 4 and 5 §§ 285, 289 (in Caesarea), vii. 3, 3 § 44 (in Antioch), and Antt. xix. 6, 3 § 300 (in Dora).

tinian Aramaic which the "Ebionites" of Epiphanius probably spoke this distinction could not be expressed; both *συναγωγή* and *ἐκκλησία* would be כנישתא. Perhaps what Epiphanius means to say is that they called their "church" by the same name which was used of the "synagogue."

It is questioned whether special edifices for the synagogue were in the first instance places of meeting for the reading and exposition of the Law, or for public and private prayer. The origin of the Synagogue itself is too obscure to warrant a positive answer, and in view of the various other uses for which the buildings served perhaps the alternative is too sharply put. Nor can it be safely assumed that the development was everywhere the same. In the period represented by our sources it was both.

Another name by which the synagogue, considered as a place of worship, could be called in accordance with common Greek usage was *ἱερόν*. In Josephus B. J. vii. 3, 3 the building in Antioch which in § 44 is called *συναγωγή* is in the immediate sequel (§ 45) called *τὸ ἱερόν*. In the letter which Onias addressed to Ptolemy and Cleopatra for permission to build a temple (*ναόν*) to the most great God after the pattern of that in Jerusalem, he says that in his observation of the Jews in various places — Coele-Syria and Phoenicia are mentioned by name — he found most of them having improper sacred places, *πλείστους εὑρὼν παρὰ τὸ καθῆκον ἔχοντας ἱερά* and in consequence on bad terms with one another, as happens to the Egyptians also on account of the multitude of temples and disagreement about the cultus (*διὰ τὸ πλῆθος τῶν ἱερῶν καὶ τὸ περὶ τὰς θρησκείας οὐχ ὁμόδοξον*). These *ἱερά* of the Egyptian Jews have been usually assumed to be synagogues, the only *ἱερόν* in the meaning 'temple' being in Jerusalem. This assumption and the prevailing opinion that there were no Jewish "temples" with sacrificial cultus outside of Palestine is contested by Krauss, *op. cit.*, pp. 72 ff., cf. p. 24. — Jos. Antt. xiii. 3, 1 §§ 65 ff.

I, 284 N 53

Besides the ascription of the Tefillot to the Men of the Great Synagogue we have another statement, which perhaps means the same thing and is at least not inconsistent with the antiquity attributed to the prayers: "A hundred and twenty elders, among whom were a number of prophets, prescribed Eighteen Benedictions in their order" (Megillah 17b; Jer. Berakot 4d.). See Vol. I, p. 32 with n. 2.

I, 284 N 54

Cf. also Tosefta Sukkah 4, 5. See Krauss, *op cit.*, pp. 66 ff.

I, 284 N **55**

The מקדש מעט (miniature sanctuary) of the prophet has frequently been taken in this way — the synagogue as a substitute in the remoteness of the diaspora for the temple. So the Targum: "and I have given them synagogues second to my sanctuary" (the Temple in Jerusalem): ויהבית להון בתי כנישתא תיניין לבית מקדשי. The prophet's words, understood in the same way, are applied more specifically to the synagogues and school houses in Babylonia, or (by Eleazar ben Pedat) particularly to the school of Rab (Megillah 29a; see Bacher, Pal. Amoräer, II, 221, cf. III, 35). Another verse which was homiletically applied in the same sense was Psalm 90, 1; the "dwelling-place" (מעון) of the Lord, is the synagogues and school-houses (Megillah l.c. See further Vol. I, p. 436).

I, 285 N **56**

On the great synagogue in Alexandria see especially Tosefta Sukkah 4, 6 (Judah ben Ila'i) and the parallels in Jer. Sukkah 55a–b, Bab. Sukkah 51b; Krauss *op. cit.* pp. 261–263. It is called דיפלסטון ('double colonnade'), and is described as a large basilica which had one colonnade within another; we may imagine two rows of columns on either side of the (higher) hall in the middle. There was a wooden platform (*bema*) in the middle of the building; the edifice was so large that the *ḥazzan* of the synagogue or master of ceremonies (*memunneh*) had to give the signal for the responses of the congregation by waving a cloth (*sudarīn*). It is noted as a peculiar feature that the people were not seated indiscriminately, but each trade (e.g. goldsmiths, silversmiths, blacksmiths, weavers, etc., etc.) by itself; perhaps places were assigned the several occupations in the bays between two columns, as they might have been in a market hall (basilica), and this, as well as the size of the edifice, may have contributed to the necessity for a visible signal for the responses. In the Palestinian Talmud it is said that this building was destroyed by Trajan (presumably in the suppression of the revolt in 116 A.D.). If so, Judah ben Ila'i as a young man might have seen the building himself, and the way in which the description in the Tosefta is introduced would make this impression.

A different explanation of דיפלוסטון is given in Kohl and Watzinger, pp. 180–183, where the "double stoa" is interpreted as a "two-story stoa," the lower row of columns supporting a gallery (presumably for the women), and the upper row carried up to the roof. The words of the Tosefta, סטיו לפנים מסטיו, have then to be taken of a colonnade across the end of the building from one of the side colonnades to the other (p. 182). Their reconstruction in perspective of the synagogues at Tell Hum and at Irbid shows this form.

The term used in Tos. Sukkah 4, 6 (ed. Zuckermandel, p. 198, l. 20) דיפלוסטון is not known in Greek, but is doubtless intended for *διπλήστοον* (cf. *τετράστοον*). It is used also of a synagogue in Tiberias (Midrash Tehillim on Psalm 93, end (ed. Buber, p. 416), where R. Haggai (an Amora of the 4th generation) tells of a visit to this synagogue, which, like others, was used as a boy's school. That a synagogue in Alexandria and one in Tiberias should be designated by this unusual name suggests that they were distinguished by something peculiar in the architecture, not that they conformed to the prevailing type, as illustrated by the Galilaean synagogues, e.g. at Tell Hum, and may be connected with the unusual size of the building in Alexandria and perhaps in Tiberias.

In Talmudic references to the temple in Jerusalem a double stoa (סטיו כפול) is mentioned in several places (see Pesaḥim 13b, 52b; Sukkah 45a, top, and parallels), and it is described as that in Alexandria is in Tos. Sukkah, סטיו לפנים מסטיו. The cloisters in הר הבית apparently consisted of two rows of columns roofed over; cf. Josephus, Bell. Jud. vi. 3, 1, and in other places, in accounts of the burning of these cloisters and especially in the description of the temple v. 5, 2, *διπλαῖ μὲν γὰρ αἱ στοαὶ πᾶσαι*. The columns were marble monoliths twenty-five cubits high, and the panelled roof was of cedar. The width of the cloisters was thirty cubits. They were enclosed on the outside by a thick wall; and the complete circuit, taking in the Antonia, was six furlongs. See further S. Krauss, Synagogale Altertümer, pp. 335–337.

It was probably this synagogue which the Alexandrian mob desecrated by setting up in it a bronze statue of Caligula in a four horse chariot (Philo, Leg. ad Gaium, c. 20 § 134, ed. Mangey, II, 565): *ἐν δὲ τῇ μεγίστῃ καὶ περισημοτάτῃ* [*προσευχῇ*] . . . [*ἱδρύοντο*] *ἀνδρίαντα χαλκοῦν ἐποχούμενον τεθρίππῳ*.

There were many other synagogues (*προσευχαί*) in the different quarters of Alexandria (Philo, In Flaccum c. 8 § 55) which were destroyed or similarly desecrated by the setting up of images (Philo, *l.c.*, cf. In Flaccum c. 6 § 41).

I. 286 N 57

שרפו כל מועדי אל בארץ. Aquila (cf. Symmachus): *ἐνέπρησαν πάσας συναγωγὰς ἰσχυροῦ ἐπὶ τῆς γῆς*. The reference is thought to be to the times of Antiochus Epiphanes; cf. the following verse, "there is no prophet more."

I, 288 ll. 22–24

On Nazareth see G. Dalman, Orte und Wege Jesu (3 ed. 1924), pp. 61–88. — The name, as was observed long ago, occurs neither in the Old Testament, nor in Josephus, nor in the Jewish writings (Talmud and Midrash), and from the silence of the sources it has been inferred that there was no such place, and still more serious things inferred from the inference. See G. F. M., "Nazareth and Nazarene," in Jackson and Lake, The Beginnings of Christianity, Vol. I, Appendix B, pp. 426–432). The name is found, however, in two synagogue poems by Ḳalir, from one of which it appears that it was the residence of priests of one of the twenty-four courses. Ḳalir's source seems to have been a list of the courses, with the places in Galilee where priests of each settled, probably after the war under Hadrian. A trace of such a source has been found in Jer. Ta'anit f. 68d, middle, where two well-known Amoraim of the third and fourth centuries respectively (Levi, Berechiah) differ in their interpretation of the obscure opening words. See Samuel Klein, "Die Barajta der vierundzwanzig Priesterabteilungen." Beiträge zur Geographie und Geschichte Galilaeas, 1909. (Text of Ḳalir's first elegy and part of the second, with a mediaeval commentary on the first, pp. 97–108.) The lines of the first elegy in which Nazareth is named are quoted by Dalman, *op. cit.*, p. 65, and of the second p. 66). The eighteenth course to which the order of the poem brings us is הַפִּצֵּץ (1 Chron. 24, 15). Some particular disaster to this course seems to be implied in the verses ending with the words: משמרת נצרת [גזרת v.l.] מזרת [Jer. 15, 7] ובשערי הארץ. The commentary (Klein, p. 107), in the way of etymological midrash, explains the "course" of Nazareth was *piṣṣeṣ* and "because they spread abroad (*paṣū*) with their mouth what they had not seen with their eyes they were dispersed abroad (*napōṣū*) by the Roman people who put faith in the Nazarene (*noṣri*) who was born in Nazareth (*Noṣrat*), and they (the Christian empire) became enemies to them (*ṣōrerīm*).

The age of this comment is not known, and what is thus drawn out of plays on words is not to be taken for authentic history, though after Nazareth became a holy place for Christians the expulsion of priests who made themselves obnoxious is not in itself unlikely. It remains to be noted that according to Epiphanius (Haer. xxx. 11) Nazareth was in his time (4th century) a purely Jewish place.

I, 288 N **58**

That they got their knowledge of the Bible by their own reading is an imagination not unnatural in an age of printed books and multiplied translations, but shows extraordinary ignorance of the conditions of the time of Jesus. That his "home library" included not only manuscripts of the Hebrew Scriptures, but "extraneous" books such as Enoch in Hebrew (or Aramaic) is to push the misunderstanding to absurdity.

By an error (corrected in the second printing, p. 289) the signal of the coming on and the close of the Sabbath was said to have been made similarly also for a "holy day." — References should have been given to M. Ḥullin 1 (end) and Josephus Bell. Jud. iv. 9, 12 § 582 (in the Temple). Cf. Elbogen in Lewy-Festschrift (pp. 173–187), and Ginzberg, Unbekannte jüdische Sekte, p. 153 [L. G.]

I. 289 NN **59** and **60**

On the officers of the synagogue, their titles and functions, see Juster, Les Juifs dans l'empire Romain, I, 438 ff., especially 450 ff. (1914); Krauss, Synagogale Altertümer, 112 ff. (1922). — For some inscriptions from Rome additional to the sources cited in these works the reader may be referred to the publications noted by La Piana, "Foreign Groups in Rome, etc." Harvard Theological Review, XX (1927), 351.

I. 290 l. 12

The תיבה was originally a portable chest, or closet, which could be carried out into the streets and open places of the town in a public fast (M. Ta'anit 2, 1). It is now usually a press, or closet, in or against the wall at the end of the building toward which the congregation faces in worship, on a platform raised by three or more steps above the level of the floor. As it is, by reason of its contents, the most sacred part of the edifice it is often highly ornate (see illustrations in the Jewish Encyclopedia, Vol. I, s.v. Ark of the Law). The name ארון הקודש, "the holy ark," in reminiscence of the ark (*'arōn*) in the tabernacle (Exod. 25), and perhaps particularly of the *'edut* in it (Exod. 25, 16). The same ignorant vulgus who invited their death by calling the synagogue "public hall" (see above, p. 89) are condemned also for disrespectfully calling the ארון הקודש in their vernacular ארנה, "box"; Shabbat 32a below.

I, 290 N **61**

See Vol. I, pp. 317 f. — Literature on the *ḥazzan*, Krauss, Synagogale Altertümer, p. 121, n. 2.

I. 290 N **62**

Krauss, Synagogale Altertümer, p. 267 (literature); pp. 317 ff. (orientation); pp. 334 ff. (architecture). See especially Kohl and Watzinger, Antike Synagogen in Galilaea, 1916.

I. 291 l. 5f.

The translation given in the text is that of the English version issued by the Jewish Publication Society, The Holy Scriptures according to the Masoretic Text (1917); Singer, Prayer Book, p. 40, 97; K. Kohler, Jewish Theology (1918), p. 57; cf. the Vulgate Latin, "Dominus Deus noster, Dominus unus est." The Authorized English Version (1611) is, "The Lord our God is one Lord." — The words have been differently construed and understood by Jewish scholars (e.g., Ibn Ezra) as well as by Christians (e.g., by Ewald and by Dillmann). The problem is somewhat disguised by the substitution of "the Lord" for the proper name, and the copula (not expressed in Hebrew) is sometimes introduced in the first clause (Jehovah *is* our God), or in the second (Jehovah *is* one), or in both.

I. 291 ll. 11–17

The ascription quoted (יוצר אור) is recited only in the morning, and the statement in the text should be corrected accordingly. For the evening an appropriate prefatory benediction is provided (אשר בדברו מעריב ערבים), "Who . . . bringest on the evening-twilight" — The differentiation of the evening service from the morning seems to have been gradual; Berakot 11b. For the history of the evening prayer, see Elbogen, Der jüdische Gottesdienst, § 14. Singer, Prayer Book, p. 96, with I. Abraham's note, Companion to the Authorised Daily Prayer Book, pp. cviii–cx. See also S. Baer, p. 164.

I, 291 l. 26f.

The first three and the last three are recited; see Vol. I, p. 295.

I, 291 N **64**

See Elbogen, Der jüdische Gottesdienst, 1 ed. p. 242, cf. 236; M. Tamid 5, 1 (in the Temple); see also *ibid.* p. 24. The Decalogue should properly have been recited in the Shema' not only by the priests in the Temple but in "the borders," i.e. outside of Jerusalem. This was discontinued on account of the "cavils of the heretics" (מפני פרענת

המינים [Bab. תערומת] Jer. Berakot 3c middle, Bab. Berakot 12a), that they might not say, "These (Ten Commandments) *only* were given to Moses at Sinai" [? Deut. 5, 19]; cf. Maḥzor Vitry, p. 12, below. See also the discussion in Sifrè Deut. § 34, ed. Friedmann, f. 74a–b, of the rightful place of the Decalogue in the Shema'. — The "heretics" are here probably Christians; in fact the Maḥzor Vitry *l.c.* (interpreting המינים) has "lest" * * * תלמידי ([the disciples of Jesus], should say, the rest of the Torah is not truth," etc. A manuscript in the hands of S. D. Luzzatto contained, after the (suppressed) name of Jesus, some additional words, mediaeval characterization of contemporary Christians, *l.c.*, footnote 8). The attitude toward the revelation of the Law ascribed to these heretics is not that of the immediate disciples of Jesus nor of the Nazarenes or Ebionites after them. Nor is it — rightly understood — the position of Paul and the Christianity which he represents; even less of the Marcionite extreme.

The testimonies in the Talmud are somewhat uncertainly datable; the Rabbis cited in connection with them are Amoraim (Palestinian and Babylonian) of the third century or later, except R. Nathan (the Babylonian) Berakot 12a.

Who the "heretics" were who held that the Decalogue alone was the revealed law of God I have not been able to recognize in the heresiographers.

I, 291 N **63**

The Shema' consists of the following passages: (1) Deut. 6, 4–9; (2) Deut. 11, 13–21; (3) Num. 15, 37–41. In the morning two "benedictions" יוצר אור and אהבה רבה) precede and one (אמת ויציב) follows these biblical passages (M. Berakot 1, 2). See Elbogen, Der jüdische Gottesdienst § 7, and the literature cited at the beginning of the section. — The passage from Numbers was introduced later than the two from Deuteronomy (Elbogen, p. 24 ff.).

The modern form of the Tefillah may be found in the Prayer Books (Singer, pp. 44 ff.); on its composition and wording see Elbogen, § 8, § 9; on the other daily prayers (Minḥah, 'Arabit), Elbogen, § 13, § 14.

An older (Palestinian) form of the Tefillah was found in the Cairo Genizah and published in Jewish Quarterly Review, X (1898), pp. 656 ff.

I, 291 N **65**

In Jewish use the name "Tefillah" is appropriated to the Eighteen Prayers (Shemoneh 'Esreh) or the short prayer which may be used instead in circumstances of danger. The "Eighteen" is also called 'Amidah, because the worshippers stand during the recitation of it. See the article "Shemoneh Esreh" in Jewish Encyclopedia.

I, 291 n. 5

It should be understood that this prescription has reference to private devotions.

I, 292 **N 66**

On this disposition see Abudraham, chap. 2 (ed. Prag, 1784, f. 2b–3a), quoting Rab Huna, Sifrè § 343 (ed. Friedmann, f. 142b, top).

I. 292 l. 21

The redactor of the prayer for the extirpation of heretics was *Samuel* the Little (so correctly in the index), not "Simeon the Little." The mistake was not observed in time for correction in the second printing.

I. 292 **N 68**

This is the Birkat ha-Minim to the use of which Epiphanius (Haer. 29, 9) and Jerome (on Isaiah 5, 18 f.; 49, 7; 52, 4 f.) refer; in both the Nazarenes are specifically named. The text in the current Prayer-Books (Singer, p. 48, with Abrahams p. lxiv f.; Baer, p. 93 f.) with the editor's note on the variants in the list and explanation of them, beginning ולמלשינים is innocuous enough, and has the appearance of having been modified more than once in the course of the centuries and adapted to new conditions and surroundings.

I, 293 **N 69**

The present texts probably derive from, or have been conformed to, Babylonian sources of the Gaonic period.

I, 293 **N 70**

The first is called in the Mishnah *l.c.* אבות on account of the repeated mention in it of "our fathers," "Our God and our fathers' God, God of Abraham, Isaac, and Jacob" etc.); the second, גבורות from the recognition of the almighty power of God ("Thou art mighty — גבור — for ever"); the third, קדושת השם, "the hallowing of the Name" ("Thou art holy, and thy name is Holy" — קדוש). — See Elbogen, Der jüdische Gottesdienst § 8 (Komposition, § 9 Wortlaut).

I. 294 l. 8 ff.

Josephus, c. Apion. ii. 23 § 196, speaking of the temple service, "At the sacrifices prayers for the common welfare come first, after them those for ourselves individually."

I, 294 N **71**

See Elbogen, Der jüdische Gottesdienst § 9b.

I, 296 l. 18–21

Jer. Megillah 75a, above; see also Josephus, c. Apion. ii. 17 § 175, Philo, De opificio mundi, c. 43 § 128; cf. Jos. Antt. xvi. 2, 4 § 43. — On Ezra see above, p. 6 f.

I. 297 N **72**

"At the end of every seven years, in the set time of the year of release, in the feast of tabernacles, when all Israel is come to appear before the Lord thy God in the place which He shall choose [Jerusalem], thou shalt read this law (cf. vs. 9) before all Israel in their hearing. Assemble the people, the men and the women and the little ones, and the stranger that is within they gates, that they may hear, and that they may learn," etc.

I. 297 n. 2

Read Deut. 31, 10–13, instead of "33, 10–13."

I, 297 N **73**

On the whole subject see Elbogen, *op. cit.*, § 25.

I. 298 N **74**

"M. Megillah 4, 4 does not refer to the regular weekly readings, but to special Sabbaths and holy days. As a matter of fact the rule given in the Mishnah, not to skip, was not observed by the high priest on the Day of Atonement; see M. Yoma 7, 1 and Megillah 24a. [L. G.]

I, 298, end, and 299, top, and N **74**

See Elbogen, p. 158 f. — Bertinoro (*in loc.*) observes that the high priests on the Day of Atonement read Lev. 16, 1 ff. and then Num. 29, 7 ff. (M. Yoma 7, 1). Though these passages are widely separated, they have the same subject, forming two parts of the proper lesson for the day. — In the prophets it was not allowed to skip from one prophet to another, except in the Book of the Twelve (Minor Prophets). Jer. Megillah 75b; cf. Megillah 24a.

I. 299 N **75**

See Elbogen, cited below (note 3).

I. 300 N **76**

The custom of reading the Torah through in three years is attributed in Megillah 29a to the Westerners (Palestinians), in evident distinction from the Babylonian one year cycle. The former division, represented by Sedarim, is observed in many of the Midrashim. As this system was superseded by the sections of the annual cycle (Parashiyot) its divisions became a matter of purely learned interest; they are ignored in most manuscripts, and the enumeration in the Massoretic sources varies from 153, 154 or 155 (the last being the greatest number of Sabbaths that can fall in three consecutive years of the Jewish calendar) to a total of 167. The annual cycle has 54 sections. It is perhaps not unnecessary to add in this connection that the *chapters* in printed Hebrew bibles are not a Jewish division: they were taken over from the Latin Bible (Vulgate), in which they had been introduced for convenience of reference in a concordance, to serve a similar purpose in a Hebrew concordance, and the differences which may be discovered in the enumeration of verses between, say, the English version and the Hebrew Bible are not departures from the "original" — they are in fact usually quite the opposite. See G. F. Moore, "Vulgate Chapters and numbered verses in the Hebrew Bible," Journal of Biblical Literature, XXX (1894).

I, 300 ll. 8–12

"On Sabbaths which fall in a festival the order of continuous reading is not observed. On these Sabbaths two different lections are read; the first is the festival reading, the second an introduction to the prophetical lesson, whence the reader of the second is known as *maftir*, i.e., the reader of the Haftarah."). [L. G.] — See also N **74** (on Vol. I, p. 298).

I. 300 N **77**

The quorum for certain religious observances specified in M. Megillah 4, 3. See Jewish Encyclopedia, s.v. 'Minyan'; Elbogen, *op. cit.*, § 53. The origin of this minimum number and its constitution (ten adult free males) are not explained. Perhaps ten was taken as the smallest unit in the Mosaic organization of the people (Num. 18, 21; Deut. 1, 15). In M. Sanhedrin 1, 6, in an explanation of the make up of the minor sanhedrin of twenty-three members, it is asked, "Whence is it learned that a congregation (עדה) consists of ten?" and Num. 14, 27 is adduced, where the עדה הרעה הזאת is taken of the (ten) spies who brought back a bad report of the land, Joshua and Caleb, who reported favorably, not being counted with them (cf. Jer. Megillah 75b, above; Megillah 23b; Maimonides, Hilkot Tefillah 8, 5 f.).

I, 300 n. 4

See Vol. I, p. 411 ff. Cf. Jerome Epist. 53 (ad Paulinum, Vallarsi I, col. 277): Tertius [Ezechiel] prinicipia et finem tantis habet obscuritatibus involuta, ut apud Hebraeos istae partes cum exordio Geneseos ante annos triginta non legantur.

I. 301 n. 2

See Vol. I, p. 303, n. 3

I, 302 l. 20f.

With the survival of the prevailing language of the Persian period and the coming and going from Palestine and more remote eastern lands, the number of Aramaic-speaking Jews in Alexandria and other parts of Egypt in this age was doubtless considerable.

I. 303 N **78**

The word מפורש so interpreted, Jer. Megillah 74d; Megillah 3a; Nedarim 37b. See Elbogen, Der jüdische Gottesdienst § 28, and the literature there cited; A. Berliner, Targum Onkelos, II, 73 ff., especially pp. 84 ff.

I. 303 N **79**

See especially M. Megillah 4.

I. 304 N **80**

Berliner, Targum Onkelos, II, 86 f., where additional examples are adduced.

I, 304 n. 4

Add Bacher, Tannaiten, II, 204 f.

I. 305 N **81**

See Vol. I, pp. 175 f. The English reader may get a notion of the freedom of the Palestinian Targums on the Pentateuch, in the forms in which they have been transmitted to us, from the translation by J. W. Etheridge, "The Targums of Onkelos and Jonathan ben Uzziel on the Pentateuch with the Fragments of the Jerusalem Targum" (2 vols. 1862, 1865). — The texts are conveniently brought together (with standard commentaries on the Hebrew, etc., etc.) in an edition, חמשה חומשי תורה, Vienna, 1794.

I. 305 N **82**

The search for precedent and authority found the exposition as well as the reading of Scripture and the translation (Targum) in Neh. 8, 8 ושום שכל ויבינו במקרא "they gave the sense, and caused them to understand the reading."

I, 306 n. 1

In some of the Midrashim, e.g. Lam. R., a good deal of Aramaic is interspersed, and some of them seem to be, at least in part, Hebrew versions of discourses spoken in Aramaic. We may compare mediaeval Latin sermons, probably delivered to popular audiences in the vernacular.

I. 306 NN **83** and **84**

Elbogen, Der jüdische Gottesdienst, § 12a; David de Sola Pool, The Old Jewish-Aramaic Prayer, the Kaddish, 1909. — See Vol. II, pp. 101, 212 f. — In the extant prayer books, the Aramaic is larded with Hebrew clauses, but this is obviously secondary. Aramaic is exceptional in prayers. Rab Judah says: "Let a man never ask for what he needs in Aramaic," and R. Johanan, "Whoever asks for what he needs in the Aramaic language, the ministering angels [who transmit his prayer] do not ally themselves with him, for the ministering angels do not understand the Aramaic language." (Shabbat 12b, Soṭah 33a.)

I, 307 N **85**

The innumerable specific precepts and doctrines (*λόγοι, δόγματα*) have two highest principles *τό τε πρὸς Θεὸν δι' εὐσεβείας καὶ ὁσιότητος καὶ τὸ πρὸς ἀνθρώπους διὰ φιλανθρωπίας καὶ δικαιοσύνης· ὧν ἑκάτερον εἰς πολυσχιδεῖς ἰδέας καὶ πάσας ἐπαινετὰς τέμνεται.* Philo devoted two treatises to these subjects (cf. Vol. I, p. 213), of which the former (*περὶ εὐσεβείας*) is not preserved; the latter (*περὶ φιλανθρωπίας*) has its place under the head of the Virtues (Mangey, II, 383 ff.). With the subsumption of the many specific precepts and doctrines under these two heads, cf. Matt. 22, 34 ff., Mark 12, 28 ff. See Vol. II, pp. 85 ff. (Testaments of the Twelve Patriarchs, ibid., p. 86); cf. pp. 173 f.

Vol. I, 308 n. 1

In Jer. 2, 8 the תפשי התורה seem to be a special class of students and interpreters of the Law, like the Scribes in our period (Vol. I, pp. 37 ff.), but those who earliest addicted themselves to these studies were probably priests.

I, 309 **N 86**

Sofer is probably a denominative from סֵפֶר, 'book,' as if we should say "bookman," with especial reference to the books of Scripture, or to the whole "Bible." Taken as a *nomen agentis* in the sense of "one who counts," the name was supposed to be given to them because of what we should call "massoretic" enumeration of words, etc. Kiddushin 30a: "The ancients were called *soferim* because they counted all the letters in the Law." The motive for such exactness is explained in the context. See Bacher, Terminologie, I, 134 f.

I, 309 **N 87**

For a translation of the whole passage see Vol. I, pp. 40 f.

I, 310 **N 88**

See Vol. I, pp. 156–158.

I, 311 l. 13

"Sacrificial worship" is perhaps too narrow a rendering for Simeon's '*abodah*; in other places I have used "cultus" (Vol. I, p. 35; Vol. II, p. 172), or "worship," and have explained the latter in Vol. II, pp. 84 f., cf. p. 217 f.

I, 311 n. 1

On בית ועד see L. Ginzberg, "Geonica I, 3, n. 3. — The phrase suggests the מועדי אל in Psalm 74, 8 (Vol. I, pp. 285 f.), which Aquila (cf. Symmachus) rendered by συναγωγαί (meeting-places): N **57**, above, p. 92.

I, 312 **N 89**

Sirach (Hebrew text), 51, 23: פנו סכלים עלי ולינו בבית מדרשי; Greek, ἐν οἴκῳ παιδείας, similarly (and probably not independently) Syriac, בית יולפנא. See further Vol. I, pp. 314 f.

I, 312 n 3

The suggestion had been made that the phrase may represent חבורת סופרים, "association," collectively "associates"; e.g., of a teacher and his colleagues and disciples (Ezra, Hillel, Johanan b. Zakkai, Meir). See Lev. R. 26.

I, 313 l. 13
"Janitor," literally "the keeper" of the Bet ha-Midrash.

I, 313 N **89**a
The name Πολλίων is perhaps conformed (? by copyists) to that of (Asinius) Pollio, a friend of Herod at Rome (Antt. xv. 10, 1 § 343). Cf. Ποπλᾶς Bell. Jud. ii. 2, 1 § 14 and Πτόλλας Antt. xvii. 9, 3 § 219 — the same man, friend of Archelaus. — It is said that Abtalion was of foreign ancestry (Vol. I, p. 347), and if he had a name which began with two consonants both the prothetic א in our rabbinical sources and the dropping of the second consonant in Josephus would be explained.

I, 313 N **90**
In fact they imagined that the antediluvians from Seth on — as well as the Patriarchs, Abraham, Isaac, and Jacob — were at the head of schools of the Law. They have a corresponding position (Enoch, Noah) in the apocalyptic tradition.

I, 313 ll. 21 ff.
"Certain statements in the Mishnah are described as having been brought from Babylonia by Hillel; cf. Ḳiddushin 75a, with reference to M. Ḳiddushin 4, 1." [L. G.] — See also Vol. I, pp. 248 f., and N **14** there.

I, 314 l. 22 *Read* Eleazar.

314 n. 4
It does not appear that when Philo writes of the "innumerable schools" (διδασκαλεῖα) open in the cities on the Sabbath he means to distinguish in a corresponding way between the Bet ha-Midrash and the Synagogue (προσευχή).

I, 315 ll. 18f. and n. 2
On Eccles. 12, 11 see also Sifrè Deut. § 41 (f. 79b, middle).

I, 315 ll. 24 ff
On the Yelammedenu problem see Vol. I, p. 170, and the Notes on that page (above, p. 48 f).

I, 316 N 91

The usual name is בית ספר; בתי סופרים, Ketubot 105a; corresponding (in number) to the בתי כנסיות and בתי מדרשות in Jerusalem. The *sofer* is here the teacher of the elementary school.

I, 316 N 92

It is said that Simeon ben Shaṭaḥ ordained that children (תינוקות — boys are meant, not girls) should go to the elementary school (בית ספר). Jer. Ketubot 32c, top. A new arrangement is ascribed to Joshua ben Gamla, who ordained that teachers should be installed in every district (מדינה) and in every city, and that boys should enter the school at the age of six or seven years, instead of sixteen or seventeen, at which age they had previously gone to the schools in Jerusalem. Baba Batra 21a (tradition in the name of Rab); Krauss, *op. cit.* III, 200 — Simeon ben Shaṭaḥ was a great figure in the days of Alexander Jannaeus and Queen Alexandra — say, in the first decades of the first century B.C. Joshua ben Gamla is usually identified with Jesus son of Gamaliel, who, with Ananus, was one of the leaders of the moderate party in Jerusalem in the early stages of the War (66 A.D.) and, with Ananus, was one of the victims of the fury of the Idumaeans and Zealots (Josephus, Bell. Jud. iv. 3, 9; 5, 2). See Jewish Encyclopedia, "Education" (Güdemann). It is obvious that if these reforms were proposed on the eve of the war, everything must have begun over again after it. Such considerations have led to the conjecture that the name of Joshua ben Peraḥiah (the contemporary of Simeon ben Shaṭaḥ) should be read, instead of Joshua ben Gamla (Bacher); see Krauss *op. cit.* III, 337, n. 10. But this seems only to be getting out of one difficulty into another.

I, 317 n. 4

See also Maimonides, Hilkot Talmud Torah, 2, 1. — Jerusalem was destroyed only because the children were allowed to play on the streets instead of attending the schools. (Shabbat 119b, quoting Jer. 6, 11). The words (of R. Hamnuna) occur in a passage in which several Amoraim of the third century give reasons for the destruction of Jerusalem: "The world is sustained in existence only on account of the breath of school children." (Shabbat, ibid., below, R. Simeon ben Laḳish.)

I, 317 l. 25

Levi ben Sisi (Vol. I, p. 290) should not have been decorated here with the rabbinical title which he is never given in the sources; apparently, notwithstanding his close relations with the Patriarch, he was not ordained by him. The famous haggadist R. Levi (Bacher, Pal. Amoräer, II, 296–436) is a different person, and belongs to a later generation.

I, 318 ll. 5–10

The neighbors complained that they could not sleep through the noise. Jer. Baba Batra 13b, below. Cf. Martial, ix. 68:

> Quid tibi nobiscum est, ludi scelerate magister?
> . . . .
> Nondum cristati rupere silentia galli,
> Murmure iam saevo verberibusque tonas.
> . . . .
> Vicini somnum non tota nocte rogamus,
> Nam vigilare leve est, pervigilare grave est.
> Discipulos dimitte tuos. Vis, garrule, quantum
> Accipis ut clames, accipere ut taceas?

I, 319 n. 4

Quoted, Vol. I, p. 161.—For other references and literature see Marmorstein, The Old Rabbinic Doctrine of God, I (1927), 7.

I, 320 ll. 23 and 29

Properly speaking rabbinical ordination did not confer the *venia docendi*, but an authorization to give decisions as jurisconsults or judges; and this authorization might be general, or restricted to certain classes of decisions, as is illustrated in the case of Rab (Vol. I, p. 105; Sanhedrin 5a–b; on the three degrees see also Maimonides, Hilkot Sanhedrin 4, 8).

I, 321 l. 8

When this kind of Jews is referred to the usual phrase is *'amme ha-'areṣ*, in distinction from non-Israelite *'amme ha-'araṣot*, who are *really* heathen.

I. 321 n. 4

The investigation could be resumed with profit. In the lack of a recent comprehensive work, the notes in the German translation of Philo (Professor Leopold Cohn), particularly on De Specialibus Legibus, will be found helpful.

I, 322 ll. 6–10

Josephus, whose knowledge of Hebrew will hardly be disputed, is capable of etymological explanations of names from which an opposite inference might be drawn.

I, 322 N 95

See C. Siegfried, Hebräische Worterklärung des Philo, u. s. w., 1868; "Philonische Studien," in Merx, Archiv fur wissenschaftliche Erforschung des Alten Testaments, II. 2 (1871), pp. 141–163. — In Greek also Philo makes etymologies more edifying than sound, e.g., De Monarchia (ed. Mangey, II, p. 219): the ἰδέαι are so-called because they ἰδιοποιοῦσι every individual thing.

I, 322 n. 2

Mathematical astronomy fell in the field of higher education, and it is uncertain how extensively or in what way it was cultivated in our period. The first scholar celebrated for his attainments in this field is Mar Samuel (end of the second century and first half of the third). — The attitude toward Greek learning and the Greek language differed with times and circumstances, and with individuals. In the end of Soṭah (f. 49 b) we read of an occasion, while Hyrcanus was besieged in Jerusalem by Aristobulus, when the practical joke of an old man expert in Greek learning — he sent up a pig for the daily sacrifice (תמיד) instead of the expected lamb — in consequence of which they said, "Cursed is the man who raises pigs, and cursed is the man who teaches his son Greek learning." In the sequel there is somewhat roundabout tradition that among Rabban Simeon ben Gamaliel's (II) reminiscences of his youth was that in the very numerous household of his father, the Patriarch, one half the boys studied Torah and the other half Greek learning. His son, the Patriarch Judah, said: "Why Syriac (סורסי) in the land of Israel? Either the holy language (Hebrew) or the Greek language!" Simeon ben Gamaliel is elsewhere reported to have said that it was not permissible to write the Scriptures (ספרים) except in Greek. On the other hand, R. Joshua, being asked about teaching one's son Greek, answered, let him teach it to him at an hour that is neither day nor night (since the son should be engaged with the Law day and night). A daughter may be taught Greek, for it is an accomplishment for her. Jer. Peah. 15 c.

I, 323 l. 3f.

Buddhism, which in these centuries was in the midst of its great age of expansion, lies outside this field, and the Mysteries did not try to convert men from the public religions, but offered their various ways of salvation within and beside them.

I, 324 l. 4f.

On the Diaspora see Th. Reinach, in Jewish Encyclopedia, s.v. Diaspora, IV, 559 ff.; Juster, Les Juifs dans l'empire Romain, I, 179–212 and the literature there cited (p. 179, n. 5); on the numerousness of the Jews, ibid., p. 209 ff. — Josephus, B. J. ii. 16, 4 (Agrippa's speech) § 398, "there is not a people in the world which does not contain a portion of our race"; vii. 3, 3 § 43; cf. Antt. xiv. 7, 2 § 115 (Strabo). On the influence of the Jewish religion and its observances, Contra Apionem, ii. 39 § 282 ff. — The Jews were exiled among the nations, in God's purpose, for the sake of increasing their numbers by converts. See Pesaḥim 87b (R. Eleazar ben Pedat — third century — quoting Hos. 2, 25, 'I will *sow* (broadcast) her for me in the earth').

I. 326 ll. 5–9

See, e.g., Josephus, B. J. ii. 20, 2 § 560 f., on the women in Damascus, who were with few exceptions addicted to Jewish observances.

I, 328. N **97**

προσήλυτος has not been found outside the Greek Bible and writers influenced by its diction, and may perhaps have been coined to distinguish גר in the later meaning of a convert to Judaism from the older and secular sense of the word, an alien living in a country and among a people not his own — the *advena legum et rituum* from the *advena regionis* (Philo, Fragt., ed. Mangey, II, 677). In the latter meaning, a new-comer or stranger in a foreign land, the classical word is *ἔπηλυς*, e.g. Herodotus iv. 197 (opposite of *αὐτόχθων*), Aesch. Persae 243 (invaders), cf. Theb. 34; Suppl. 195; *ἐπηλύτης* Thuc. i. 9; cf. *ἐπήλυτος* Dion. Hal. iii. 72; LXX Job 20. 26 (for שריד). Similarly *προσήλυτος* is opposed to *αὐτόχθων* (Lev. 16, 29; 19, 34; 24, 16) or *ἐγχώριος* (Lev. 18, 26; 24, 22).

I, 328 n. 4

One of the leaders of the revolutionaries in the War was "Simon son of Giora," from Gerasa, one of the Hellenistic cities east of the

Jordan in the Decapolis (Josephus, B. J. iv. 9, 3 § 503), and, as the patronymic "son of the proselyte" shows, of non-Jewish extraction.

I, 329 ll. 1–10

Torrey (The Second Isaiah, pp. 257, 427 f.) regards Isa. 56, 2–6 as an insertion by a later hand; cf. 58, 13 f. It would not be questioned, however, that it was in the text long before the period with which we are concerned. In the Greek translation 56, 6 is rendered: *καὶ τοῖς ἀλλογενέσι τοῖς προσκειμένοις κυρίῳ δουλεύειν αὐτῷ, κ. τ. λ.* (cf. vs. 3, *ὁ ἀλλογενὴς ὁ προσκείμενος πρὸς κύριον*). The reference to proselytes is evident.

I, 329 l. 20

On *advena* in a religious sense see Apuleius, Metamorphoses, xi. 26: Eram cultor denique assiduus, fani quidem advena, religionis autem indigena — as already an initiate of Isis – xi. 23–25. See also Reitzenstein, Hellenistische Mysterienreligionen, 3 ed., p. 19 and p. 193.

I, 330 N **98**

Esther 8, 17: ורבים מעמי הארץ מתיהדים כי נפל פחד היהודים עליהם. This reflexive denominative, of which there is apparently no other instance, is equivalent to *ἰουδαΐζειν*; see the Greek version, *καὶ πολλοὶ τῶν ἐθνῶν περιετέμοντο καὶ ἰουδάιζον διὰ τὸν φόβον τῶν Ἰουδαίων.*

I, 331 N **99**

See the story of Shammai and the heathen inquirer in Sabbat 31a: the inquirer asks, "How many laws have you?" "Two, the written law and the traditional law." "About the written law I trust you; but about the traditional law I do not trust you. Make me a proselyte (ניירני) with the understanding that you shall teach me the written law." Shammai chode him angrily and sent him off with a smart rebuke. (Hillel, to whom he went, received him: and next day convinced him by a lesson on the alphabet that tradition is the indispensable condition of learning.)

I, 332 N **100**

M. Keritot 1.2, R. Eleazar ben Jacob: The proselyte is in default a piaculum until the blood of the victim is splashed upon him. Cf. Tos. Shekalim 3,20: a proselyte who is prevented from eating of sacrificial flesh until he brings his bird (dove or pigeon) may bring a [single] bird in the morning and eat of sacrificial flesh in the evening.

See Keritot 8b. It is remarked that in other cases when a pair of birds is offered, one of them is a so-called "sin-offering," the other a burnt-offering; but in the propitiation of the proselyte, if two birds are offered, both are burnt-offerings (Sifrè; cf. Keritot 8b). Since in his case there is no sin-offering, some authorities held that only one bird, for a burnt-offering, was required (Tos. Shekalim 3, 20, quoted above, p. 108). The legitimacy of sacrificing a single bird, notwithstanding the fact that in the laws they are always offered in pairs, is affirmed in Sifra, Wayyikra, Par. 7, but denied in Sifrè Num. § 108.

I, 333 l. 12

In filling out the ellipsis I have followed Rashi *in loc.* (f. 47a), who continues the suppletion, "but would that I might deserve this."

I, 333 N **101**

According to Simeon ben Yoḥai, as reported in the Talmud (Soṭah 12b, Megillah 13a), the motive of Pharaoh's daughter in going down to the Nile to bathe was to cleanse herself from the idols of her father's house; and since Jewish legend discovered Moses' foster-mother in Bithiah (daughter of Job) in 1 Chron. 4, 18 (Wayyikra Rabbah, 1, 3 *et alibi*) this bath was taken to be, in her intention, proselyte baptism. (See Rashi on Soṭah 12b, etc.) It need hardly be said that the original meaning of baptism cannot be learned by such tortuous combinations, as some scholars still think (see Jewish Encyclopedia, II. 500).

I, 333 n. 2

Three witnesses are required.

Yebamot 46b; Johanan gives an explanation of this number: it was the number of judges in the lowest court. In the sequel (f. 47a) the case of the proselyte who has been made one in such and such a court and one who claims to have become a proselyte by himself are discussed; according to R. Judah (ben Ila'i) the latter is not a proselyte at all, on account of the absence of proof. Assimilation to the rule that sessions of a court are not to be held at night produced the rule that baptism of converts should not be at night. Yebamot 46b, end. Cf. Jer. Yebamot viii. 1.

I, 333 N **102**

The rite is presumed in the Mishnah (Pesaḥim 8, 8), and a difference between the schools of Shammai and Hillel about the right of a proselyte baptized on the eve of Passover to partake of the

Passover is reported, which would take us back to a time before the fall of Jerusalem. There is, so far as I know, no earlier evidence; but there is nothing to indicate that proselyte baptism was of recent introduction.

I, 334 N 103

The opinion of R. Eliezer (ben Hyrcanus, first generation of the second century) is sometimes quoted, that a man who had been circumcised but not baptized should be treated as a proselyte. His habitual opponent in such questions, R. Joshua ben Hananiah, matched this opinion by as good a one, namely that one who had been baptized but not circumcised was a proselyte. The one proved it from the fathers in Egypt and the other from the mothers. Such *jeux d'ésprit* did not impress the majority, who ruled that a man was not a proselyte until both rites had been duly performed. (Yebamot 46a).

I. 335 l. 2

The point of the discussion in Yebamot 62a would have been more correctly stated if I had written "Whether a son born *after* his conversion is his first born son." This correction, which I owe to Professor Ginzberg, was made in the second printing of the volume, Nov. 1927. As to inheritance, the rule is that a proselyte is not an heir-at-law of a heathen father, even if the latter also has become a proselyte (Ḳiddushin 17b); see Maimonides, Hilkot Naḥalot 6, 9 and 10.

I, 335 ll. 12–14 and n. 2

It should be noted that this is the implication of R. Jose's opinion in a controverted question, not a generally accepted principle, still less a "doctrine." That the proselyte is like a newborn child, see also Yebamot 22a, below; Bekorot 47a, above. Cf. also Jer. Bikkurim 65b, top — all his transgressions are forgiven to a proselyte, — the same thing is affirmed of others who enter on a new sphere of life — an "elder" newly elected, a bridegroom. The exegetical argument is unusually subtle, and the conclusion not to be taken dogmatically. In Midrash Samuel, c. 17, the point of departure is 1 Sam. 13, 1, בן שנה שאול במלכו (Saul was a year old when he became king).

I, 335 l. 19

The proselyte is a fourth category also in the schismatic Damascus sect. Ginzberg, Unbekannte jüdische Sekte, pp. 124–126.

I, 337 l. 29 f.

The Idumaeans who were summoned to support the Zealots profess to be very patriotic Jews: they are come to defend the liberty of Jerusalem; they are of the ἔθνος, συγγένεις, συγγενέστατοι (kinsmen, nearest kinsmen), and resent finding themselves shut out of the city which they name τὴν κοινὴν πόλιν; they will fight in defense of the house of God and our common country, against the invaders from without and the traitors within, etc., Josephus, B. J. iv. 4, 4, cf. also Antt. xiii. 9, 1, end. — On compulsory circumcision at a much later time, as a condition of living among Jews, see Josephus, Vita i. c. 23 § 113; i. c. 131 § 149.

I, 338 ll. 6 ff.

The ambiguity of the phrase 'righteous' might be avoided by saying an 'upright proselyte'; צדק is frequently used where we should say genuine, or colloquially 'real.'

I, 338 (l. 19)–339 top

In the Pentateuch *toshab* is such a resident, and the word is often conjoined with *ger* (*ger we-toshab*). The distinction between the two names or classes designated by them is not clear. In one place only in the Pentateuch (Lev. 25, 47), the phrase *ger toshab*, without the conjunction, occurs in the Massoretic text, perhaps merely by accident. (The Samaritan Hebrew and the ancient versions all present the usual *ger we-toshab*.) However that may be, Jewish jurists made it a technical term in the sense to be defined.

I, 339 ll. 1 ff.

On the גר תושב see Sifrè Deut. § 259 (on Deut. 23, 16 f., the fugitive slave); more fully, Midrash Tannaim, ed. Hoffmann, p. 149. [L. G.]

I, 339 l. 7

For "Jewish courts," "established courts" was substituted in the second printing; see Vol. I, p. 274 and note 4. Cf. Jewish Encyclopedia, s.v. Laws, Noachian (VII, 648 ff.).

I, 340 ll. 15–20

"The question is whether Exod. 20, 10 refers to work done by a גר for a Jew, in which case it is the גר תושב, or to work done for himself, in which case it means the גר צדק." [L. G.]

I, 340 n. 1

In the second printing the last words ("a Jew in slavery to such an alien") were deleted. The nature of the case contemplated by R. Simeon ben Eleazar ('Arakin 29a) is a question which it is unnecessary to pursue here. — That the year of Jubilee was not observed after the exile is agreed; that it was given up much earlier is said in 'Arakin 32b near the end. See also Jubilees 50, 5, where the possession of all the land is the condition of the observance of this year, as in 'Arakin 32b. It is evident that the reversion of landed estates to the heirs of those to whom they were originally allotted is dependent on the occupation of the whole territory thus divided into allotments by tribes, clans, and families.

I, 340 **N 104**

The legislation about the resident alien (*ger toshab*) is rather of an academic than practical character, for it is applicable only under circumstances in which the Jews were lords in their own land, and had only to do with the particular conditions on which foreigners should be allowed to dwell in the land. That the jurists were aware of this unreality appears from the statement that the class of institutions existed only so long as the law of the Jubilee was in operation, and as by common consent the celebration of the Year of Jubilee had not been held since the Babylonian exile, the casuistry about the *ger toshab* could become actual law only in the future golden age, when the Jews in their own land should again be a nation making and executing laws for foreigners domiciled among them.

I, 341 ll. 1 ff.

On the so-called "proselyte of the gate" (גר שער) see Schürer, Geschichte des jüdischen Volkes, u. s. w., III, 127. Schürer opines that this distinction makes its appearance in the literature with Salomon Deyling, De σεβομένοις τὸν Θεόν (in his Observationes Sacrae, II, 460 ff.). It may be so; though Deyling's pages would not suggest it. His σεβόμενοι are גרי תושב or גרי שער "qui dicebantur," proselytae portae — two names for the same class. He gives no references to Jewish sources or Christian predecessors in this phraseology or identification. — The correct opinion is expressed by Lardner: "There was but one sort of proselytes among the Jews. They were circumcised," etc. (Works, VI, 216 ff.; cf. X, 300 ff.).

I, 341 ll. 13 ff.

On the attitude toward proselytes see Israel Lévi in the Hebrew periodical הגורן, IX, 5–30; L. Ginzberg, Unbekannte jüdische Sekte, pp. 124–126.

I, 342 N **106**

The מלשינים who now appear in the twelfth of the Eighteen Prayers do not occur in the oldest texts of the Tefillah, and probably have their origin in Christian or Persian surroundings rather than under Roman rule. The report of Simeon ben Yoḥai's comment on the selfish motives of the Roman public works, greatly admired by one of his colleagues but which coming to the ears of the government forced him to flight and long hiding (Sabbath 33b), is not represented as a case of delation. Judah ben Gerim (i.e., of proselyte ancestry, not himself a proselyte), who incautiously repeated the words of R. Judah (ben Ilai') and R. Simeon outside the school, was a rabbi who is found elsewhere in the school of R. Simeon (Mo'ed Ḳaṭon 9a; Pesiḳta ed. Buber, 87b).

There is an anecdote which suggests how proselytes might be employed as detectives: two Roman military officers were instructed by the government to become proselytes and investigate the Jewish law. In this character they studied all branches of the law under Rabban Gamaliel at Usha, and finding in it only one thing to take exception to, left, promising not to report that point to the authorities. See Sifrè Deut. on 33, 3 (§ 344).

A relapsed proselyte was an "apostate" no less than a born Jew who had gone over to another religion. That some found the obligation they had assumed to keep the whole law too much for them is what we should expect, and is attested by Josephus, c. Apion. ii. c. 10 § 123: εἰσὶ δ' οἱ τὴν καρτερίαν οὐχ ὑπομείναντες πάλιν ἀπέστησαν.

I, 343 l. 3

In Isa. 46, 1 קורס is a verb (כָּרַע בֵּל קֹרֵס נְבוֹ, "Bel has crouched down, Nebo bends double" (?). That קרס is a verb is recognized by all the ancient versions, however variously they render it (the same verbs, in the plural, in vs. 2; קרס is not found elsewhere in the Bible). In the quotation of this passage in Mekilta, l.c., "Yesterday you were worshipping Bel, Ḳores, Nebo," a proper name seems to be required (cf. Sifra, Ḳedoshim Pereḳ 8, 2, on Lev. 19, 33), even if it be a mistake (to which the change of tense may have contributed).

I, 344 N **107**

Num. R. 8, 2 (on Num. 5, 6).

I, 346 n. 7 end

See the same author's הרעיון המשיחי וגו' (1927), p. 276.

I, 347 l. 25

On the combination which makes Akiba a descendant of Sisera, see Jewish Encyclopedia, I, 304, note. — On Meir (Vol. I, p. 95), above, Note p. 35.

I, 348 l. 7

On Elisha and Gehazi see also L. Ginzberg, Legends of the Jews, IV, 244–246 and VI, 346 f. — Ibid. l. 10 f. (Joshua ben Peraḥiah and Jesus). Joshua b. Peraḥiah is one of the second "Pair" (Vol. I, p. 255), colleague of Nittai of Arbela; their successors were Judah b. Tabai and Simeon b. Shaṭaḥ, in the days of Alexander Jannaeus and Queen Alexandra. The Palestinian Talmud tells the story of Judah ben Tabai and one of his disciples, unnamed (Jer. Hagigah 77d, mid.). In both stories the scene is laid in Alexandria. The anachronism in the Babylonian Talmud which gives the name "Jesus the Nazarene" to this disciple is obvious.

I, 348 **N 107**

Num. R. 8, 2 (Num. 5, 6).

I, 349 n. 1

Cf. Suetonius, Domitian c. 15. — Others, also, *ἐς τὰ τῶν Ἰουδαίων ἤθη ἐξοκέλλοντες* were convicted on the same charge of *ἀθεότης* (Dio, l.c.). "Atheism" in law was not the theoretical denial of the existence of gods, but, like *ἀσέβεια*, covered various and ill-defined offenses against the religion of the state. Christians were called "atheists"; they would not take oath by the emperor nor say *Κύριος Καῖσαρ* nor offer sacrifice. (Mart. Polycarpi). From these demonstrations of loyal piety the Jews were exempted, but presumably not proselytes to Judaism (see Vol. I., p. 350). Dio's description of the offense as "driving ashore (and making shipwreck) on *τὰ τῶν Ἰουδαίων ἤθη*, suggests addiction to Jewish observances and customs, rather than the monotheistic doctrine which Christians derived from the Jews and shared with them.

I, 357 ff.

On this and the following chapters, cf. Josephus, c. Apion. ii. 16 ff., especially § 164 ff.

I, 359 l. 28f.

See A. Marmorstein, The Old Rabbinic Doctrine of God. I. The Names and Attributes of God. 1927.

I, 360 n. 1

Gen. R. 26, 6 (on Gen. 6, 3) with Theodor's note (p. 252 f.) citing also Pesiḳta ed. Buber, f. 68b, Lev. R. 28, 1, Eccles. R. on Eccles. 1, 3.

I, 361 N **108**

Monotheism in this, the proper sense of the word, is the central doctrine of the "theologian among the prophets" in Isa. 40–66. See C. C. Torrey, The Second Isaiah (1928), pp. 67 f.; R. Smend, Alttestamentliche Religionsgeschichte, pp. 356 ff. This *only* God had been from the beginning the God of Israel, and Israel was the only people that acknowledged and worshipped him and obeyed his revealed will. See Vol. I, pp. 219 ff. (Nationality and Universality). It is in this sense that the words of the Shema', Adonai Eḥad, were understood and professed (Vol. I, p. 291, n. 1).

I, 362 l. 24

Read *αὐτὸς*.

I, 363 n. 2

To the references in Josephus on Egyptian theriolatry may be added: Contra Apionem, i. 25 § 225, ii. 6 § 65 f., ii. 7 § 80 f.; on the statues (cf. Wisdom of Solomon, l.c.), ibid. ii. 6 § 74 f.

I, 364 N **109**

The whole subject of the intercourse of Jews with adherents of other religions is covered in the Mishnah with the Talmuds, and the Tosefta, and in the codes, under the head of 'Abodah Zarah. (The abbreviation עכו״ם "Worship of the Stars and Constellations.") came in with the Christian censorship.

I. 364 N **110**

Dualism, of one origin and kind or another, was in the atmosphere of philosophical and religious thought in the period with which we are concerned. The references given in note 3 could be multiplied indefinitely. To that from Plato I add only one (Laws x. 896 E), where the question of Soul as controlling heaven is raised — "One, or more than one? . . . More than one; at least two must be assumed, the beneficent (soul) and that which is capable of bringing about effects of the opposite kind." See also Aristotle, Metaphysics 986 A–B. Dualism of a Platonic kind pervades Plutarch's interpretation of the Egyptian as well as the Persian religions in the De Iside et Osiride. Dualism of this sort is found in Paul (*ὁ Θεὸς τοῦ αἰῶνος τούτου*, 2 Cor. 4, 4; Eph. 2, 2; 6, 12) and in the Gospel according to John: *ὁ ἄρχων τοῦ κόσμου τούτου*, 12, 31; cf. 14, 30; 16, 11; cf. also 1 John 5, 19. A dualism, not of contrariety but of subordination ("one God, the Father . . . and one Lord, Jesus Christ"), is the specific difference between Christianity as a religion distinct from polytheistic heathenism on the one hand and strictly monotheistic Judaism on the other (see, e.g., 1 Cor. 8, 5 f.). The early controversy of Judaism was with this type of dualistic theism; the trinity (שלוש), which became the distinctive peculiarity of Christianity in Jewish apprehension, belongs to a later development of dogma.

Dualism of the good-and-evil kind is found also in the Christian Gnostic systems which have made whole mythologies out of it, generally with a further premise, that *matter* in and of itself is evil; but the proper characteristic of "gnosticism" is not its dualism but its plan of salvation by transcendental "knowledge" (*γνῶσις*). All dualists were heretics in the eyes of Jewish orthodoxy, but that the pre-Christian Jewish dualists were therefore "gnostics" is not to be inferred in default of other evidence.

The literature on Jewish "Gnosticism" from Krochmal (ed. Lemberg 1851, pp. 226 ff.) and Graetz down to 1903 may be found in Blau's article (Jewish Encyclopedia, V, 686). See also Weiss, Dor II, 125 f.

I, 365 N 111

See Bacher, "Die Gelehrten von Caesarea," Monatschrift für Geschichte und Wissenschaft des Judenthums, XLV, 298 ff.; on Abahu in particular, Bacher, Agada der palästinensischen Amoräer, II, 88 ff. — Two sayings attributed to Abahu may be quoted. On Exod. 20, 2 (I am Jehovah, thy God): A human king may be king though he has a father or a brother or a son (living). God says, I am not so. "I am first," for I have no father; "and I am last," for I have no brother; "and besides me there is no God," for I have no son (Isa. 44. 6. Exod. R. 29, 4). "If a man says to you, 'I am a god,' he is lying; 'I am the Son of Man,' he will end by being sorry for it; 'I am going up to heaven,' he will not fulfil what he said." (Jer. Ta'anit 65b, bottom.)

I, 365 N **112**

Perhaps these are only the initial words of longer formulas which were interpolated in the recitation of the prayers of the congregation. The errors which are condemned in them are pointed out in the commentaries on M. Berakot 5, 3.

I, 366 ll. 4 ff.

R. Nathan is an authority of the second century who held a high place in the Academy of R. Simeon ben Gamaliel and was afterwards closely associated with the Patriarch Judah. He was a native of Babylonia, but most of his life was passed in Galilee.

I, 367 ll. 9 ff.

Cf. Marmorstein, Old Rabbinic Doctrine of God (1927), pp. 105 ff., *sed quaere*.

I, 368 ll. 1 ff.

See Boll, "Hebdomas," in Real-Encyclopädie der classischen Altertumswissenschaft, VII, 2547 ff., esp. 2561 ff. — On the seven heavens and what is in them see L. Ginzberg, Legends of the Jews, V, 10 f.

I, 368 n. 5

Cf. Pesaḥim 94b, attributed to R. Johanan ben Zakkai (f. 94a, bottom).

I, 369 l. 14

Hence an oath by the Temple, the abode of God, Ḳiddushin 71a (Rashi); cf. המעון הזה M. Ketubot 2, 9 (Bertinoro; see also Yom Ṭob, *in loc.*).

I, 370 ll. 11 ff.

On the omnipresence of God, Marmorstein, Old Rabbinic Doctrine of God, pp. 148 ff. and on His omniscience, pp. 153 ff. — As a Greek parallel it may suffice to adduce Aratus, Phaenomena, 1 ff. *μεσταὶ δὲ Διὸς πᾶσαι μὲν ἀγυιαί, πᾶσαι δ' ἀνθρώπων ἀγοραί, μεστὴ δὲ θάλασσα καὶ λιμένες·* . . .

I, 371 N **113**

In the sequel in the Mekilta a distinction is drawn from other texts between the messengers who are sent to execute a decree of God favorable to Israel and those sent on an evil decree; but this does not affect the preceding argument. The messengers of a human ruler always have to return in order to render their report. — The omniscience of God is recognized in the prayer in the 'Amidah of the Day of Atonement (Singer, p. 259; Baer, p. 416): Thou knowest the secrets of eternity, and the hidden things of the secrets of every living being. Thou searchest the inner chambers of the body, and triest the reins and the heart. Nothing is concealed from Thee and nothing is hidden from Thine eyes, — followed by prayer for forgiveness and the individual confession of sins (*'al ḥeṭ*). This form of prayer is known to Rab, if it is not meant that he is the author of the first clause, Samuel of the second, and so on (Yoma 87b, middle; see Baer's note, l.c., and, as a commentary, Abudraham (Prag, 1784, f. 88b.)

I, 373 **N 113a**

On the omniscience of God in Philo cf. also De Somniis, c. 15 § 90 f., ed. Mangey, I, 634 (the most secret thoughts of men). — On God as Τόπος in Philo see Drummond, Philo Judaeus, II, 20; on מקום in rabbinical sources, Marmorstein, *op. cit.*, pp. 92 f. (literature on its relation to Greek, p. 91, n.), cf. pp. 127 ff. This author's thesis is that for the מקום of the older sources substitutes were later introduced, especially, הקב״ה.

I, 374 ll. 15 ff.

On the omnipotence of God, Marmorstein, pp. 82, 127, 160 ff.

I, 374 **N 114**

For additional references see Marmorstein, pp. 158 f.

I, 374 **N 115**

Numerous other occurrences of גבורה, especially in connection with the giving of the Law, e.g., Mekilta, Beshallaḥ 1 (ed. Friedmann, f. 26a); Cf. Jer. Sanhedrin 28a, bottom: "not as though he heard it from the mouth of a shepherd (Moses), but as though he heard it from the mouth of the Almighty," *et alibi*. See Aruch Completum, s.v. (II, 230).

I, 376 ll. 11 ff.

On miraculous events of later times brought into existence at the close of the creative week, see Abot 5, 6 (cf. Pesaḥim 54a; Sifrè Deut. § 355, ed. Friedmann, f. 147a–b; Mekilta, Beshallaḥ 4, ed. Friedmann 30a, Weiss 37a). Mediaeval Jewish philosophers found support in these passages for their view that miracles were not after-thoughts or innovations, but had been implanted in nature from the beginning.

See Maimonides commentary on M. Abot, l.c., and Moreh Nebukim, ii. 29; Jewish Encyclopedia, VIII, 607, with references.

I, 377 N **116**

Additional references of the same tenor: Berakot 4a, Sanhedrin 94b.

I, 377 N **117**

Honi (Ὠνίας) is a caritative for more than one Hebrew name (Johanan, Neḥunya). The rain-making saint is referred to in Josephus, Antt. xiv. 2, 1 §§ 22–24; in the war between Aristobulus and Hyrcanus with his ally the Arab king Aretas, he prayed that God would hear the prayers of neither party, and was killed by those who had invited him to turn his effectual prayer into imprecation against Aristobulus and the priests who were besieged with him in the Temple. The rabbinical references which connect the name of Simeon ben Shaṭaḥ with this importunity in prayer for rain (Vol. II, p. 222, 235 f.) are not incompatible with the date in Josephus.

I. 378 l. 8

New Testament examples: cures, Acts 3, 6, cf. 16; 4, 7, 10; exorcisms, Matt. 7, 22; 9, 38; Luke 10, 17; Acts 16, 18; 19, 13–16. Rabbinical: Jacob of Kefar Sekanya, Tos. Ḥullin 2, 22 f.; Jer. ʻAbodah Zarah 2, 2; Jer. Shabbat, 14, end; ʻAbodah Zarah 27a–b. See in general on the efficacy of names in incantations and in prayer, Pfister, in Encyclopädie der classischen Altertumswissenschaft, XI, 2154–2156; Heitmüller, Im Namen Jesu (1903).

I, 379 N **118**

"In Shabbath 32a, Taʻanit 20b, it is said that the miracle wrought for one will be deducted from his merits, that is, he will in this way have drawn on his bank account in heaven!" [L. G.]

I. 379 n. 8

Heraclitus: *ἥλιος γὰρ οὐχ ὑπερβήσεται μέτρα· εἰ δὲ μή, 'Ερινύες μιν Δίκης ἐπίκουροι ἐξευρήσουσιν.* Diels, Fragmente der Vorsokratiker, 94 (3 ed., I, 96).

I, 380 N **119**

Bacher, in Jewish Encyclopedia, XI, 641a–b.

I, 382 N **120**

Creation *ex nihilo* is discovered by some (see Charles, Apocrypha and Pseudepigrapha, II, 493 note) in Apoc. Baruch 21, 4: "Who didst call from the beginning of the world to that which till then did not exist and they (*plural*) obey thee"; but the inference does not seem to be warranted by the words. Cf. Philo, De justitia, c. 7 (De special. legibus, iv. § 187, ed. Mangey, II, 367): *τὰ γὰρ μὴ ὄντα ἐκάλησεν εἰς τὸ εἶναι τάξιν ἐξ ἀταξίας καὶ ἐξ ἀποίων ποιότητας καὶ ἐξ ἀνομοίων ὁμοιότητας . . . ἀεὶ γάρ ἐστιν ἐπιμελὲς αὐτῷ καὶ ταῖς εὐεργέτισιν αὐτοῦ δυνάμεσι τὸ πλημμελὲς τῆς χείρονος οὐσίας μεταποιεῖν καὶ μεθαρμόζεσθαι πρὸς τὴν ἀμείνω.* As Philo elsewhere expressly includes the material (the four elements) as one of the conditions that must concur in every creative act (De Cherubim, c. 35 §§ 125–127, ed. Mangey, I, 161–162), it is plain that he does not here imagine creation *ex nihilo*.

I, 383 N **121**

On the end of God in creation see Ginzberg, Legends of the Jews, V, 67 f.

I, 384 ll. 5 ff.

See Marmorstein, Old Rabbinic Doctrine of God, p. 102.

I, 384 n. 6

The Yoṣer (Singer, p. 37, Baer, p. 76; Elbogen, Der jüdische Gottesdienst, § 7) is the first of the Benedictions introductory to the recitation of the Shema' and the Tefillah in the daily morning ritual. The clause, "And in his goodness renews every day continually the work of creation," is found in a different context in Ḥagigah 12b, middle, with Isa. 40, 22, as scripture for it.

I, 385 N **122**

God's providence is not confined to human beings: Even a bird is not caught in a fowler's snare without (the decree of) Heaven. Pesiḳta ed. Buber, f. 89a, in a story about R. Simeon ben Yoḥai; other references and readings in Marmorstein, Old Rabbinic Doctrine of God, p. 91; cf. Matt. 10, 29.

I, 387 N **123**

On the two מדות see Gen. R. 33, 4 (on Gen. 8, 1): . . . בכל מקום שנ׳ י״י מדת הרחמים י״י י״י אל רחום וחנון . . . בכל מקום שנ׳ אלהים מדת הדין וגו׳. The occurrences which seem contrary to this rule are explained as cases in which men by their conduct have turned the attribute of mercy into judgment or vice versa.

See Marmorstein, Old Rabbinic Doctrine of God (1927), pp. 43 ff. Other terms are מדה טובה and מדת פורענות ('punishment') (ibid. 45);

e.g., Mekilta Yitro 10, ed. Friedmann, f. 72b, ed. Weiss, f. 79b — one should give thanks to God for both alike — Akiba, in a significant contrast with the attitude and custom of the heathen; cf. the words of R. Ishmael reported in Mekilta Bo 16, ed. Friedmann, f. 19b, top, ed. Weiss, f. 23b–24a. — The reason why the attribute of mercy is associated with the name Yahwe is that Yahwe is the proper name of the God of Israel; He is expressly qualified as יי׳ אל רחום וחנון (Exod. 34, 6), Sifre Deut. § 27 init.; cf. also Rosh ha-Shanah 17b. Philo, who read his Bible in Greek was led by the substitution of *Κύριος* for יהוה, to connect with it the idea of sovereignty in its judicial aspect, and *θεός* conversely with the beneficent power (Quis rerum divinarum sit haeres, c. 6, ed. Mangey, I, 476 f.; De somniis i. 26 § 163, ed. Mangey, I, 645).

I, 387 l. 26–388 l. 1 ff.
Marmorstein, pp. 181 ff., cf. pp. 196 ff.

I, 388 N **124**
Upon condition of repentance. Hence the sentence pronounced at New Years is not sealed until the Day of Atonement, in order that in the intervening ten days a man may have opportunity and occasion to repent. See Vol. I, p. 533, Vol. II, pp. 62 f.

I, 389 ll. 1 ff.
For other references see L. Ginzberg, Legends of the Jews, V, 73.

I, 390 N **125**
See Vol. I, p. 396.

I, 391 N **126**
Compare 1 John, 2, 1; Rom. 8, 33 f. In general, in the rabbinical sources, almsgiving and personal charity "are a great advocate (paraclete), and great peace is between Israel and their Father who is in heaven" (Jer. 16, 5, Tos. Peah 4, 21), or repentance and good works are the great advocates (פרקליטין); though nine hundred and ninety-nine testify that he is guilty and only one bear witness in his favor, he will be saved (Shabbat 32a). Cf. R. Eliezer b. Jacob, Abot 4, 11, and the numerous places quoted by Moses Kobryn on this saying (f. 96b–100b).

I, 393 N **127**
Men asked wisdom (philosophy) what is the penalty of the sinner? Its reply was: 'Evil pursueth sins' (Prov. 13, 31); they asked prophecy

the same question, and were answered: 'The soul (person) that sins shall die' (Ezek. 18, 4); [they asked the Law, and got the response: 'Let him bring a trespass-offering, and atonement shall be made for him' (cf. Lev. 1, 4)]; they asked God, and He said, "Let him repent, and it shall be forgiven him." — There are variations in the tradition, the most important of which I have added in brackets from the Pesiḳta; but the substance is the same, and God's answer is always forgiveness on condition of repentance. — The omission of sacrificial atonement after the destruction of the temple in not strange; but the symmetry of the scheme obviously requires the answer of the Torah as well as those of Wisdom and Prophecy.

I, 393, end.

On the suffering of God in his people, see L. Ginzberg, Legends of the Jews, VI (1928), 25 f. — many and old occurrences, e.g., Mekilta, Bo 14, ed. Friedmann, f. 16a, ed. Weiss, f. 10b–11a.

I, 394–395

On the goodness of God extending to the animals see Baba Meṣiʿa 85a (quoting Psalm 145, 9). [L. G.] This Psalm is recited in the Daily Prayers (see Berakot 4b), and in fact thrice (Singer, pp. 29, 71, 94; I. Abrahams, Companion to the Daily Prayer Book, xxxvi; Baer, 126). On Psalm 145, 9 see Gen. R. 33, 3. See also Psalm 104. The doctrine is so common in the Bible that it needs no further illustration. On the goodness of God to all his creatures see also Marmorstein, *op. cit.*, pp. 196 f.

I, 396 N **128**

Particularly חסד, manifestly undeserved goodness (like χάρις).

I, 396 N **129**

Note especially חשק, Deut. 7, 7; 10, 15. R. Simeon ben Laḳish includes דבק, Deut. 4, 4; חפץ, Mal. 3, 12; Gen. R. 80, 7.

I, 397 ll. 16 f.

See Vol. I, p. 395 (Jer. Ḥagigah 77c); also pp. 393–394, and with the references there, R. Meir, M. Sanhedrin 6, 5.

I, 399 N **130**

In the period from which our sources come "Esau" and "Edom" were taken to apply to the Roman empire. See Vol. I, p. 400.

I, 401 ff.

Inasmuch as it was my purpose in the volumes on Judaism to set forth the teaching of the Tannaim, not the imaginations or superstitions of the Jewish masses, I have not made place for either the mythical angelology or the popular demonology. For the latter the reader may now be referred to an Excursus, Zur altjüdischen Dämonologie, in Strack-Billerbeck, IV, 435–501, observing that the range of sources is much wider than in my "Judaism." Cf. also Bousset, Religion des Judentums (3 ed. Gressmann, pp. 331–342), "Der Dualismus. Die Dämonologie," in which title the author's unhistorical point of view is indicated.

I, 402 N **131**

There are places where אלהים ("divinities") itself has been understood in ancient and modern times to be applied to angels (Psalm 8, 6; 82, 1; 97, 7; 138, 1) in all which except 82, 1 (where it construes differently, and renders *θεούς*) the LXX has *ἄγγελοι*. — In Enoch 6, 2 (Gk.), *οἱ ἄγγελοι υἱοὶ οὐρανοῦ* (cf. 13, 8; 14, 3), *οὐρανός* is probably a metonymy (שמים for אלהים, as was already noted by Lods (1892).

I, 402 N **132**

Angels, or a class of angels, are named עירין (wide awake, unsleeping), commonly rendered "watchers" (Dan. 4, 10, 14, Aramaic), frequent in Enoch (*ἐγρηγοροί*); epithets expressive of might or majesty are poetically appropriated to them, Psalm 78, 25, לחם אבירים אכל איש, the manna, which R. Akiba interpreted "the bread which angels eat," cf. LXX *ἄρτον ἀγγέλων* (see Vol. I, p. 405 and N **137**; pp. 408 f.).

I, 402 N **133**

Etymology would suggest that the primary sense of מלאך might be best expressed in English by 'agent.' In later Hebrew שליח (literally 'one sent') is commonly used for an agent empowered to act for his principal — a converse evolution of meaning.

I, 403 l. 12

Names of angels (and of demons, e.g., Azazel) are usually compounds the second element of which is אל.

I, 403 n. 1

Nor is Gabriel the only angel who is the medium of revelation; Michael, as the patron and guardian of Israel, naturally brings to them the message of God.

I, 403 n. 4

See also Ḥullin 60a end, שר העולם.

I, 404 **N 134**

"Whether good or bad, whether inadvertent or presumptuous," the angel appointed over a man takes it down, and God is apprised of it (Mal. 3, 16). See also the references in Strack-Billerbeck, III, 840, IV, 1041.

I, 405 **N 135**

See Vol. I, p. 412, below, the ephemeral angels who are created from the river of fire.

I, 405 **N 136**

Observe that in Jubilees 16, 1 ff. the meal that Abraham prepares for his visitors in Gen. 18, 8, which they ate, is not mentioned at all. See also L. Ginzberg, Legends of the Jews, V, 236.

I, 405 **N 137**

Bacher gives the parallel references, with diverse attributions.

I, 406 ll. 11–13

The much discussed words of Paul in 1 Cor. 11, 10 have sometimes been interpreted in a contrary sense.

I, 407 **N 138**

The demons which of their own ill-will and by their own power cause disease and death are thus subordinated to God and taken up into the moral order, without change of function or disposition. In becoming tormenters of the damned they extend their activity to the existence after death.

I, 407 **N 139**

For additional references to the "household above" and the "household below" the reader may consult the index to Strack-Billerbeck, s.v. "Familie" (IV, 1225).

I, 408 ll. 1 ff.

Acts of the High Court Below confirmed by the High Court Above, Makkot 23b. Three instances of a legislative kind are adduced; one of them the use of the Divine Name in salutation (Vol. I, p. 427).

I, 409

"In the liturgy the Ofannim and the Ḥayyot are the only ones named [L. G.]. — See the Ḳedushah at the end of the Yoṣer (Baer, p. 79, top).

I, 410 n. 5

In Isa. 63, 9, 'The angel of his presence delivered them' (singular) is interpreted by Rashi traditionally of Michael (שר הפנים). See Tanḥuma ed. Buber, Bereshit § 23, where R. Johanan interprets פלמוני in Dan. 8, 13 of Michael ("notarikon" for לפני מי). Cf. also Jubilees 1, 27, and 1, 29, where the angel of the Presence who went before the hosts of Israel is presumably Michael the patron and guardian of Israel. See Buber's note no. 176, and on this method of interpretation, Bacher, Terminologie I, 125 f.

I, 410 **N 140**

On the four — or seven — chief angels see L. Ginzberg, Legends of the Jews, V, 23 f. (n. 65).

I, 411 **N 154**

On the Ma'aseh Merkabah see Bousset, Religion des Judentums, 3 ed. (Gressmann) 520 f.; note the reference to Dio Chrysostom.

I, 411 n. 1

Cf. Toṣ. Ḥullin 2, 18 (quoted Ḥullin 40a; animal slaughtered לשם מיכאל שר צבא הגדול ולשם שלשול קטן). M. Ḥullin 2, 8 (where Michael is not named), corresponds, but with noteworthy differences, and the absence of Michael and the earthworm hardly proves that angels are purposely ignored in the Mishnah.

I, 412 l. 9

Read: "one excels in teaching but not in *practising*."

I, 413 l. 23 f.

What is meant by the enigmatical report that Aḥer קיצץ את הנטיעות is unknown. The rationalistic explanation, he went around among the schools persuading the pupils to abandon the study of the Law and take up practical trades is not a solution (Jer. Ḥagigah 77b, top). The figure may remind us of Plato, Euthyphro 3 A, cf. Apol. 24 B.

I, 413 n. 4

The reference should be corrected to Ḥagigah 14b.

I, 415 N **146**

Hence the common phrase signifying God מי שאמר והיה העולם. Marmorstein, The Old Rabbinic Doctrine of God, p. 89: "This is one of the characteristic Tannaitic terms for God." It is superfluous to cite a "Sumerian Psalm" as an antecedent through which "we can trace the origin of this term to the oldest stage of religious thought."

I, 416 N **147**

For Philo's conception of the nature of God and of the Logos, and for the literature on the subject reference may be made to Praechter, in Ueberweg, Grundriss der Geschichte der Philosophie, Erster Teil, 12 ed., 1926. — The metaphysical idea of transcendence makes mediation necessary. The Hermetic tracts are to be compared. See Wilhelm Kroll in Encyclopädie der classischen Altertumswissenschaft, VIII, 803 ff. (The transcendent God is in essence Nous; but the secondary Nous or Logos is dynamic, demiourgos, etc.)

I, 417 N **148**

See Josef Kroll, Hermes Trismegistos, pp. 55 ff., besides the older monographs, M. Heinze, Die Lehre vom Logos in der griechischen Philosophie (1872); Aall, der Logos, u. s. w. (1896).

I, 418 n. 1

For a contradictory opinion see Bousset, Religion des Judentums, 3 ed. (Gressmann), p. 343.

I, 419 l. 14 f.

The Aramaic מימר (determined, מימרא) formally corresponds to a Hebrew מאמר, e.g., Gen. R. 4, 6 (on Gen. 1, 7, citing Psalm 33, 6); cf. Abot. 5, 1: בעשרה מאמרות נברא העולם (the ten occurrences of ויאמר in Gen. 1). In the Midrash (in Hebrew contexts) the word דיבור is sometimes used in the same sense, e.g., Lev. R. 1, 1, Moses only heard קול הדיבור, "the sound of the utterance," cf. Targums on Deut. 5, 21 ff. (e.g., קל מימרא דיי).

I, 420 ll. 16–21

כבוד in a similar circumlocution in the Yalkuṭ (כבוד הב״ה), and so in a fragmentary manuscript from the Cairo Genizah (L. Ginzberg, Yerushalmi Fragments, I, 312), compared with our texts in Jer. Yoma 42c. [L. G.].

I, 421 ll. 21–24

Seder 'Olam ed. Ratner p. 70, and additional references in Ratner's notes.

I, 422

Common phrases are, "they heard a *bat ḳol*," "a *bat ḳol* issued," ("said," etc.), e.g., Toṣ. Soṭah 13, 3; Abot 6, 2; Jer. Berakot 3b; Shabbat 88a and often. It is a "daughter of a sound," a secondary, or derivative, sound; so Tosafot on Sanhedrin 11a. The idea of a *faint* sound may perhaps come from 1 Kings 19, 12. — In Abot 6, 2, "Every day a *bat ḳol* issues from Mount Horeb (the mountain of the law-giving) and cries abroad and says, "Woe to mankind on account of their contempt of the Torah" (neglect of study). R. Joshua ben Levi. — Note also Jer. Soṭah 24b (Simeon the Righteous and other examples). — In the case of Simeon the Righteous, who heard a *bat ḳol* issuing from the Most Holy Place (the *adytum* of the Temple) saying, "Gaios Koligos is killed and his edicts are annulled," the reference to the death of Caligula (Jan. 41 A.D.) and the frustration of his orders for the setting up of his statue in the temple (Josephus, B. J. ii. 10, 1–5; Antt. xvii. 8, 1–9) is unmistakable. Simeon "the Righteous" (ca. 200 B.C.) is out of the question; the epithet may be an erroneous gloss, though the position of the anecdote (before the oracle received by John Hyrcanus, Vol. I, p. 422) shows that the connection with Simeon the Righteous determined the order in the compilation of instances in the Talmud. The recipient of this oracle "from the Holy of Holies" was presumably a high-priest; the only Simon among the high-priests mentioned in Josephus whose incumbency falls near the time of Caligula's death is Simon son of Boethus (Antt. xix. 6, 2), who was, however, appointed by Agrippa, after the accession of Claudius.

I, 424 n. 1

The absence of the name in the poetical parts of Job (except 38, 1; 40, 6) is dramatically appropriate to the scene and the speakers; it is used freely in the prose prologue and epilogue. The author of Ecclesiastes employs the cosmopolitan "god." In Esther there is no mention of God at all. Daniel has the proper name only in the prayer (chapter 9; but observe אדני האלהים 9, 3), which is noteworthy in view of the national-religious character of the book.

I, 424 n. 2

The use of the words for God in the Psalms is thus summarized by Driver: In Book I (Psalms 1–41), יהוה occurs 272 times; אלהים (absolutely) 15 times. In Psalms 42–83 אלהים occurs 200 times; יהוה 43 times; but in the rest of Book III (Psalms 84–89) יהוה is found 31 times; אלהים 7 times. In Books IV and V (Psalms 90–150), finally, יהוה is used almost exclusively, the only exceptions being Psalm 108 (taken from Psalms 57 and 60), and one other solitary instance, Psalm 144, 9. Psalms 42–83 therefore once existed as a separate collection, the editor of which had a strong preference for אלהים. The natural tendency of scribes would be to introduce the name יהוה and thus to diminish rather than increase the significant preponderance of אלהים. In 45, 7 אלהים was put in the place of the verb mistaken for יהוה in an early form of the square alphabet. The inference probably to be drawn from these statistics is that when the bulk of that collection (Psalms 42–83) was compiled and edited, יהוה was pronounced when it was written, but that, in the circle to which the editor belonged, if not generally, there were scruples about the free use of the name, in deference to which the appellative אלהים was substituted in the text. That in the considerably later compilation, Books IV and V, יהוה only is used, shows that by that time the custom of substituting אדני (or אלהים) for the proper name *in reading* was fully established; exactly as in the Targums יהוה could be written everywhere, *because* no one dreamed of pronouncing it.

I, 424 ll. 11–15

Baudissin maintains the thesis that the substitution of *Κύριος* in the use of Greek-speaking Jews and in translations made for them *preceded*, not followed, the customary substitution in reading of אדני for יהוה in regions where the lessons were read in Hebrew. See his (posthumous) Kyrios als Gottesname im Judentum und seine Stelle in der Religionsgeschichte, edited by Otto Eissfeldt (1926 seqq.). In Baudissin's book this thesis is, so to speak, incidental; the whole is conceived as a contribution to the history of religion, and carried through, on a large scale, with the massive learning, the laborious accuracy, and the insight into the nature of the problems and the approaches to their solution which characterize all his work.

Inasmuch as in the LXX *Κύριος* is not put exclusively for יהוה, but very often for the appellatives אדני, אל, אלהים (with frequent variants in the manuscripts), it cannot be inferred from the occurrences of *Κύριος* in extracanonical books translated from Hebrew that יהוה stood in the Hebrew original. It should be needless to say that in a translation at two removes, like the Ethiopic Enoch, inferences to what the author wrote are doubly unsafe.

I, 425 N 154

On the utterance of the ineffable Name, Marmorstein (The Old Rabbinic Doctrine of God, pp. 17–40, The Pronunciation of the

Tetragrammaton) has collected the rabbinical texts and discussed them with his habitual ingenuity. He sees in the disuse of the proper name influences flowing from the Hellenistic doctrine of the namelessness of God. (See further the Note below on Vol. I, p. 427.)

I, 425 n. 2

Outside the temple (בגבולין, במדינה), in the synagogue service, the priest pronounced the blessing not with the Name, but בכנוי. See also Mekilta, Yitro 11, ed. Friedmann, f. 73b, and Sifrè Num. § 39 (on Num. 6, 23), Num. R. 11, 10 (near the end), cf. 11, 21. The substitution of אדני, Ḳiddushin 71a; Sanhedrin 28b (בעה״ז נכתב בי״וד ה״י ונקרא באל״ף דל״ת.)

I, 425 n. 3

A definition is given in Sifrè Deut. § 48 (on Deut. 11, 22, ed. Friedmann, f. 83b, below), פורץ גדרים של חכמים (here the cause is lazy ignorance, and on the consequence Eccles. 10, 8b is quoted). In the Damascus sect (Schechter, Fragments of a Zadokite Work, p. 20, line 25), וכל אשר פרצו את גבול התורה; cf. Daniel 11, 14, and on these passages see E. Meyer, Ursprung und Anfänge des Christentums, II, 127 f. — The colloquial "breachy" (of cattle), given to breaking fences, would be etymologically an equivalent.

I, 425 N **155**

See Blau, Das altjüdische Zauberwesen, pp. 93 ff. (1898.) The belief that men who knew the Name could by pronouncing it work all manner of wonders had, apparently under the influence of the Cabbala, a recrudescence in more recent centuries. Cf. in general R–E. der classischen Altertumswissenschaft, XIV, pp. 330 ff.)

I, 426 N **154**

In Sanhedrin 101b followed by the words, תנא ובגבולין ובלשון עגא (Aruch אגא, on which see Tosafot *in loc.*, and Kohut, Aruch Completum, p. 20). The word אגא occurs in the Samaritan Targum of Lev. 14, 11 translating Hebrew ויקב. — See the story of R. Ḥanina ben Teradion, Abodah Zarah 17b–18a. Possibly הוגה should be understood "spells out" (by its letters, *Yod-he-waw-he*) rather than "mutters."

I, 427 n. 1

What Theodoret got from the Jews was Ἀϊά; perhaps they were putting him off with אהיה (Exod. 3, 14).

I, 427 **N 155**

On the use of the Name in salutation and response see Marmorstein, Old Rabbinic Doctrine of God, pp. 22 ff., and the sources there cited, particularly Makkot 23b; Jer. Berakot 14c–d. R. Nathan transposes (מסורס) the clauses. Instead of 'it is time for the Lord to do something; they have nullified Thy Law,' he made it: 'They have nullified Thy Law; it is time to do something for the Lord.' — At the end of the paragraph I have interpreted the דור השמד of the persecution under Hadrian, after the Bar Kocheba war. This is not, however, expressly said; the persecution under Antiochus Epiphanes is an alternative; so David Cassel in a footnote to his edition of Me'or 'Enayin, p. 245. This is the view of Marmorstein also (*op. cit.* p. 27, the change instituted by the Zeḳenim, the early Ḥasidim, to counteract Hellenistic influence). — It has been suggested, by other scholars, referring the ordinance to the time of Hadrian, that the measure was in opposition to Judaean Christians who appropriated the title "Lord" to Jesus; with their complete separation from the synagogue the need for a profession of Jewish orthodoxy such as is implied in the salutation with the Name no longer existed. I have expressed in the text the opinion that the saying of R. Abba bar Kahana in Midrash Tehillim is a play of exegetical ingenuity, not an historical tradition (see Buber, notes 25 and 26). Even if there were better warrant for taking this wholly isolated statement — there is not even the remotest parallel — historically, I should doubt whether those who entertain the opinion in question are not attributing to the Nazarenes ("Judaean Christians") such an ambiguous use of the Lord (Κύριος) as we find, for example, in Paul. The whole subject of what is called "Jewish (or Judaean) Christianity" has been so confused by writers on the beginnings of Christianity that Jewish scholars may well be excused for falling into the same confusion. On interpretation by way of inversion of clauses (or of letters in a word) see Bacher, Terminologie, I, 136; II, 144.

I, 428 **N 156**

In the preliminary examination of the witnesses in a trial for blasphemy the testimony is given יכה יוסי את יוסי, בכינוי (יוסי in place of the proper name of God); in the formal proceeding, behind closed doors, the eldest of the witnesses is bidden to say precisely (בפירוש) what he heard, i.e., the Tetragrammaton, whereupon the judges rend their garments, etc. As the commentators observe, יוסי not only has four letters but is numerically (= 86) equivalent to אלהים.

I, 428 N **157**

A distinction is made between זה שמי לעלם (the Tetragrammaton) and זה זכרי לדור דור (Adonai); in the World to Come there will be no reason for such discrimination, and the Name will be written and read in the same way (with Yod-He).

I, 428 N **158**

Not of what we call "profane swearing."

I, 428 n. 6

"Jer. Berakot 10a does not give a reason for the periphrastic benediction, but (cites the opinion of R. Tanḥum bar Judan) that if a man has recited a benediction containing the name of the Lord that was not called for, he should immediately add the benediction "Blessed be his name," etc., thus turning the benediction into an ascription. See Maimonides, Hilkot Shebu'ot 12, 11." [L. G.]

I, 429 ll. 4 ff.

A list of over ninety such substitutionary words and phrases, with references and comments, may be found in Marmorstein, The Old Rabbinic Doctrine of God, pp. 54–107 ("The Rabbinic Synonyms for God"). See Bousset, Religion des Judentums, 3 ed. (Gressmann) pp. 310 ff.

I. 429 N **159**

On the utterance of the "name of Heaven" idly (לבטלה) see also Temurah 3b, below; Maimonides, Hilkot Talmud Torah 6, 14 (13).

I. 429 N **160**

See Note **157** for additional references.

I, 430 ll. 1–4

Marmorstein (*op. cit.*, pp. 108 ff.) maintains that הקב״ה was not commonly used by the Tannaim, and in our texts is usually a substitute for המקום.

I. 430 N **161**

For עליון (עלאה), מרום, whether associated with God or not, the Greek translators generally give Ὕψιστος, which is used as a name of God by authors who wrote in Greek (Wisdom of Solomon 5, 15; 6, 3; 2 Macc. 3, 31; Sibyll. iii, 519, 580; Frag. 1, 4; etc. It is frequent in the Testaments of the XII Patriarchs. Probably *Altissimus*, which is very common in 4 Esdras, represents a Greek ὕψιστος. Ὕψιστος is frequent in Ecclus., but in only a half-dozen places does it correspond to עליון in the Hebrew fragments; it often stands for simple אל. This fact enjoins caution in dealing with translations of translations such as the Ethiopic Enoch. — Ὕψιστος was a current word in the Gentile religious vocabulary of the time, and therefore peculiarly useful to Jewish writers who had an eye to possible Gentile readers. On Ὕψιστος see Cumont in Real-Encyclopädie der classischen Altertumswissenschaft, IX, 444–450.

I, 430 N **162**

On Shamaim for God in Jewish use it is hardly necessary to multiply examples. The religious motive is for a man to do what he does לשם שמים (Vol. II, p. 98); the goal of all endeavor, the world as it ought to be, is מלכות שמים, the sovereign rule of God.

I, 431 N **163**

The multiplication of honorific names and titles is condemned by R. Ḥanina (see Vol. II, p. 229); but the man whom he censured was probably not a solitary offender against reverence by such piling up of epithets.

I, 434 n. 2

For the universalistic conception of the kingdom of God see especially the prayer מלוך על כל העולם כלו בכבודך in the Musaf for New Years after the ʻAlenu and the Malkuyot (Baer, p. 399; Singer, p. 249):

Our God and God of our fathers, reign thou in thy glory over the whole universe, and be exalted above all the earth in thine honour, and shine forth in the splendour and excellence of thy might upon all the inhabitants of thy world, that whatsoever hath been made may know that thou hast made it, and whatsoever hath been created may understand that thou hast created it, and whatsoever hath breath in its nostrils may say, The Lord God of Israel is King, and his dominion ruleth over all. Sanctify us by thy commandments, and grant our portion in thy Law; satisfy us with thy goodness, and gladden us with thy salvation. O purify our hearts to serve thee in truth, for thou art God in truth, and thy word is truth, and endureth for ever. Blessed art thou, O Lord, King over all the earth, who sanctifiest Israel and the Day of Memorial. (Singer's translation.)

I, 435 l. 2

"Shekinah is found in the Mishnah several times, though הקב״ה and המקום occur more frequently." [L. G.] See also Marmorstein, *op. cit.*, pp. 103 f., and below, Note on p. 436, end.

I, 435 ll. 12–17

Ten descents (of God) are mentioned in the Law, Mekilta, Baḥodesh 3 (on Exod. 19, 11); Sifrè Num. § 93 (on Num. 11, 17); Gen. R. 38, 9. The count of ten is attributed in Gen. R. to R. Simeon ben Yoḥai. In Abot de Rabbi Nathan 34, 5 they are enumerated, but the last (Gog and Magog) is not in the Pentateuch. Ed. Schechter, f. 51b.

I, 435 N **164**

Inasmuch as R. Jose ben Ḥalafta elsewhere teaches that God is not in any place (Tanḥuma ed. Buber, Ki Tissa 16; Bacher, Tannaiten, II, 185, with notes 1 and 2), perhaps that is his meaning here. It has been suggested (Bacher, Tannaiten, II, 185) that the words quoted in the text had a polemic point against Christian dogma — the incarnation and the resurrection of Jesus. But it is uncertain whether Jose b. Ḥalafta came in contact with that kind of Christian dogma in Galilee in the generation after the Bar Kocheba war.

I, 436 N **165**

There is a considerable lacuna in the printed text here; see Buber's note 66. — The interpretation in the name of Isaac takes עצר in the sense of 'assemble' (שמיני עצרת, so understood); cf. Joel 1, 14 קראו עצרה (cf. Yalkuṭ I § 782 ואין עצירה אלא כניסה). For the way in which this meaning was associated with the ordinary meaning of עצר ('keep in, shut up') reference may be made to Kimḥi, Shorashim, s.v. (לפי שנעצרי״ ומתעכבים במקום אסיפתם). — In the sequel in Pesikta, the same in other expression, כל זמן שישראל מקוין בבתי כנסיות ובבתי מדרשות הקב״ה מקוה שכינתו עמהם.

I, 436 N **166**

The midrash is somewhat subtle in that it extracts two inferences from אלהים נצב בעדת אל (Psalm 82, 1), first the place (cf. במועדי אל Psalm 74, 8 and Rashi), and second the congregation, the minimum number (*minyan*) of which for concerted prayer was ten (Numbers 14, 27, the twelve spies, Caleb and Joshua excepted, verse 6); see above, p. 99 f. For judges the minimum bench was three. — With this passage (Berakot 6a) compare Abot 3, 2 (Ḥanina ben Teradion); see also

Abot 3, 7; Mekilta, Yitro 11 (ed. Friedmann, f. 73b; ed. Weiss, f. 80b). The enumeration in Berakot 6a is the most complete, and perhaps the latest form of this commonplace; observe also the climactic order given it. — On the exegetical derivation see Bacher, Pal. Amoräer, II, 220 f., n. To the same homilist Song of Songs 2, 8 f. suggested God's springing from synagogue to synagogue and from school to school to bless the Israelites (Pesiḳta Rabbati, ed. Friedmann, f. 72a; less complete text, Pesiḳta, ed. Buber, f. 48b).

I, 437 **N 167**

Frequently this interchange is due to copyists; a good example of this is Mekilta Beshallaḥ 2 (on Exod. 14, 13, ed. Friedmann, 28b, above; ed. Weiss, 34a, above): see Friedmann's note on the variants. Sometimes כבוד interchanges with שכינה. A more significant variant is הקב״ה and שכינה.

I, 438 n. 2

In Hebrew סרסור, 'a go-between,' especially in business transactions. Chiefly in the Jerusalem Talmud and the Midrashim.

I, 438 **N 168**

In Philo the Logos is intermediate in nature between God and man, *οὔτε ἀγένητος ὡς ὁ Θεὸς ὢν οὔτε γενητὸς ὡς ὑμεῖς, κ. τ. λ.* (Quis rerum divinarum haeres, c. 42 § 205 f., ed. Mangey, I, 501–502). The words of Moses (Deut. 5, 5, 'I stood between the Lord and you') are appropriated to him (ibid. § 206).

I, 438 **N 169**

On Metatron in this office see "Intermediaries in Jewish Theology," Harvard Theological Review, XV (1922), 74 f.

I, 439 **N 170**

Michael and Gabriel were peculiarly the patron angels of the Jews, and that Jews may have sought their intercession is conceivable enough, though not necessarily to be inferred from the passage quoted. It has been thought that in Colossians 2, 18 the *θρησκεία ἀγγέλων* against which the Christians are warned was borrowed from Jews (cf. vs. 17), perhaps particularly from Jews of Essene proclivities, e.g., Lightfoot, Commentary on Colossians, "The Colossian Heresy." But if this were more certain than it is, it would prove nothing for what may be called orthodox Jewish belief or practice. In Tos.

Ḥullin 2, 18 (see above Note on I, 411, n. 1) the flesh of an animal slaughtered in the name of the highest archangel or of a little earthworm is זבחי מתים.

I, 440 N **171**

Another homilist has God sitting and (figuratively) making ladders — making one man go up and another down, as it is written — (Psalm 75, 8), 'For God is judge; one he abases and one he exalts' (Gen. R. 68, 4). Or Moses finds him putting the finishing strokes on the Law, making 'crowns' for the letters (Menaḥot 29b; see above, p. 76, Note **20**; cf. above p. 83). Or he sits and teaches school children who have died before they had opportunity to learn Torah. 'Abodah Zarah 3b, quoting Isa. 28, 9. — To many, in whose imagination of God portentous dignity is a dominant attribute, such occupations seem unbecoming, and, for want of a sense of humor, they have set them down to the "rabbinical idea of God," all the more absurd in association with the "transcendence" which the rabbis were supposed to ascribe to him.

I, 441 N **172**

The words ביה שמו gave rise to divers midrashic ingenuities, in one of which it is taken for the Greek *βία*; Jer. Ḥagigah 77c; Gen. R. 12, 10 (see Theodor's note there).

On man's creation and endowment see Ecclus. 17, 1–15, and in other places cited below.

I, 445 N **173**

See also the Baraita in Ḳiddushin 40b (near the top; Eleazar ben R. Simon): Inasmuch as the world is judged according to the preponderance (of good or evil) and the individual is judged in the same way — if a man fulfils one commandment, blessed is he, because he has tipped the balance to the side of merit for himself and the whole world; if he commits one transgression, woe to him because he has tipped the balance to the side of guilt for himself and the whole world, for it is said, 'One sinner destroys much good' (Eccles. 9, 18). For this one sin of the individual which he has committed destroys much good for himself and the whole world. Cf. Tosefta Ḳiddushin 1, 13.

I, 446 N **174**

See Bacher, Tannaiten, I, 417 f., with references also to modern writers on Jewish ethics.

I, 448 **N 175**

The "two ways" (respectively of life and of death) are from Deut. 30, 19; these two ways were set before Adam (Gen. 2, 17). On the ingenious twist by which Akiba found this in Gen. 3, 22 see Bacher, Tannaiten I (2 ed.), 319, note 1. (He took ממנו not as one "of us," but "of himself" (ממנו), that is, by his initial choice of evil, he became as one who has only *one* way before him. See Gen. R. 21, 5 (on Gen. 3, 23) with Theodor's note on the variants and on the competing interpretations of Pappos and Akiba, substantially as in Bacher, l.c.

I, 448 **N 176**

The moral likeness to God is brought out in Tanḥuma on Gen. 3, 22 (§ 7) by way of Eccles. 7, 29: God created man to be righteous and upright (צדיק וישר) like Himself. (There follows a discussion of the question why, if this was His intention, He created the evil impulse, with the argument that it is man himself who makes the impulse *evil.*)

I, 449 **N 177**

That the image of God is the intellectual soul is the conception of later Jewish philosophers also need hardly be said; see Maimonides, Moreh Nebukim i, 1. The haggadah in Berakot 10a which recounts the points in which the soul of man (נשמה) resembles God (cf. Vol. I, p. 370) does not seem apposite.

I, 449 end, and n. 6

On the notion that the world was made for Israel, and for other Christian parallels, see L. Ginzberg, Legends of the Jews, V, 67 f.

I, 451 **N 178**

That the ministering angels do not understand the vulgar tongue, Aramaic, is a reason for the use of Hebrew in prayer. Shabbat 12b; Soṭah 33a (R. Johanan). Private petitions are meant; the Tefillah may be recited in any language. In Soṭah, l.c., instances of a *bat ḳol* heard in Aramaic are cited. The same dissuasive from praying in Aramaic is enounced also by Rab Judah (Babylonian). That the angels will not ally themselves with the petitioner because they do not understand him has a bearing on the belief in the function of angels in presenting prayers. See above, Notes **83, 84** (p. 101).

I, 452 **N 179**

Other haggadic matter about angels, Gen. R. 8, 11 and 14, 3 (Aha).

I, 452 l. 7 ff.

Cf. Josephus, Bell. Jud. iii. 8, 5 § 372: "All of us, it is true, have mortal bodies, composed of perishable matter, but the soul lives forever, immortal: it is a portion of the deity housed in our bodies" (Thackeray's translation).

I, 453 N 180

That Adam somehow represented the whole world was discovered by taking the letters of the proper name ΑΔΑΜ for the initials of the four cardinal points, *ἀντολίην τε δύσιν τε μεσεμβρίην τε καὶ ἄρκτον*, Oracula Sibyllina, ii [iii], 26. — For Christian parallels see Geffcken's note, p. 48.

I, 453 N 181

The midrash operates with Gen. 2, 21, אחד מצלעתיו, interpreted as "one of his (two) sides," as in Exod. 26, "the side" of the tabernacle. Another way of coming at it was through Psalm 139, 4 אחור וקדם צרתני, "Thou didst fashion me behind and before" (back and front), Berakot 61a; 'Erubin 18a; Tanḥuma ed. Buber, Tazri'a 2; see Rashi on Berakot l.c. — Plato's description of these androgynous creatures is as follows: The form of each of the species was completely round, having back and sides encompassing it; it had four hands and a corresponding number of legs, and two faces (*πρόσωπα δύο*) exactly alike on a cylindrical neck; for both faces, looking in opposite directions, there was one head and four ears, and two sets of sexual organs, and, all the rest as may be imagined from the preceding." The gods were perplexed what to do with these creatures until Zeus proposed to slice each one of them in two from top to bottom. The consequent plastic surgery was entrusted to Apollo as assistant, and is described at some length.

It should not be forgotten that all this passes among a small group of friends spending the night over their wine (a symposium, etymological and actual, see 223 B–D), discussing *ἔρως* in all its varieties and consequences. The description of the facing-both-way monsters and what came of them is humorous, and it is part of the humor that it is the contribution of Aristophanes. It must not be taken out of its setting and treated as if it were Plato's own theory, quoted, say, from the Timaeus. — For Philo, as a serious Platonist, the man who was created *κατ' εἰκόνα* in contrast to the man made of the dust of the earth (cf. § 76), was *ἰδέα τις ἢ γένος ἢ σφραγίς, νοητός, ἀσώματος, οὔτ' ἄρρεν οὔτε θῆλυ*. (De opificio mundi, c. 46 § 134, ed. Mangey, I, 32).

I, 454 n. 4

Thus Maimonides, Hilkot Teshubah 5, 2 ff. "Power (of self-determination) is given (by God) to every man. If he chooses to turn himself to a good way and to become righteous, the power is his; if he chooses to turn himself to an evil way and become wicked, the power is his. This is what is written in the Law, 'Behold, the man is become like one of us, to know good and evil' (Gen. 3, 22). That is to say, this species, mankind, has become unique in the world; there is no second one resembling it in this respect, that of itself, by its intelligence and reflection knows what is good and what is evil, and does whichever it chooses, and there is no one who restrains it from doing the good or the evil." The author goes on to assert man's unrestricted power of self-determination and his sole responsibility for his character and conduct against the alien (Christian and Moslem) doctrine of predestination and similar opinions entertained by many uneducated Jews (גולמים), and against astrological fatalism.

I. 455 **N 182**

Cf. Plato, Rep. 617 E (of the initial choice of returning souls) *αἰτία ἑλομένου· θεὸς ἀναίτιος*. The Hebrew Sirach exhibits a doublet: וישיתיהו ביד חותפו | ויתניהו ביד יצרו; cf. the Syriac version: ואשלם אנון ביד יצרהון. In the first member of the doublet חותפו corresponding to *διαβουλίου αὐτοῦ* is unintelligible and perhaps corrupt. For *διαβούλιον* in Ecclus. see 17, 6 (no corresponding Hebrew).

I. 455 **N 183**

Καὶ πίστιν ποιῆσαι εὐδοκίας, which may be construed by any one who thinks he can do it.

I, 455 n. 6

The Midrash supplies שאת after ואם לא תטיב also — שאת ברכה, שאת קללה. For the former meaning is cited Lev. 9, 22 ('Aaron lifted up his hands on the people and blessed them'), for the latter, Lev. 22, 16 ('And cause them to hear iniquity involving guilt'). These proof texts are probably afterthoughts. The point is the ambiguity of נשא without an object. The incomplete construction of שאת without a complementary genitive is remarked in Mekilta, Amalek c. 1 (ed. Weiss, f. 61b–62a) and parallels, for which see Weiss's note or Theodor on Bereshit Rabbah, on Gen. 4, 7 (p. 209 f.). Others understood, "If thou doest well, I will forgive thee, and if not thy sin is heaped up and accumulated" (again two senses of שאת, Bereshit Rabbah, l.c.)

I, 456 l. 8
Read Exod. 15, 26.

I, 457 N **184**
In this very difficult sentence the text presents its own problems; for δοκῆσαν τῷ Θεῷ κρίσιν γενέσθαι some codices and editions κρᾶσιν. In my translation I have taken the latter, on the ground that κρᾶσις is more likely to have been displaced by κρίσις than vice versa, and have, with many doubts, rendered it, in the light of the context, by 'concurrence,' rather than 'combination.' — On Heimarmene in the philosophy of the age see Encyclopädie der classischen Altertumswissenschaft, s.v., VII, 2622–2645 (Gundel). It was what Cicero calls *fatalis necessitas* (De natura deorum, i. 20, 55), or as, in another place, he lets an exponent of the Stoic doctrine say: "Fatum autem id appello, quod Graeci εἱμαρμένην, id est, ordinem, seriemque causarum, cum causa causae nexa rem ex se gignat" (De divinatione, i. 55, 125). This concatenation of causes in Stoicism is the eternal causal nexus of the universe itself. The divination, to which the Stoics were addicted, undertook to read the future in the sky, and the belief in astrological determinism was wide-spread outside — or on the outskirts of — philosophical circles.

Attempts were made to evade the fatalistic consequences of this doctrine (the irresponsibility of man) and to compromise with Platonism. The best-known of these is the treatise *De fato* among the writings of Plutarch, but presumably not by him. See Praechter, in Ueberweg, Geschichte der Philosophie, I (12 ed. 1926), 555. With a mediating conception of this kind the account in Josephus is not irreconcilable; man's choice is his own and free, but the consequences are completely determined. And it is possible that such compromises were made much earlier than the writings through which we know about them. — My impression is that the characterization of the Jewish "philosophies" in the War by their conflicting doctrines about Heimarmene comes from a non-Jewish source (Nicholas of Damascus?); how Josephus would naturally express himself may perhaps be gathered from what he says about the Essenes in Antt. xviii. 1, 5 § 18: Ἐσσηνοῖς δε ἐπὶ μὲν Θεῷ καταλείπειν φιλεῖ τὰ πάντα ὁ λόγος, compared with xiii. 5, 9 § 172: τὸ δὲ τῶν Ἐσσηνῶν γένος πάντων τὴν εἱμαρμένην κυρίαν ἀποφαίνεται καὶ μηδὲν ὃ μὴ κατ' ἐκείνης ψῆφον ἀνθρώποις ἀπαντᾶν (cf. ταύτην ἔθετο τὴν ψῆφον ὁ Θεός, B. J. ii § 359?) The passage in xviii. 1, 2 ff. seems to be an attempt to explain the attitude of the Pharisees as it is briefly stated in B. J. ii. 8, 14 § 162.

It is not without significance that this notion cannot be expressed in Hebrew. The recent Hebrew translation of Josephus' Jewish War from the Greek by Shimḥoni can come no nearer to it than 'decree' (גזרה, in such a connection the divine decree), putting the Greek word in parentheses and explaining it by השגחה ('providence'). But this makes the writer say that the Pharisees made everything depend on "a (divine) decree *and on God*." — On the Essenes see Realencyclopädie der classischen Altertumswissenschaft. Supplementband IV (1824), 386–430 (Bauer). — In the accounts of the differences between the "Jewish philosophies" about εἱμαρμένη it may be assumed that the word is used in the sense in which it was employed in the current Greek philosophy, but there are many other occurrences of the word where it is more loosely used of the inevitable; see, e.g., B. J. ii § 297; vi. 84, 108, § 267, etc. It may interchange with πρόνοια, as in the Stoics: see Titus's escape from imminent peril. See also "Fate and Free Will in the Jewish Philosophies according to Josephus," Harvard Theological Review XXII (1929), 371–389. On Philo's use of the word see the references in Leisegang's Index Verborum (1926), p. 226.

I, 461 ff.

See Köberle, Sünde und Gnade im religiösen Leben des Volkes Israel bis auf Christum (1905).

I, 461 N **186**

"Though the Halakah quite correctly limits the חטאת to inadvertent transgressions and to things which have of themselves no moral quality, the Haggadah — and Tannaites earlier — attempt to explain all the cases for which a sin-offering is prescribed as involving *sin*. See [childbirth] Gen. R. 20, 7 [R. Simon in the name of R. Simeon ben Yoḥai]; Niddah 31b; [nazirite] Sifrè Num. § 30; Nazir 19a; Jer. Nazir, i. 5 [f. 51c]; [leper] Lev. R. 16, 6 to the end. See L. Ginzberg, Legends of the Jews, V, 122, note 128, with reference to Apocalypse of Moses 25." [L. G.] — In these passages the Haggadah is trying to find a reason for the prescription of a "sin-offering," and naturally connected the חטאת with חטא; in the case of child-birth (Simeon ben Yoḥai) particularly for the prescription of a bird as sin-offering.

I, 462 l. 4–11

See Note **189**, below (on Vol. I, p. 464).

I, 462 l. 25

Read *non* punirentur.

I, 463 N 187

"Accidental sin" is to our way of thinking a contradiction in terms; but where the revealed will of God comprehends the whole field of clean and unclean it is a real and large category. "Sin" may even attach to inanimate objects, as to the stones of the altar in Ezekiel, which have to be "unsinned." Ezek. 43, 20, 22, 23; (cf. 1 Macc. 4, 43–46). To express it in logical terms, the Hebrew חטא has a much wider extension than the English "sin" by which it is customarily translated. The חטאת (specific "sin-offering"), the *piaculum* by which man's relation to God (and thus to the cultus and to society) is redintegrated, is not made for what we call "sin." — For the Tannaite point of view one may profitably read Sifra on Lev. 4, 2 (ed. Weiss f. 15b *seq.*; Sifrè Num. § 111, on Num. 15, 22).

I, 463 N 188

See Wissowa, Religion und Kultus der Römer § 61 (1 ed. pp. 329 f.): Ist der Verstoss wissentlich und absichtlich geschehen, so ist für ihn persönlich eine Wiederherstellung des zerstörten Verhältnisses zur Gottheit ausgeschlossen, er hat sich seinerseits ausserhalb des *ius divinum* gestellt und ist darum, ohne die Möglichkeit einer Sühnung, als *impius* zwar nicht weltlicher, wohl aber göttlicher Strafe verfallen. Ist dagegen die Verfehlung unwissentlich und versehentlich begangen worden oder ist sie erfolgt unter dem Zwange einer unausweichlichen Notwendigkeit, so geschieht die Ausgleichung durch eine sühnende Darbringung, die ebenfalls *piaculum* heisst.

I, 463 n. 6

Cf. Cicero, De legibus ii. 8, 22: Sacrum commissum, quod neque expiari poterit, impie commissum esto (quoted by Wissowa, l.c.).

I, 464 N 189

In these pages (460–467) and elsewhere in various connections (e.g., Vol. II, pp. 5–10, 79 f.) I have tried to make it plain that the Jewish teachers clearly distinguished between things to be done or left undone for the doing or avoidance of which there was an evident moral reason — such as not harming our fellow men in person or reputation, or property, and those in which a moral reason is not obvious, such as not eating rabbits. Nor have I anywhere implied that the former were not regarded as intrinsically more important than the latter, so that in cases of conflict the duties of humanity were given the precedence — if I had thought it worth while to emphasize the self-evident, I might have added to the citations I have made in various connections (e.g., Vol. II, pp. 30 f.) some drastic examples from M. Yoma 8, 5 f. with the Talmud (ff. 82–83) on satisfying the craving of a pregnant woman, or feeding a sick man, or one afflicted with ravenous hunger (bulimy), on the Day of Atonement, a day of the strictest fasting, even with food unclean every day such as a pork stew.

Here as elsewhere (e.g., Vol. II, pp. 7 f.), however, I have maintained that in the logic of a revealed religion — Judaism is not peculiar in this respect — the ground of obligation is the will of God as known through revelation; moral precepts have not an independent ground of obligation in what we call ethical principles.

The religious man believes that in giving those particular statutes for which he discerns no rational or moral reason God was actuated by a wisdom and goodness that pass our understanding; he does not exempt himself from them because of the limitations of his own understanding. — In Judaism morals are an integral part of religion, and I have endeavored to show how this side of the religion was developed beyond the letter of Scripture by the Scribes and the teachers who succeeded them (חכמים); but they did not dissociate it from religion.

I, 464 n. 4

The word זדון conveys the idea of impudence, insult; it is sin conceived as an affront to God; מרד is disobedience in the spirit of revolt against His authority, and in a manner defiantly provoking (cf. להכעיס). — That one who sins unwittingly is nevertheless a trasgressor (עובר) of the commandments of God is proved from Lev. 4, 2 (Tanḥuma ed. Buber, Wayyiḳra 11). In Buber's edition [כאילו] עובר על מצות ה׳, "as it were a transgressor"; so also in the Old Tanḥuma (without the critical brackets).

I, 465 N **190**

מרד of rebellion against God, Ezek. 2, 3; 20, 38; Num. 14, 9; Josh. 22, 18–29. It is from the collocation of the words in these places as well as in 2 Kings 3, 5 and 7, that the definition in Sifra is derived which makes פשע equivalent to מרד, not from reflection on the nature of sin or analysis of the use of פשע in the Bible. To this conception of the heinousness of sin, in association with the radical sin of apostasy, additional emphasis was given by the conflict with hellenizing tendencies in the period when the revolt against God was not the worship of other gods but the ignoring or neglecting of the law of God and the denial of providence and retribution. It was perhaps in this way that it came to be typical of sin gone its whole length, and of the direction and goal of all deliberate sin.

I, 465 N **191**

On the two "yokes" (of the Law and of subjection to heathen rule) see also Pesiḳta ed. Buber, f. 200 a–b (on Deut. 33, 3). Of diligent students, "who bruise their feet (in going from city to city and from province to province) and sit and labor in the Law" God says, "I will break off from them the yoke of (human) empire" (cf. Baba Batra 8a, above; Tanḥuma ed. Buber, Berakah § 4.

I, 466 N **192**

פורק עול ומפר ברית ומגלה פנים בתורה (cf. Tos. Sanhedrin 12, 9). — On פורק עול see above. הפר ברית is frequent in the Scriptures of nullifying (in act) God's covenant, or law; e.g., Lev. 26, 15; Deut. 31, 16 and 20; Isa. 24, 5; Jer. 31, 32; Ezek. 16, 15. In the context of Sifrè, l.c., it is more specifically the "covenant of Abraham" (circumcision); see 1 Macc. 1, 15; Josephus Antt. xi. 5, 1. — The figure of speech in מגלה פנים is similar to that in the English "bare-faced" (impudence). In Sifrè Num. § 112 (on Num. 15, 30) the 'audacity' of one who sins ביד רמה is thus described: זה מגלה פנים בתורה, and illustrated by the example of king Manasseh, of whom it is said that he sat and made derogatory remarks on the Pentateuch before God — Moses should not have written in it the story of Reuben and his mandrakes (Gen. 30, 14 ff.), nor "Lotan's sister was Timna" (Gen. 36, 22) — the objection is based on vs. 12, Timna was the concubine of Eliphaz son of Esau (cf. Sanhedrin 99b). On this phrase, see further, Bacher, Terminologie, I, 149–151, with the reference there (p. 150, n. 1) to Guttmann's articles in the Monatsschrift for 1898. For a definition of this offense see also Maimonides, Hilkot Teshubah 3, 11.

I, 466 N **193**

"Attention should be called also to the (Tannaite) Halakah in Ḥullin 5a: Sacrifices are not accepted from a Jew who has apostatized to heathenism (מומר ומנסך היין) or from one who openly profaned the sabbath." [L. G.] Though they are accepted even from the wickedest men (פושעי ישראל), since such may repent of their misdeeds.

I, 467 N **194**

Other illustrations. In Tos. Shebu'ot 3, 6 (on Lev. 5, 21, 'If a man . . . deal fraudulently with his neighbor in the matter of a deposit,' etc.): "No man deals fraudulently with his neighbor until he denies the root" (כופר בעיקר); Jer. Peah 16a, above. "No man speaks slanderously of another (אומר לשון הרע) until he denies the root" (Johanan. Note the proof following, from Psalm 12, 3–5). The infidelity may be, not the implicit premise, but the outcome, e.g., Sifra, Beḥuḳḳotai Pereḳ 2, end (ed. Weiss, f. 111c, on Lev. 26, 15): If you find a man who does not learn and does not do, and despises others and hates scholars, and does not allow others to do, he may profess to accept the commandments delivered from Sinai, but will end by disbelieving them; and one who has all these characteristics will end by denying the root.

The relation of conformity and belief is here clearly brought out; observe in the preceding examples especially the relation of man's sins against his fellow and his real belief in God. The substance of it is that no man whose faith in God is more than an idle profession will slander or defraud his fellowman; and conversely, that, no matter what professions he may make, and however he may delude himself about his faith, if he ignores the law of God, he will end in practical atheism, though he might be shocked by the very thought.

I, 467 N **195**

For a definition of heinous (חמורות 'grave') and venial (קלות, 'lighter') sins see Maimonides, Hilkot Teshubah 1, 2; the former are those to which the penalty of death by the sentence of a court is affixed or extirpation by God (כרת) is denounced; others fall into the category of lighter sins. The distinction, so far as the כרת is concerned, is made by Hillel in his argument before the Bene Bathyra, Jer. Pesaḥim 33a, above; Pesaḥim 66a; Tos. Pesaḥim 4, 2. See Vol. I, pp. 498 and 507 ff. 'Heinous' and 'venial' sins of commission or omission are not those which the conscience of the individual or the community at any time may regard as major or minor; which they are in God's judgment is to be learned from the penalties He has attached to them, and this is the basis of the classification in rabbinical law. The gravity of an offense does not depend on the element of intention: both חמורות and קלות may be done either בשגגה or ביד רמה (בזדון).

I, 468 n. 5

On patriarchs and saints who died without sin see below, Note to Vol. I, p. 474.

I, 470 ll. 1 ff.

Schechter's quotation is by a typographical error in his work attributed to "Sifra"; it is actually from Sifrè Deut. § 187.

I, 472 n. 4

See the editor's notes on Echa Rabbati, ed. Buber, l.c. (f. 35b).

I, 473 n. 1

Read הוחל. On the beginning of idolatry in the days of Enosh see Maimonides, Hilkot עכו״ם, init.; L. Ginzberg, Legends of the Jews, I, 122–124, V, 151.

I, 474 N **196**

The quotation in Pugio Fidei is attributed to "Siphre," but the first half of it is actually found in Sifra, ed. Weiss, f. 27a. In the sequel in the Pugio (not in Sifra) the question is raised whether the attribute of goodness or of punishment predominates, and the answer given that the attribute of goodness is augmented and that of punishment diminished, for which Isa. 53, 5 and 6 are alleged; the King Messiah who was humiliated and afflicted for the sake of the wicked — how much more shall he justify all generations! The Christian origin of this interpolation is evident. Martini compares Romans 5, 15, where the same figure of argument (ק״וח) is employed.

I, 474 n. 4

On sinless individuals (cf. Vol. I, p. 468) and on the relation of death to the sin of the individual there are different opinions. The reader may be referred to L. Ginzberg, Legends of the Jews, I, 74 with V, 95 f., 128–131, with the texts there cited. That there is no death without sin and no chastisement without guilt is a view attributed to Rab Immi (Shabbat 55a–b); note the discussion between the ministering angels and God about the death of Moses and Aaron (ibid. 55b) and the long following passage. The seemingly conflicting utterances in Scripture about the suffering of posterity for the misdeeds of their progenitors (e.g., Exod. 20, 5, Deut. 5, 7 and Deut. 24, 16) are confronted in Berakot 7a, and harmonized by a distinction derived from Ezekiel's doctrine of retribution. — On a similar point of view in the Apocalypses see Vol. I, p. 478 (Adam's sin entailed death on all his posterity, and Adam was not the cause except to himself alone, etc.).

I, 476 l. 28

Read ἑνὸς.

I, 477 N **197**

Propter eos enim feci saeculum. Et quando transgressus est Adam constitutiones meas, iudicatum est quod factum est. — What was judged (condemned), as the sequel shows, was not the world (*mundus*) but the *saeculum* (*αἰών*, עולם), and *quod factum est*, not inanimate nature, but (human) creatures (הבריה).

I, 477 N **198**

O tu, quid fecisti, Adam! Si enim tu peccasti, non est factum solius tuus casus, sed et nostrum, qui ex te advenimus. — *Casus* is here not to be rendered "thy fall," with the understanding that "Adam is here charged with being the cause of the perdition of the human race" (Box). See, 4 Esdras 3, 10: Et factum est in uno casus eorum; sicut Adae mors, sic et his diluvium. "Adam's fall" *cannot* be divested of the associations it has contracted in Christian theology! The ancient versions understand correctly, *malum*, *calamitas*, etc.

I, 478 N **199**

In the passages quoted the author of 4 Esdras is in accord with the rabbinical teaching of his time about the 'evil imagination' (impulse, יצר הרע) or 'heart' (mind). See Vol. I, pp. 479 ff., with the Notes on those pages.

I, 479 n. 2

In this note the phrase "image of God" is employed in the sense it has acquired in Christian theology; on the Hellenistic Jewish notions see Vol. I, p. 448. That the dominion over the animal kingdom which was conferred on man (Gen. 1, 26) was no longer possessed by his descendants in its whole extent was evident, and Scripture was found for it: "A wild beast does not have power over a man until the man seems to him like a domestic animal, as it is written 'Man abideth not in honor; he is like the beasts (בהמות) that perish'" (Psalm 49, 13), Shabbat 151 f. The words have sometimes been thought to imply the loss of the divine image. On the relations between man and the animals see L. Ginzberg, Legends of the Jews, V, 119 f.

I, 479 N **200**

On the יצר see F. C. Porter, "The Yeçer Hara. A Study in the Jewish Doctrine of Sin," in Biblical and Semitic Studies, 1902. — The word is found in the Hebrew Sirach 15, 14 (on the variants in Hebrew text and versions see Smend, Die Weisheit des Jesus Sirach erklärt (1906, p. 142): אלהים מבראשית ברא האדם ויתנהו ביד יצרו. Ecclus.: αὐτὸς ἐξ ἀρχῆς ἐποίησεν καὶ ἀφῆκεν αὐτὸν ἐν χειρὶ διαβουλίου αὐτοῦ. Other expressions for the same idea may be διαλογισμός (27, 6), ἐνθύμημα καρδίας (27, 7), but מזמה is in these and similar cases at least equally probable.

I, 480 N **200** (bis)

An example of the metaphor in another connection, Mekilta, Beshallaḥ 2 (on Exod. 14, 11), ed. Friedmann, f. 28a, bottom; ed. Weiss f. 33b: מאחר שנתנו שאור בעיסה (the Israelites began to murmur against Moses).

I, 481 N **201**

תבלין are 'spices.' The translation 'antiseptic' is suggested by the preceding parable in Sifrè (see Vol. I, p. 490) and by the use of aromatics in plasters or poultices applied to open wounds; cf. the words in the same context (before the parable), שנמשלו דברי תורה בסם החיים.

I, 481 N **201a**

In the preceding context, Gen. 4, 6 (God's words to Cain) is quoted, and Prov. 25, 21 f.: ('If thine enemy be hungry, give him bread to eat' — the bread of the Law, etc.).

I, 481 N **202**

See above, N **200**

I, 483 N **203**

On the "sons of God" in Gen. 6, 2, in Jewish and Christian sources, see L. Ginzberg, Legends of the Jews, V, 153–156, and 172 f. (note 14).

I, 484 n. 4

R. Alexander's prayer, Vol. II, p. 216. See also the prayer of Rab Ḥamnuna to be delivered from the יצר הרע and other evils, Berakot 17a. R. Tanḥum (bar Iskolastika — this name only here) prays: "May it be Thy will, O Lord my God and the God of my fathers, to shatter and bring to an end the yoke of the evil impulse from our heart; for Thou didst create us to do Thy will and we are under obligation to do Thy will. Thou desirest it and we desire it. And what hinders? The leaven in the dough. It is perfectly well-known to Thee that there is in us no power to resist it; but may it be Thy will, O Lord, my God and the God of my fathers, to cause it to cease from ruling over us and bring it into subjection; and we shall do Thy will as our own will, with a perfect heart." Jer. Berakot 7d, below. (Against the supposition that this Tanḥum is no other than the well-known Tanḥuma bar Abba see Bacher, Pal. Amoräer, III, 470.) On the impulses of animals, and their difference from the passions of men, cf. Seneca, De ira, i. 3, 4 ff.

I, 485 N **204**

R. Jose the Galilean said: Righteous men, good impulse (יצר טוב) judges them, as it is said, 'And my heart is wounded within me' (Psalm 109, 22); wicked men, evil impulse judges them, as it is said, 'Transgression speaketh to the wicked man, in the midst of my heart, there is no fear of God before his eyes' (Psalm 36, 2); intermediate men, one and the other judges them, as it is said, 'he will stand at the right hand of the needy to save him from them that judge his soul' (Psalm 109, 31). The application and appositeness of the proof-texts is dubious enough, but the only point with which we are are here concerned is that לב ('heart') is used in the first two texts as equivalent to יצר. Berakot 61b; in Yalkuṭ, Psalms § 725, mistakenly ascribed to Eleazar ben Pedat. A different version with the same proof texts, Abot de-R. Nathan c. 32. See Bacher, Tannaiten, I, 368; and compare Gen. R. 34, 10, quoted Vol. I, p. 486, n. 2.

I, 487 N **206**

In Sankhya texts the relation of the soul, which has intelligence but no power of action, and the body, which has all active powers but no intelligence, is illustrated by a lame man mounted on the shoulders of a blind man, both of whom thus escape from the jungle in which singly they were helpless. See Garbe, Die Sâṃkhya-Philosophie, 1894, p. 164. In the Buddhist Visuddhi-Magga the same illustration is used for the combination of 'Name' and 'Form,' each of which individually is impotent, but when they support each other can do things. (See Warren, Buddhism in Translations, p. 184 f.) In the Greek Anthology (ix. 11, 12, 13, B), the lame man on the shoulders of the blind man is only an example of how two imperfections may complement each other. In Mohammedan tradition it is applied, as in the Jewish sources from which it is doubtless derived, to the common responsibility of soul and body. (See Goldziher, Vorlesungen über den Islam, p. 43 ff, and references, *ibid.* p. 74, note 4, 1). A variation is found in Ikhwan al-Ṣafa (Dieterici, Philosophie, u. s. w., I. 115 f.)

I, 485 n. 1

According to another Baraita in the same context (Berakot 61a, end) man has two reins (כליות, kidneys) one of which counsels him to good, the other to evil; the good counsellor is the *right* kidney, as is shown by Eccles. 10, 2, 'A wise man's heart (לב) is on his right side, a fool's on his left.' Cf. the expression בחן כליות ולב God tests 'reins and heart' (Jer. 11, 20, *et alibi*.).

I, 486 N **205**

The notion that the soul (often as a manikin exactly reproducing in miniature the form of the owner's body) tenants the chambers of the heart, which being empty after death seems made on purpose for such occupancy, is common. Thus in India the *manas* (soul as mind and will) is "the little winged thing in the heart" (Atharva Veda vi. 18, 3); so, as a manikin (*purusha*), in the Upanishads, etc. On similar notions in the Talmud (Berakot 61a, end) see Schechter, *op. cit.*, p. 256.

I, 492 N **206** (bis)

On this variety of permutation of letters (מנון = סהרה) by אטב״ח see R. Hananel and Rashi on Sukkah, l.c. Other interpretations in the Talmud, l.c. The rendering of the English version, "shall have him become his son at length" connects the word with נין; see Ibn Ezra on Prov. 29, 21.

I, 493 N **207**

R. Judah (ben Ila'i). See Vol. II, p. 370. — To the righteous it will seem very large ("like a high hill") and to the wicked very small ("like a single hair"); "the former will weep, saying, How could we subdue this high hill! the latter will weep, saying, How could we not subdue this strand of hair!"

I, 493 N **208**

This is sometimes held up as evidence of the moral confusion caused by 'legalism,' whereas it is only an instance of mental confusion caused by translation. The English 'sin' differs from the Hebrew חטא both in extension and connotation; but instead of recognizing that the terms do not match, it is inferred that the Jews had a defective idea of 'sin'! It would be equally intelligent to assert that Aristotle had an erroneous idea of 'form' because we translate his εἶδος by 'form' while he uses εἶδος for a conception that does not fall in with our notion of *form* at all.

What I may call the dictionary fallacy, namely, that a Hebrew or a Greek word *means* a word in English or German, is one to which doctrinal interpreters are peculiarly addicted. Having substituted their own word, with its peculiar history and associations, for the author's, they imagine that they are interpreting his term, when they are only naïvely assuming that he thought in theirs. Jewish theologians are sometimes caught in the same fallacy, and to prove that the rabbis had a correct, i.e., a modern, idea of sin and righteousness set themselves to prove that their distinctions were strictly "ethical."

I, 495 N **209**

Paul's argument rests on two premises equally alien to Jewish thought and repugnant to its spirit: *First*, as we have seen, that the righteousness which is under the Law the condition of salvation in us is nothing less than perfect conformity to the law, see, e.g., Gal. 3, 10–12. *Second*, that God, in his righteousness, cannot freely forgive the penitent sinner and bestow upon him a salvation that is of grace, not of desert. This second assumption is less explicitly developed than the first; on it rests, however, the whole necessity of the expiatory death of Christ; see, e.g., Rom. 3, 25. It is to be noted that Paul shifts the whole problem from forgiveness to "justification." The rhetorical form in which he puts this argument, especially in the seventh chapter of Romans, has led interpreters to take it as his own experience, and to generalize it as the normal experience of a conscientious seeker of salvation in Judaism — inescapable conviction of the impossibility of justification by the works of the law, and the despair of knowing that there was no other way. To Jews, on the other hand, it is a perpetual amazement how a Jew, on his own testimony brought up in an orthodox home, a professed Pharisee, for a time, it is reported, a student in the school of the elder Gamaliel, evidently well-versed in the Scriptures and the hermeneutics of the day, should ever have come to make such assertions or assumptions. To his overstrained definition of the requirements of the Law in Gal. 3, 10, "Cursed is everyone who does not abide by *all* the things written in the book of the law to do them," a verbal parallel is found, indeed, in the utterance of the younger Gamaliel when he read Ezek. 18, 1–9: "Only he that does *all* these things shall live." But Akiba quoted to him Lev. 18, 24: 'Do not defile yourselves with all these things,' does not mean that a man must commit *all* the abominations enumerated in the preceding part of the chapter to be defiled, but *any* of them. Sanhedrin 81a. In a parallel narration, Makkot 24a, the cause of Gamaliel's searching of heart was Psalm 15. Compare also Midrash Tehillim on Psalm 15.

How a Jew of Paul's antecedents could ignore, and by implication deny, the great prophetic doctrine of repentance, which, individualized and interiorized, was a cardinal doctrine of Judaism, namely, that God, out of love, freely forgives the sincerely penitent sinner and restores him to his favor — that seems from the Jewish point of view inexplicable.

From that point of view it is in fact inexplicable. The two propositions we are dealing with are not given premises from which Paul draws his conclusion; they are the postulates which the predetermined conclusion demands. His thesis is that there is no salvation but by faith in the Lord and Saviour, Jesus Christ. The Jews were equally positive that the only way of salvation was the religion which God had revealed to them in Scripture and tradition, with all its teachings and observances, and they were diligent to make proselytes even among Gentiles who had embraced Christianity. Paul had therefore to prove that Judaism is not a way of salvation at all, neither by man's merit in the works of the law nor by God's grace forgiving the penitent. He can hardly have expected the argument to have effect with Jews, who would deny both premises. He was, in fact, not writing to convince Jews but to keep his Gentile converts from being convinced by Jewish propagandists, who insisted that faith in Christ was not sufficient to salvation apart from the observance of the law.

It is perhaps Christians who are meant in Tanḥuma ed. Buber, Naso 30, by the Minim who say that God does not receive repentant sinners, with the reply of Resh Laḳish; but the tenor of the passage as a whole does not favor so specific a reference. In Pesiḳta Rabbati (ed. Friedmann, f. 184b) those who doubt the reception of the penitent are called "fools" (שוטים).

I, 497 N 210

M. Shebu'ot 1, 2–5; M. Yoma 8, 8 f.; Jer. Yoma f. 45b; cf. Tos. Yom Kippurim 5 (4) 6–8 (Ishmael), and 9. In M. Shebu'ot the principal point of the controversy about the public sin-offerings, in which the chief authorities of the generation after the war under Hadrian participate, is over the relation of the sin-offerings at the festivals (Num. 28; 29) and new moons (Num. 28, 15) to the supplementary sin-offering on the Day of Atonement (Num. 28, 11) and the specific sin-offering of the Day whose blood was carried into the inner sanctuary (Lev. 16, 15 ff.). R. Meir held, as we have seen above, that all the goats (sin-offerings) without distinction expiate uncleanness affecting the sanctuary and the holy flesh of sacrifices. All agree that the public sin-offerings avail for the individual only when this intrusion of the unclean into the sphere of holiness was not deliberate. For wilful violations of this holiness "the goat (sin-offering) which is made in the inner sanctuary and the Day of Atonement expiates." On the whole subject see Encyclopaedia Biblica, s.v. Sacrifice (Vol. IV, cols. 4223–4226). See also Shebu'ot 12b–13a. The opinion there ascribed to Rabbi, viz. that the Day of Atonement atones, with or without repentance, for all sins except those of the man who פורק עול ומגלה פנים בתורה ומיפר ברית בבשר: for *these* it atones only on condition of repentance, did not prevail. (See Rashi, *al.*)

I, 498 N **211**

On the אשם תלוי see Maimonides, Hilkot Shegagot 8, 1 ff. — M. Keritot 1, 1 enumerates thirty-six cases in which the Pentateuch denounces the penalty of extirpation (כרת), all except two (observance of the Passover and circumcision) attached to express prohibitions, ranging from incest, blasphemy, and the defilement of the sanctuary and holy food, to the so-called dietary laws. The rule (M. Keritot 1, 2) is that if any of these is transgressed wilfully (זדון) the *Karet* is incurred; if inadvertently (שגגה) a sin-offering (חטאת) is required; if על לא הודע (Lev. 5, 17, 'though he know it not'), an אשם תלוי (with exceptions which we need not here pursue). The uncertainty may arise in various ways, for instance a man may be in doubt whether he has eaten suet (חלב, Lev. 7, 25) or ordinary fat (שומן), or has eaten more or less than the minimum necessary to constitute a transgression of the law; eye-witnesses may contradict each other on the facts, and so on. On the derivation of this interim *asham* from Lev. 5, 17 see Sifra *in loc.* Pereḳ 20 f., ed. Weiss, ff. 26–27.

I, 499 ll. 17–19

The legitimacy of sacrifices by proxy is here assumed as it is in several places in the Mishnah. The Babylonian Talmud (Giṭṭin 28b), in restricting this to certain kinds of sacrifice or to the sacrifices of women, represents a later theory; see the Tosafot *ad loc.* [L. G.] The difficulty raised is about the סמיכה (cf. Menaḥot 63a; and especially Sifra on Lev. 1, 4, ed. Weiss, f. 5c: ידו לא יד בנו ידו לא יד עבדו ידו לא יד שלוחו). What I have said in the text refers only to the practicability of such offerings.

I, 500 N **212**

Sifra, Aḥarè Perek̤ 8, ed. Weiss, f. 83a: "Whence do we prove that, although there are no sacrifices and no scape-goat, the Day atones?"

I, 500 N **213**

That in animal sacrifice it is the blood that atones stands in the Law (Lev. 17, 11 f.), and that there is no atonement (כפרה) without blood is deduced in Sifra, Aḥarè Perek̤ 10, ed. Weiss, f. 84b; Yoma 5a; Zebaḥim 6a as well as in Heb. 9, 22. From the Hebrew word כבש, 'lamb,' the victims in the daily morning and evening sacrifices in the Temple (Num. 28, 3), the school of Shammai inferred by way of etymology, or rather play on words, that they 'pressed down' (כבש) the iniquities of Israel, according to Mic. 7, 19; the school of Hillel, remarking that what is pressed down (submerged) comes to the top again, held that the lambs 'washed off' (כבס) the iniquities of the Israelites (Pesik̤ta, ed. Buber, 61b; cf. Pesik̤ta Rabbati, c. 16, ed. Friedmann, 84a). In the 'Aruk̤, where this passage is quoted, the text is more completely preserved, and continues: Ben Azzai says, 'Lambs a year old,' for they wash off the iniquities of Israel, and make them like an infant a year old, which has no iniquity. The difference between the two schools is also quoted in slightly different form from the (lost) Midrash Yelammedenu. The scripture of the Hillelites is Isaiah 1, 18 ('like snow'). These alternative paronomastic etymologies are the nearest approach to a theory in the rabbinical literature. With the etymology of כפר which has filled so much space in Christian speculation the rabbis seem never to have played. See "Sacrifice," Encyclopaedia Biblica IV, col. 4226; "Atonement," Jewish Encyclopedia II, 277 B.

I, 500 ll. 25 f.

It is hardly necessary to add that this applies only to the people of God. Those who are not of the true religion have no claim upon its promises. For such, repentance is primarily conversion to the true religion, according to Philo exemplified by Enoch (Vol. I, p. 516); cf. Acts 20, 21; 26, 20.

I, 501 N **213a**

See Pesik̤ta Rabbati, ed. Friedmann, f. 183b: "All the prophets call Israel to repentance, but not like Hosea" — the difference from Jeremiah and Isaiah illustrated in the sequel. Observe also in Pesik̤ta de-R. Kahana that the section שובה (f. 157 ff.) begins with Hos. 14, 2

(Haftarah to the Parashah האזינו, Deut. 32, 1 ff.) and frequently recurs to it. On the doctrine of Repentance in Hosea see Köberle, Sünde und Gnade im Alten Testament, pp. 147 ff.

I, 503 n. 2

Note should be made also of a saying of R. Johanan ben Zakkai (Baba Batra 10b): "As the sin-offering atones for Israel, so almsgiving (צדקה) atones for the Gentiles." Sin-offerings are prescribed — and accepted — only for Israelites; for the בני נח there is no requirement of such a sacrifice; see Vol. I, p. 504, n. 2.

I, 503 **N 214**

See also Makkot 24a–b, and Ekah Rabbati on Lam. 5, 18. Two occasions are named, one on a mission of the rabbis to Rome, the second in Jerusalem. The others wept over the destruction of Jerusalem and the Temple; Akiba showed by his behavior that he was glad, extracting both from the prosperity of Rome and the desolation of Jerusalem the assurance of the better future in store for the Jews and their sanctuary.

I, 504 **N 215**

That the gods cannot be bribed to condone wrong-doing through gifts is emphasized by Plato in the Laws (x, 905 D seq.; 907 A–B, watch-dogs and ordinary men would never betray the right for the sake of gifts impiously offered by bad men — much less the gods; cf. iv, 717 A (the great pains that ungodly men take about the gods is in vain). Other places in Philo are cited in Encyclopaedia Biblica, l.c.

I, 505 n. 1

The words quoted in the text are also in M. Menaḥot 13, 11.

I, 505 **N 216**

In Sifrè, l.c., there is a variant; for the לעשות רצוני of the editions from Venice (1546) f. 25 to Friedmann, Horovitz, with manuscript authority and derivative Midrashim, has בשביל לעשות לך רצונך, which is supported by the proof-text adduced (Lev. 22, 29, לרצונכם). Sacrifice was not demanded because of any need on God's part, but to satisfy or gratify the worshippers; cf. Pesikta Rabbati f.195a. See Schechter, Aspects of Rabbinic Theology, p. 298 n., who is not inclined to think that the rabbis entertained any such "rationalistic views . . . in regard to sacrifices."

I, 505 N **217**

"In our time, when there is no temple and no altar, there is no atonement there but repentance. Repentance atones for all iniquities; even the man who has been wicked all his days and at the last repents, no whit of his wickedness is remembered against him (Ezek. 33, 12). . . . The Day of Atonement itself atones for the penitent (Lev. 16, 30)." — See, to the same effect, from the supposed situation in the Exile, the Prayer of Azarias in the Greek Daniel 3, 38–40.

I, 505 N **218**

Tanḥuma ed. Buber, Aharè 16 f. God made provision for the state of things that would arise when the Temple was destroyed and piacular sacrifices could no more be made. He bids man study diligently the words of the Law, "for they are made like to offerings, and they atone for you" (Lev. 17, 2, וזה הדבר), etc. Cf. Berakot 5 a–b.

I, 507 N **219**

Hence the literal equivalent is ἐπιστρέφω (intrans., compare the New Testament use). When the change of mind and purpose are in the foreground of the thought, μετανοέω (cf. μετάνοια).

I, 508 N **220**

This phrase has sometimes been taken to imply that repentance was "wesentlich als Tun aufgefasst." What such naïve linguists do with the Christian *agere poenitentiam* or "Busse tun," is not apparent.

I, 509 N **221**

Tos. Ta'anit 1, 8: If a man have an unclean reptile in his hand, though he bathe in the waters of Shiloah or in all the waters of creation, he will not be clean; if he casts the reptile away, a bath of forty *seahs* (the minimum measure for ritual ablutions) suffices for him, for it is written, 'He who confesses and forsakes [his sins] shall receive mercy' (Prov. 28, 13) and 'Let us lift up our hearts as well as our hands (to God in heaven)' (Lam. 3, 41). — Abot de-R. Nathan c. 39 (cf. Bacher, Tannaiten I, 336, n. 3): "There are five for whom there is no forgiveness: he who repeatedly repents and repeatedly sins . . . he who sins relying on repentance, and he who is guilty of profaning the name of God." The compiler apparently attributes the saying to Akiba; see Bacher, l.c. — Abot de-R. Nathan c. 40: "One who sins and repents and walks in his integrity is forgiven on the spot; one who says, I will sin and repent, is forgiven unto three times and no more" (R. Eleazar ben Jose). Cf. Yoma 86b, middle, where the somewhat different question of the repetition of a transgression once repented of and confessed is raised. — In the Shepherd of Hermas the possibility of repentance is more narrowly limited; see especially Mandate 4, 3. See also Shebu'ot 12b, below.

I, 510 N **222**

Maimonides, in his definition of perfect repentance, adds that, opportunity and ability being given, a man refrains from yielding to the temptation "because of his repentance" (Hilkot Teshubah 2, 1).

I, 510 N **223**

See also N **219**. The usage of the Greek words in the LXX does not support the precise discrimination of synonyms sometimes attempted.

I, 511 N **224**

On the cultivation of repentance by special seasons and exercises see Vol. II, pp. 58–61, 62 f.; cf. also Vol. II, p. 14. — That man should always be in the attitude and spirit of repentance is the meaning of the saying, "Repent one day before thy death" (Abot 2, 10); Shabbat 153a, since no man knows but that this day is his last, therefore repent today. For this reason the petition that God will bring his worshippers back in perfect repentance has its place among the first in the Daily Prayer (Tefillah; Singer, p. 46; Baer, p. 90) immediately preceding the petition for forgiveness.

I, 512 N **225**

For an older form of confession see Jer. Yoma, end, f. 45c (R. Berechiah in the name of R. Abba bar Abina, 3d cent.): "My Lord, I have sinned and done wickedly, I have continued in an evil frame of mind, and have habitually walked in a far-off way; but as I have done I will do no more. May it be Thy will, O Lord my God, to forgive me (שתכפר לי על וגו') for all my wickednesses, have mercy on me for all my sin." Cf. Lev. R. 3, 3 (as a formula for individual confession on the Day of Atonement). — On the confession to the injured party in the case of wrongs done to a fellow-man, and reconciliation with him, see Jer. Yoma 45c; Yoma 87a. Cf. Vol. II, p. 154. — Whether in the confession it is necessary to specify (פרט) the sin or sins was a disputed point (Yoma 86b). R. Judah ben Baba held that it was necessary, alleging Exod. 32, 31, 'This people has sinned a great sin, and have made them golden gods'; Akiba held the opposite, quoting Psalm 32, 1, 'Blessed is he whose trasgression is forgiven, his sin concealed.' See Maimonides 2, 3, and 5. In case of a wrong done to a fellow-man, however, it is laudable to confess it publicly before others, with specification of the person and the offense, and expressions of regret. Offenses against God, on the contrary, should not thus be proclaimed (Maim. 2, 5). Misdeeds of common notoriety, however, should be publicly confessed. In Pesiḳta (ed. Buber 163b) R. Juda bar Simon (end of 4th cent.) teaches that God accepts a repentance that is between the sinner and himself alone, even for public insult and blasphemy.

I, 513 **N 226**

The confession of Samuel (1 Sam. 7, 6, חטאנו לי״י) is adduced, and the lesson drawn: "Lord of the worlds, Thou dost not judge (condemn) a man at all, except in case he says, I have not sinned."

I, 514 **N 227**

Repentance and good works (מעשים טובים) are like a shield against God's punishments (Eleazar ben Jacob, Abot 4, 11); repentance and good works are man's advocates (פרקלטין, *παράκλητοι*) in judgment (and secure his acquittal), Shabbat 32a. Better is one pang of compunction (מרדות, fig.) in a man's heart than a hundred (legal) floggings, as it is said, (Hos. 2, 9). Berakot 7a.

I, 515 **N 228**

Yoma 86b. Both eulogies of repentance are attributed to R. Simeon ben Laḳish. In Hosea, 'Return O Israel, unto Jehovah thy God (repent), for thou hast stumbled through thine iniquity,' the inference is drawn from the very mild word (unintentionally) 'stumbled' (כשלת); in Ezekiel, 'When the wicked man turns from his wickedness and does justice and righteousness. . . . none of his sins that he has committed shall be remembered against him; he has done justice and righteousness, he shall surely live.' The two utterances are harmonized by the distinction between repentance out of love and repentance out of fear. See Bacher, Agada der palästinensischen Amoräer, I, 356. With the first of these sayings compare Yoma 36b, where Moses prays (cf. Exod. 34, 7 and 9): Lord of the world, whenever Israelites sin before Thee, and repent, do Thou make for them wilful sins (זדונות) like unwitting (שגגות). We may be reminded of the Catholic doctrine: By penitence mortal sins become venial. The second is Philo's teaching also: The Day of Atonement (the "Fast day") is a day of purification and of turning from sins, for which forgiveness is granted through the grace of the merciful God, who holds penitence in as high esteem as guiltlessness. De spec. legg. i. § 187; cf. § 188, end: The scapegoat takes upon it the curse of the sinners who by turning to the better way have made atonement for their former sins and have purified themselves by their new piety. (Apparently Ezek. 33, 14 ff., 18, 21 ff. are in the author's mind.) Cf. De Abrahamo c. 18, ed. Mangey, II, 4 (on Enoch as a type of repentance): 'He was not found,' to intimate that the former sinful life was effaced and destroyed and no more found, as though it had never been. Elsewhere Philo regards the state of the repentant sinner as inferior to that of the righteous man (De virtutibus: De paenitentia § 177; De Abrahamo § 26: but in both places he is thinking chiefly of those who have turned from false religion to the true. In an earlier passage in De spec. legg. (i. § 103, end), he remarks that in the soul of the repentant man scars and marks of his former sins remain — almost verbally reproducing a saying of the Stoic Zeno in Seneca, De ira i. 16, 7. From Isa. 57, 19 R. Abahu (end of third century) inferred that not even completely righteous men stand in as high a place as repentant sinners (Berakot 34b, Sanhedrin 99a: God bestows the greeting of peace first on those who are afar off, and then on those that are near). Bacher, Pal. Amoräer, II, 104. Cf. Luke 15, 6: There will be more rejoicing in heaven (cf. vs. 10) over one repentant sinner than over ninety-nine righteous men who have no need of repentance. — See also the following verses.

I, 516 N **229**

Πλὴν μετανοοῦσιν ἔδωκεν ἐπάνοδον καὶ παρακάλεσεν ἐκλείποντας ὑπομονήν. The *ἐπάνοδος* is here a return to friendly relations, a reconciliation; see 22, 21 f.

I, 516 n. 2

The Greek of Ecclus. 44, 16, as given in the text, is supported by substantially unanimous manuscript tradition; only cod. 23 according to Lagarde's collation, has *διανοίας* (see Smend, Die Weisheit des Jesus Sirach, p. 421). The Hebrew (only one manuscript contains the passage) has אות דעת לדור ודור. In the Syriac the whole verse is lacking, probably by accident. Philo extracts from *μετέθηκεν* a metathesis or *μεταβολή* to the better (*μεταβαλεῖν*), repentance, De paenitentia, c. 1, Mangey, II, 405; see also De monarchia, c. 7, ed. Mangey, II, 219; De praemiis et poenis, c. 3, ed. Mangey, II, 411.

The Palestinian haggadists did not think well of Enoch; see Gen. R. 25, 1; cf. also Wisdom of Solomon, 4, 10 f., where the verb *μετετέθη* suggests that Enoch is in mind.

I, 517 N **230**

For other references see Bousset, Religion des Judentums, u. s. w., 3 ed. (Gressmann), pp. 389 f.

I, 518 N **231**

In his brief treatment of the subject in De paenitentia, Philo has primarily in mind conversion from mythological polytheism to the pure monotheism of Judaism, from creature-worship to the worship of the eternal creator, and, in consequence, from bad political constitutions ("ochlocracy") to the best form of government ("democracy"), from ignorance to well-established knowledge, from licence to self-control, from wrong-doing to uprightness, from cowardice to bravery — in short from vice to virtue. Such a reformation is a second-best good, indeed, such as is restoration from illness to health compared with unimpaired sound health (cf. De Abrahamo, c. 3); but never to sin at all is peculiar to God — or perhaps to a godlike man. For others there remains only the way of repentance. Philo is thinking primarily of proselytes, whose character, formed by their new religion, he contrasts with their former way of life (c. 2 § 182). See also De monarchia, c. 7, ed. Mangey, II, 219.

On the nature and effect of repentance Philo discourses more generally in De fuga et inventione, c. 18 (see especially § 99), Mangey I, 560 f. — On the Day of Atonement, De specialibus legibus, i, c. 3 § 187 f., ed. Mangey, II, 240: The Day has a double character, as a festival and as a day of purification and banishment of sins, on condition of which amnesty (dismissal from memory; Ezek. 18, 21 f.) is granted by the free gift of the propitious God, "who estimates repentance as equivalent to not sinning at all." See also § 188, end: the scape-goat is sent away into an untrodden and inaccessible wilderness, "taking upon itself the curses of those who have done wrong, who are purified by reformation (*μεταβολαῖς ταῖς πρὸς τὸ βέλτιον*), having washed away their former sin by new rectitude (*εὐνομίᾳ καινῇ παλαιὰν ἀνομίαν ἐκνιφάμενοι*). See also De Abrahamo § 19, ed. Mangey, II, 4: by repentance (as in the case of Enoch) "the old and culpable life is erased and made disappear and no more be found, as if it had originally never been." Cf. Justin Martyr, Trypho, c. 47: God, as Ezekiel says, holds the man who repents from his sins as a righteous man and without sin (also c. 141). To the same effect, Tanḥuma ed. Buber, f. 47b: No matter how many iniquities a man has, if he repent before God, He imputes it to him as if he had not sinned (Ezek. 18, 22).

An even higher rank is accorded to repentant sinners by R. Abahu: "The righteous do not stand in the place where penitents (בעלי תשובה) stand, as it is said — 'Peace, Peace, to him who is afar off and to him who is near' (Isa. 57, 2); first the far off and after that the near." (Sanhedrin 99a; see the sequel; Berakot 34a, *et alibi*). Cf. Luke 15, 7, "There will be joy in heaven over one repentant sinner more than over ninety-nine righteous men who have no need of repentance."

I, 519 N **232**

See, e.g., the terminology of Philo, N **231**.

I, 522 N **233**

On the possibility of repentance at the last moment cf. M. Sanhedrin 6, 2 — the exhortation to a man condemned to death on his way to the place of execution; confession assures him of a share in the World to Come. — The extension to death-bed repentance is a consequence of Ezekiel's doctrine applied to a later eschatology. — An example of the death-bed repentance of an atheist, the Cynic Bion of Borysthenes, is related by Diogenes Laertius, iv. 7, 54 f.

I, 523 N **234**

The sentence passed and sealed is not to be understood as man's eternal destiny. The sentence passed at New Year's and sealed at the Day of Atonement, e.g., might be that a man should die in the course of the year. The firm belief in retribution in this life was not superseded by the annexation of another sphere of retribution beyond death.

I, 524 N **235**

חתר לו חתירה. The loophole was found by a play upon ויעתר לו, 2 Chron. 33, 13 (E. V. "He (God) was entreated of him," sc. Manasseh); taken as equivalent to ויחתר לו, "he made an opening for him." R. Eleazar, son of Simeon ben Yoḥai, adds that "in Arabia" they say עתירתא for חתירתא — not the last excursion into Arabia for Hebrew etymologies. Galileans are censured for their slovenly pronunciation in general ('Erubin 53a) — they pronounced חלב so that you could not tell whether they said 'milk' (*ḥalab*) or 'suet' (*ḥeleb*, prohibited) it was that you were invited to eat, and particularly ridiculed their confusion of the gutturals — when a Galilean said *amar*, nobody could tell whether he meant an ass (חמור) or wine (חמר) or wool (עמר) or a lamb (אימר). 'Erubin 53b.

I, 524 N **236**

A modern instance is alleged: the repentance of R. Eleazar ben Durdaya, an infamous lecher, who having in vain besought the mountains and hills, heaven and earth, sun, moon, and stars, to intercede for mercy on him — they had need to seek it for themselves, since they were all doomed to annihilation — said, It all depends on me, and putting his head between his knees cried aloud till his soul went out. A mysterious voice (*bat ḳol*) was heard saying, R. Eleazar ben Durdaya is summoned to life in the World to Come. Rabbi (Judah the Nasi) said, One man gains his World in ever so many years, and another gains his World in a single hour. 'Abodah Zarah 17a.

I, 526 n. 7.

"In Gen. R. 1, 4 the matter is presented as if the earlier authorities did not count repentance among the seven (Gen. R.: *six*) things created before the world. Compare, however, L. Ginzberg, Genizah Studies, p. 476, where it is shown that repentance (as one of the seven) is a Tannaitic tradition." [L. G.] — The count of *six* in Gen. R. is arrived at by splitting בראשית into ברא שית, cf. Sukkah 49a (Theodor; see his whole note on Gen. R. *ad loc.*; cf. Buber's note in his edition of Midrash Tehillim on Psalm 93, 2, p. 414, n. 11).

I, 527 n. 1

Read pp. 528 f.

I, 528 n. 3

On Noah as a preacher of repentance see L. Ginzberg, Legends of the Jews, V, 174, n. 19.

I, 528 N **237**

The passage cited from the Mekilta adduces the generation of the flood, the tower of Babel, the men of Sodom and Gomorrah, the ten plagues in Egypt, to show that God puts off his intervention to give opportunity for repentance, and causes destruction only when men have brought their wickedness to a consummation (לא נמרת עליהם כלייה עד שהשלימו רשעם לפניך is the refrain of each example). It is natural that such utterances should be more common in the homiletic midrash of the synagogues, but the Mekilta is evidence that the teaching is old and current in the schools of the second century.

I, 531 N **238**

The same Midrash has a parable in part resembling the Prodigal Son: "'Return, O Israel, to the Lord thy God' (Hos. 14, 2). It is like the case of a king's son who was a hundred days journey away from his father. His friends said to him, Go back to your father. He replied, I have not the strength to do so. His father sent word to him, Come as far as your strength permits, and I will come to you the rest of the way. So God said to them, 'Return to me and I will return to you' (Mal. 3, 7)." Pesiḳta Rabbati, ed. Friedmann, f. 184b–185a.

I. 532 N **239**

For Philo on Repentance see further above N **228** and **N 231**.

I, 535 N **240**

To the places cited in the footnotes on I, 393, many others might be added. Perhaps the most significant is R. Joshua ben Levi's inclusion of the heretic (מין) who vexed him with Bible texts — perhaps messianic texts applied to Jesus — among the works of God over whom his mercy extends (Psalm 145, 9. 'Abodah Zarah 7b; Bacher, Pal. Amoräer, I, 147 f.).

I, 537 N **241**

A contemporary of the Patriarch Judah, R. Jose ben Zimra reported by Johanan, generalizes: "When a man depends on his own desert (זכות) he is made to depend on the desert of others; when he depends on the desert of others, he is made to depend on his own desert." Moses is an example of the latter (Exod. 32, 13 and Psalm 106, 23); Hezeḳiah of the former (2 Kings 20, 3 and 2 Kings 19, 34). Berakot 10b; cf. Pesiḳta ed. Buber, f. 167b.

I, 537 N **242**

In a long parallel between Elijah and Moses (Pesiḳta Rabbati, ed. Friedmann, f. 13b) Elijah's invocation in 1 Kings 18, 36 f. (O Lord, God of Abraham, Isaac, and Israel) is interpreted in the same way; both Moses and Elijah laid hold of the good desert of the Patriarchs in their intercession for the sins of the people. Similarly, Exod. R. 44, 1. — It may be noted that the appeal to the merit of the Patriarchs has a large place in Exodus Rabbah, as in Pesiḳta Rabbati, and in later elements in the liturgy.

I, 539 N **243**

The cleaving of the Red Sea is connected with the covenant with Abraham by verbal analogy with Gen. 15, 17 (גזרים). The parting of the waters of the Jordan on his account is elicited from Josh. 3, 16 (אדם העיר = אדם הגדול, *sc.* Abraham, Josh. 14, 15). — Correct the reference note 2 to *read* Yalḳuṭ on Josh. 3, 16 (instead of 13, 16). — On the cleaving of the sea for the sake of Jacob cf. also Mekilta on Exod. 14, 15 (Beshallaḥ 2, ed. Friedmann, f. 28a–b, with the editor's notes; ed. Weiss [3] f. 35a).

I, 540 N **244**

The Mekilta on Exod. 12, 13 (Bo 7, ed. Friedmann, f. 8a, ed. Weiss, f. 11b), in connection with the blood on the door posts and lintels of Israelite houses in the Passover in Egypt, speaks of the *blood* of Isaac's Akedah. In the Pirḳè de Rabbi Eliezer (c. 31), Isaac's soul left his body when the knife drew near his throat, but returned when the voice said to Abraham 'Do not stretch out thy hand to the lad' (Gen. 22, 12), an illustration of the revivification of the dead.

I, 541 N **245**

The blowing of the ram's horn in the New Years liturgy (Shofarot; Vol. II, p. 64) is ordained by God, "that I may remember the binding of Isaac, son of Abraham, and impute it to you as though ye bound yourselves in my presence." Rosh ha-Shanah 16a, end.

I, 541 N **246**

On the Akedah see L. Ginzberg, Legends of the Jews, I, 279–286, V, 249–251.

I, 543 N **247**

See also Tosafot on Shabbat 55a (lemma ושמואל). Rabbenu Tam said: The זכות אבות came to an end, but the covenant of the Fathers did not come to an end (Lev. 26, 42) even after the exile; therefore we now do not make mention (in the liturgy) of the good desert of the Fathers, but of the covenant. Others endeavored to harmonize the apparently contradictory statements in the Talmud.

I, 544 n. 4

Read circumspectio tua.

I, 545 N **249**

זכות is virtue, righteousness, good desert, as in Abot 2, 2 (Gamaliel, son of the Patriarch Judah): All who exert themselves in the interest of the community should do so with a religious motive (לשם שמים), for the virtue (זכות) of their fathers helps them (coöperates with them), and their (*sc.* the Patriarchs') righteousness (צדקה) abides forever. And as for you, I (God) will reckon to you a reward as though you (alone) did the work. — בזכות is, however, often used in a prepositional way, without thinking of the desert, or merit, of the object, as we use 'by virtue of' without any thought of the usual meaning of the noun. Similar cases are the Greek χάριν, δίκην, Latin *gratia* with a genitive, equivalent to *propter*. When we read, for example, that the world was created בזכות התורה (Gen. R. 12, 2; Tanḥuma ed. Buber, Bereshit § 10) or בזכות השבטים (Gen. R.), or בזכות ישראל (Tanḥuma, l.c.), the natural rendering is 'for the sake of the Torah,' 'for the sake of the tribes' (of Israel); 'for the sake of Israel,' not on account of the excellence of the Torah' or 'on account of the good desert of the tribes' or 'of Israel.' So the Red Sea was divided בזכות ירושלים 'for Jerusalem's sake' (Mekilta on Exod. 14, 15, ed. Weiss, f. 35a; citing Isa. 51, 9 f.); the world was created בזכות ציון (Tanḥuma, Buber, Bereshit § 10). — In other places the זכות אבות is a good inheritance which Israel has from its forefathers. Thus Israel is compared to an orphan maiden who has been brought up in a palace. When it came time for her to be married, people said to her, you have nothing at all (no inheritance). She replied, I have something from my father and from my grandfather. So Israel has זכות from that of Abraham and from our father Jacob (Isa. 61, 10; Pesiḳta ed. Buber, f. 147b). Frequently the phrase בזכות אבות is best translated the same way: for the sake of the Patriarchs God opened the well in the desert, for the sake of the Patriarchs Israel was given the manna to eat, etc. (Tanḥuma ed. Buber, Wayyera 9, f. 45b, 46a; Ḥuḳḳot 48; Beshallaḥ 24, etc.).

I, 547 N **250**

It must not be supposed that the idea that the death of the righteous atones for others was actually derived from the juxtaposition remarked in the narratives of Exodus and Numbers. As so often in the Midrash, a commonly accepted notion is discovered by homiletic ingenuity in some such recondite association. That is the way in which the teacher's originality is exhibited. Another illustration of the notion that the death of the righteous atones is the inference from

2 Sam. 21, 14, 'they buried the bones of Saul and Jonathan . . . and after that God was entreated for the land.' (Tanḥuma ed. Buber, Aḥarè 10.)

I, 548 N **251**

To the references given may be added the Midrash on the Ten Commandments (Jellinek, Bet ha-Midrasch, I, 68 f.). When God was about to give the Law, he demanded of the Israelites securities that they would fulfil its requirements. They offered in succession Abraham, Isaac, and Jacob, but these were succesively declined, because each of them was culpable (מחויב) for some (specified) wrongdoing or other. Then they offered their innocent children, and God at once accepted the proposal. They presented the infants at their mother's breast and those still in their mother's womb. To each of the Ten Words these answered with a chorus of Yes, Yes! or No, No! etc. — There seems to be no early trace of this particular bit of Haggadah; but that children die for their parents' sins, see Vol. II, p. 249.

I, 549 N **252**

The story is told in Sifrè Num. on 25, 7 f, cf. vss. 14–16 (§ 131, ed. Friedmann, f. 48a) and in several other places with variations and embellishments. (For a composite narrative reference may be made to L. Ginzberg, Legends of the Jews, III, 383 ff. and VI Notes). The point with which we are here concerned is that when Phineas had impaled Zimri and his Midianitish paramour, Zimri's Simeonite tribesmen sought to kill him. The quotation from Isa. 53, 12 is meant to bring up the following context, 'and was numbered with the transgressors; he bore the sin of many, and intervened on behalf of transgressors.'

I, 549 N **253**

This is probably to be connected with the opinion which identified Phineas with Elijah on the ground of the zeal for God displayed by both (cf. 1 Kings 19, 10, קנא קנאתי לי״י וגו׳ with the reiterated קנא in Num. 25, 10 f.). The Palestinian Targum on Num. 25, 12 runs: "I will make him a messenger of the covenant (Mal. 3, 1; 3, 23 f.), and he shall live forever to proclaim the deliverance at the end of days." The priesthood of Phineas is a כהונת עולם (cf. Num. 25, 13). See also Pirkè de-R. Eliezer, c. 47 (God changed Phineas's name to Elijah).

I, 550 **N 254**

Simlai (second half of the third century) is remembered in Palestinian tradition especially for his replies to Christian controversialists who deduced a plurality of divine persons from certain modes of expression in the Bible (see Bacher, Pal. Amoräer I, 555 f., and above, N 111), and it is surmisable that the application of Isa. 53, 12 to Moses was a tacit parrying of the use made of that passage by Christian apologists (see, e.g., Justin Martyr, Apology, c. 50).

I, 551 **N 255**

It would be a misunderstanding of the whole method of midrash to say that the Rabbis interpreted the passage in Isaiah of Phineas or of Moses. The modern interpreter first fixes the limits of the passage (52, 13–53, 12), and then seeks some figure, historical or ideal, singular or collective, which the whole description fits. The Rabbis did nothing of the kind. The opening verses (52, 13–15) they not unnaturally referred to the Messiah, as in the Targum, but they felt no constraint to extend this interpretation to the following. Similarly, if 53, 12 reminded them of Phineas or of Moses, it did not draw the preceding verses with it. Nor had such an application of the verse any other authority than its plausibility; whoever could suggest another was free to display his ingenuity by doing so. So again, when in a catalogue of the names or titles of the Messiah (Sanhedrin 98b) 'the leprous one,' or 'the sick one,' appears, with quotation of Isaiah 53, 6 (cf. Matth. 8, 16), the application goes no farther than the quotation. All that may legitimately be inferred from such passages is that it was a generally accepted opinion that the suffering of righteous men and their willingness to sacrifice life itself was accepted by God as an atonement for the sins of the people.

At the instance of E. B. Pusey an almost exhaustive collection of Jewish interpretations of Isa. 53, from the earliest down to the seventeenth century, was made by Adolf Neubauer, "The Fifty-Third Chapter of Isaiah according to the Jewish Interpreters" (1876), and accompanied by a volume containing translations by Driver and Neubauer with an introduction by Pusey (1877). Of recent monographs on the "Suffering Messiah" it is sufficient here to refer to August Wünsche, Die Leiden des Messias (1870), and Gustaf Dalman, Der leidende und der sterbende Messias (1888); and to the discussion by J. Klausner, הרעיון המשיחי וגו׳ (1927), pp. 158–160.

I, 551 n. 3

See Note on Vol. I, p. 474, above, p. 145.

II, 6 l. 13

Read (as in the second impression), *by the* horn-blowing.

II, 7

That the Jewish teachers recognize the intrinsic difference between the distinctive observances of Judaism in the sphere of the cultus and the support of the ministry, or of domestic life, and universal moral laws, I have tried to make sufficiently plain here (II, 6–10) and in other places (II, 70–78). What I have maintained is that they also recognized that in a revealed religion which includes both kinds of duties or prohibitions the ground of obligation is the same for both, namely that thus and so is the revealed will of God. The gravity of the offense, in case of neglect or transgression, is dependent not on our natural notions, but upon revelation, which affixes the doom of extirpation (כרת) not solely to vile crimes such as incest but to eating flesh with a remainder of blood in it or the suet of certain animal kinds (p. 6). It belonged to the Jewish faith in God's wisdom and goodness to believe that in prohibiting the flesh of a "hare" (ארנבת) and in similar cases for which there was no reason apparent to men, God had reasons which were beyond human understanding, but that all such things were ordered for the good of his people. Philosophers, from Philo on (see Vol. I, 213 f.), endeavored to discern and explain the divine motive, but he would not admit that the discovery of the goodness and reasonableness of the laws (see, e.g., De specialibus legibus, iv. cc. 4 ff., ed. Mangey, II, 352 ff.) was the reason why Jews should observe them (Vol. II, p. 9). In the sphere of morals, so far as I can see, the Tannaim had no notion of a rationalistic ethics, still less of an intuitive ethics — "thus saith the Lord" was the beginning and end of their wisdom; 'He hath taught thee, O man, what is good; and what doth the Lord require of thee' (Micah 6, 8). Between this attitude and a rationalization like that in Maimonides' "Eight Chapters" lies Aristotle. Without ignoring that morality is integral in Judaism in a sense that cannot be affirmed, for example, of the religions of the Greeks, it may be said that attempts to define Judaism as essentially an "ethical religion," like similar definitions of the essence of Christianity (often in contrast not only to contemporary heathenism but to Judaism), are modernizations which belong to apologetics, not to history.

II, 10 ll. 13–18

Consequences, which when they were put in practice, shocked Paul greatly (see, e.g., his first epistle to the Corinthians, almost throughout).

II, 11 ll. 17–21

This restriction of the sacrificial cultus to one sanctuary had not always existed. Worship at the local "high places" was in its time general and entirely legitimate (e.g., 1 Sam. 9 f.). Deuteronomy 12 (cf. Lev. 17, 3–9) proposes to make an end of all this, and 2 Kings 22 f. narrates how Josiah put in force the provisions of the law in 622/621 B.C. (according to the generally accepted chronology). Doubts about the historical character of this account and about the age of the law itself have not been lacking. We know of a temple with a priesthood and sacrifices at Elephantine, a military colony garrisoned by Jews far up the Nile, which was destroyed by the Egyptians with the connivance of the local Persian governor in 410 B.C. and by the account of the Jews on the spot had existed there before the Persian conquest of Egypt in 525 B.C., and it may be suspected that there were such ἱερά in other places in Egypt before the Onias temple. The latter was erected, or at least reconstructed, under the lead of Palestinian refugees in the days of Antiochus Epiphanes, with a legitimate priesthood of the old Jerusalem line (Josephus, Antt. xii. 9, 7 § 387 f.; xiii. 3, 1–3; Bell. Jud. vii. 10, 2). See Valeton, "Jahwe-Tempels buiten Jerusalem" in Teyler's Theologisch Tijdschrift, 1910, pp. 33 ff.; S. Krauss, Synagogale Altertümer, pp. 72–92, and the literature there cited. — It is sufficient for our present purpose that rabbinical authorities agree in recognizing Jerusalem as the one place where public sacrifice can legitimately be offered.

II, 11 ll. 28–30

As the expansion of Islam made obsolete the annual attendance on the Feast at Mecca (*ḥajj*). Nowadays a man who has made such a visit once in his life adds to his name *hajji*, like a title of nobility. — Ceremonial uncleanness would not exclude from admission to the sacrificial rites and mingling with the throng of worshippers (Ḥagigah 4b), but distance might prevent a man from appearing in Jerusalem at all.

II, 12 ll. 1–4 and n. 1

See also Tos. Pesaḥim 4, 3: Once King Agrippa wanted to take a kind of census, and instructed the priests to save for him one testicle from each passover victim. There proved to be 600,000 pairs of testicles — twice the number of the Israelites who came out of Egypt (Exod. 12, 37) — and there was no passover company numbering less than ten persons; those who were on a far journey, or who were unclean were not included in the numeration. It is added that the "mountain of the house" would not hold them all, and that it was called the "Passover when men were crushed to death." But on this name see Levy III. 190. The resulting number of those present was 1,200,000. Cf. Pesaḥim 64b; Lam. R. on Lam. 1, 1, ed. Buber, f. 23a for the text and the editor's notes). For the name "Passover of the Crushed" a Baraita in Pesaḥim 64b gives another origin, referring it to an occasion in the time of Hillel when an old man was crushed to death by the crowds in the court of the Temple.

II, 12 ll. 16–24

On the prayers and readings in the Temple see M. Yoma 6, 1; Tos. Yom Kippurim, 4, 18; Jer. Yoma, vii. 1; Yoma 70a [L. G.]

II, 12, end, 13 ll. 1 ff.

On the lay deputation (*ma'amad*) see Malter's note in his edition of Ta'anit (1928) on Ta'anit 15b (p. 105, n. 230), also pp. 198 f. (on M. Ta'anit 4, 1–4). — A private sacrifice was presented either by the offerer or by his representative (שליח).

I, 13 n. 5

Cf. Ta'anit 27b, where the purpose of these fasts is specified. Note also the reasons there given for not including Sunday. R. Johanan (third century) said מפני הנוצרים, etc.

II, 14 ll. 1–7

The blowing of the ram's horn and the waving of the palm branches were observed in the synagogues and at home before the destruction of the Temple, cf. M. Rosh ha-Shanah 4, 1; M. Sukkah 3, 12, but outside the Temple the ram's horn was not blown on the Sabbath, and, after the destruction of the Temple, the palm branches, which previously had been manipulated outside the Temple only on the first day of Tabernacles, were used on all the seven days. [L. G.]

II, 14 ll. 25 ff.

One may perhaps surmise that the idea had its starting point in the readings prescribed for the *ma'amadot* (the creation of heaven and earth, Gen. 1), rather than in the Haggadah about Abraham as is alleged in the Talmud. Or did the designation of Gen. 1 for the lessons rest on some such a connection? — In the days of the Amoraim named the temple-worship had long since ceased, but *ma'amadot* had an established place in the synagogue, which was long maintained. Baer, 'Abodat Israel p. 495 cites testimony of Rab Amram to the continuance of the custom in the voluntary practice of individuals, and gives reasons for its discontinuance as part of the synagogue service.

II, 15 n. 1

Reference should be made also to Menaḥot 110a, where the general principle is applied particularly to the various species of sacrifice. In the preceding context it may be noted that on the heavenly altar the great prince Michael offers sacrifice. It is perhaps such studious substitutes for material sacrifice that Rab has in mind.

II, 17 ll. 5–10.

This passage in Herodotus is quoted by Josephus, C. Apionem, i. c. 22 §§ 168–171; cf. Antt. xvii. 10, 3 §§ 260–262.

II, 18 ll. 22–27

R. Akiba would not admit any such delay.

II, 19 l. 15

The term *ger ṣedeḳ* is never applied to the manumitted slave, who is always described as עבד משחרר. . . . The second baptism admitted him to full standing in the Jewish community, including the *connubium*, and imposed upon him the religious obligations, which as a slave he had been exempt from. [L. G.]

II, 19 ll. 19 ff.

See Note on Vol. I, p. 198, n. 3.

II, 22 ll. 19 f.

The inference from 2 Kings 4, that in old Israel people were accustomed to demit their ordinary occupations on the New Moon, and might use the opportunity to visit a "man of God" like Elisha, is one which I should not be inclined to press; our knowledge of what was customary in Israel in the ninth century is too small to warrant confidence.

II, 23 n. 2

Labor was not forbidden on the New Moon, but some made a voluntary or customary holiday of it; see also Megillah 22b. — In Jer. Pesaḥim 30d, top, reference is made to a woman's custom, to refrain, at least partially, from work on the New Moon; cf. Pirkè de-R. Eliezer, c. 45, where an historical origin is attributed to the custom. [L. G.] This is perpetuated and commended in the Codes: see Shulḥan 'Aruk, Oraḥ Ḥayyim § 417.

II, 24 n. 1

Unleavened bread at the Passover season could be the rule everywhere, as doubtless it had been before the destruction of the Temple (cf. Vol. II, p. 40). Other features of the festival rites were taken over, with adaptation, into the synagogue and the home; but the sabbatical observance was the main thing.

II, 26 ll. 3–8

In their wars with the Romans we find it the established rule that defensive operations were licit, but not *offensive*. Josephus, Bell. Jud. i. 7, 3 § 146 (Pompey); cf. ii. 16, 4 § 392 (Agrippa's speech); ii. 17, 10 § 456; iv. 2, 3 § 100. — The Jews represent that they are forbidden to take up arms, even in defense; but they are trying to deceive Titus. The Romans themselves had *feriae publicae* on which it was *nefas* "hostem lacessere bello." (Wissowa, Religion und Kultus der Römer; Festus p. 226). — In Titus's siege of Jerusalem the factions within the city were as little deterred by such scruples from breaking the Sabbath as from desecrating the Temple. — For the rabbinical rules of defensive and offensive military operations references may be made to Maimonides, Hilkot Shabbat 2, 23–25 and the passages of the Talmud there cited in the commentaries ('Erubin 45a; Shabbat 19a).

II, 28 ll. 4–11

This connection of the "thirty-nine" species of labor prohibited on the Sabbath with Deut. 25, 2 f., is very far-fetched, and should not have been asserted as if it were an authenticated fact — the combination seems, on the contrary, to be modern. — For other ways in which the number 39 was ciphered out, see Strack-Billerbeck, I, 617 (paragraph c).

II, 29 n. 2

According to Beṣah 12b, rubbing out the heads of grain in the hands is not threshing, and is therefore only rabbinically prohibited. [L. G.]

II, 31 n. 3

According to Joshua ben Levi "combinations of courts" were ordained only for the sake of peace (friendly relations in the neighborhood). Jer. 'Erubin 20d, below; and 24c, end; Tanḥuma ed. Buber, Noah 22. The rule has, however, been interpreted as a cautionary restrictive measure.

II, 35 n. 2

In the Morning Prayer on the Sabbath of Penitence to the same purport (ישמח משה,' in the fourth 'benediction'): "And thou didst not give it, O Lord our God, unto the Gentiles of the (other) lands, nor didst thou, O our King, make it a heritage of the worshippers of images, and in its resting place the uncircumcised do not abide; but to thy people Israel thou didst give it in love, to the seed of Jacob whom thou didst choose." (Singer, Prayer Book, p. 139; Baer, p. 219, and Baer's note with citations from Talmud and Midrash). Abrahams, Companion to the Daily Prayer Book, pp. cxlvi ff., calls particular attention to the resemblance to Jubilees as illustrating the antiquity of features of the liturgy which otherwise are known to us only from the Gaonic age or after it. Cf. also the Ḳiddush of the day, on the eve of the Sabbath (Singer, p. 124; Baer, p. 198).

II, 35 l. 31

The three meals are obligatory, even for a pauper who is dependent on alms. There seems to be no authority for making of the third a *light* repast; the codes treat them all alike, each of them presuming the regular provision of wine and the breaking of the two loaves (Maimonides, Hilkot Shabbat 30, 9). The Shulḥan 'Aruk, however, contemplates the case of a man who has eaten to satiety at the previous meal; he may satisfy his obligation by eating a quantity no greater than an egg, and if he cannot do even that, he is not bound to force himself (Oraḥ Ḥayyim § 291, 1). A wise man will look out not to fill his belly at the forenoon meal, so as to have room for the third meal (ibid.).

II. 36 ll. 5–8

The statement about the sabbath lamp was corrected in the second printing to read as follows: "It was an ancient custom . . . on Friday afternoon before dark to light a lamp which was to be left burning through the evening of the holy day."

II, 36 ll. 15 ff.

This Kiddush belongs in the home, where the table has been spread for the family meal. In Tannaite times there were no congregational prayers in the afternoon, and the eve of the Sabbath was not an exception. The introduction of a Ḳiddush into the synagogue service on Friday afternoon, like this service itself, is later, and is thought to have begun in Babylonia. There is mention, however, of a Ḳiddush in the synagogue building, and over wine, in Mekilta Baḥodesh 7 (ed. Friedmann f. 69a–b; ed. Weiss f. 76b–77a; cf. Pesaḥim 106a), and on the other hand we hear from Samuel (Babylonia, 3d cent.), אין קדוש אלא במקום סעודה. The place of the Ḳiddush and Habdalah in the congregational prayer is a very tangled history, into which there is, fortunately no necessity to penetrate here. See I. Elbogen, "Eingang und Ausgang des Sabbats nach talmudischen Quellen," in Festschrift zu Israel Lewy's siebzigstem Geburtstag (1911), pp. 173–187; L. Ginzberg, REJ. LXVII (1914), pp. 133 f., 150. Ginzberg thinks that the Ḳiddush (קדושא רבא, Pesaḥim 106a, to which he would refer the passage in the Mekilta) originally had its place in the Sabbath morning service in the synagogue, the transposition to the eve of the Sabbath was later, since it presumes a Friday afternoon service.

The Ḳiddush in the home on the eve of the Sabbath is usually pronounced over the wine. It is permissible, however, to say it, omitting, of course, the blessing on the wine, over the two loaves of bread, if the householder likes it better than wine, or if he has no wine (Pesaḥim 106b; Maimonides, Hilkot Shabbat, 29, 9; Shulḥan 'Aruk, Oraḥ Ḥayyim § 271, 12).

II, 36 ll. 22 f.

This symbolism is a homiletic afterthought.

II, 36 n. 3

The form of blessing over the lights found in the prayer-books is mediaeval.

II, 36 n. 7

This note should be cancelled. — The כוס של ברכה is the cup following which the grace after meals (ברכת המזון) is said. On the Sabbath the grace after meals is expanded by the insertion of a prayer appropriate to the day, known from its initial word as רְצֵה (Singer, p. 281 f.; Baer, p. 557), which is in substance very old.

II, 37 ll. 11–14, n. 3

The text is not as clear as it should be: fasting on the Sabbath is never permissible (except when the Day of Atonement falls on a Sabbath); M. Ta'anit 3, 7 names certain emergencies in which an alarm may be sounded on the Sabbath (cf. Ta'anit 22b), but has nothing to say about fasting on that day.

II, 40

On the rules for Passover and Unleavened Bread a century or more before the Christian era, see Jubilees 49. The prescriptions closely follow the biblical laws and interpret them strictly (see especially 49, 20); nothing sectarian is discoverable in them.

II, 40 ll. 12–14

The obligation to partake of the *maṣṣot* on the eve of the fifteenth is treated as an independent requirement of the Law, binding everywhere and in all times. Maimonides, Hilkot Ḥamaṣ u-Maṣṣah, 6, 1; see also the discussion, Pesaḥim 120a. — "There can be no doubt that long before the destruction of the Temple, the Passover meal became a home ceremony entirely independent of the sacrifice. In the description of this ceremony in M. Pesaḥim 10, 1–7, though composed before 70 (cf. Hoffmann, Die erste Mischna, pp. 16–17), the sacrifice plays a very subordinate part." [L. G.]

II, 40 n. 4

As at the other pilgrim festivals, when all male Israelites were required to appear before the Lord at the sanctuary of his choice (Jerusalem), Exod. 23, 14, 17; Deut. 16, 16, the actual participation of women is not questioned. On the whole subject see M. Pesaḥim, 8, 1; cf. Pesaḥim 91a (discussion by disciples of R. Akiba).

II, 42 ll 1–21

The modern rule corresponds; see Shulḥan 'Aruk, Oraḥ Ḥayyim § 476, 1.

II, 42 ll. 21 f.

The cup of Elijah owes its origin to a misunderstood phrase. In Pesaḥim 117b (bottom) some authorities in the Middle Ages read, 'the fourth 'cup (רביעי) and others 'the third' (שלישי, see Tosafot *in loc.*). This question, like many others, Elijah would have to settle when he came. [L. G.] See below, Note on Vol. II, p. 359, n. 4.

II, 43 ll. 12 ff.

"The exact time of this procession is nowhere given. I am inclined to assume that it took place before Musaf, as is now the custom among Sephardim and has the authority of Sa'adia." (See Genizah Studies, II, n. 18). On p. 44, l. 1, for "the people" *read* "the priests." — "It is also very doubtful whether they marched with palm-branches; the text of the Mishnah rather favors the view given in Sukkot 43b that the weeping-willow was carried and not the palm-branches." [L. G.]

II, 45 ll. 7 ff.

See Feuchtwanger, "Die Wasseropfer und die damit verbundenen Zeremonien," Monatsschrift, LIV–LV.

II, 45 ll. 25 ff.

For a different interpretation ("Fackelhaus") which would explain the name of the illumination of the Temple, see Kohut, Aruch Completum, I, 85, where it is etymologically associated with the Syriac *shauba*, 'burning heat, *simmum* wind' (Bar Baḥlul, ed. Duval, 1939); it is employed to render the Greek καύσων (see Payne Smith, s.v., col. 4085 f.). That the word was ever used of a light or a torch, I find no evidence.

II, 49 ll. 5–10

The name *Simḥat Torah* is mediaeval; the earliest authority to mention it is Hai Gaon. Previously this day (23d of Tishri) was indicated merely as the second of Shemini 'Aṣeret. The one year cycle of Pentateuch lessons which ended and recommenced on this day is Babylonian, though it has become universal. Elbogen Der jüdische Gottesdienst, pp. 167, 200.

II, 49 ll. 25–30

Josephus, Antt. xii. 7, 7 § 325; cf. c. Apionem, ii. 9 § 118. Apart from the reported difference between the Shammaites and the Hillelites (Shabbat 21b), there is not much about the Ḥanukkah lights in Palestinian sources, though Palestinian Amoraim are quoted in the Babylonian Talmud (Johanan, Joshua ben Levi, al.). The provision for putting them out of sight, or in a position where they might seem to be ordinary household lights, in case of danger, seems to point to countries under Sassanian (Zoroastrian) rule in the third century.

II, 56 n. 2

In M. Yoma 6, 8, the place is called בית חדודו (cf. Enoch, 10, 4, Dudael); in the editions of the Pal. Targum, בית חדורי. In the Mishnah of the Jer. Talmud (10, 9) בית חורון is not the *terminus ad quem*.

II, 59 l. 10

On the observance of the day, see Philo, De septenario c. 23, ed. Mangey, II, 296 f.; on the all-day supplications, § 196.

II, 59 l. 23

For *after* read *before* [Perles].

II, 61 ll. 18–21, and n. 4.

The quotation of Cant. 3, 11 in the Mishnah is the answer of the young man (*read* וכך הוא אומר, so Mishnah, ed. Lowe); see Malter, Ta'anit (1928), p. 203, n. 389. — The match-making of the day left its traces in the reading of the פרשת עריות at the afternoon service; Megillah 31a. [L. G.]

II, 62 ll. 5–10

In the liturgy note the prayer אתה זוכר in the Musaf service on New Years (Singer, p. 249 f.; Baer, pp. 400–402); cf. Elbogen, Der jüdische Gottesdienst, pp. 142, 143 f., 204. The age of this prayer prefatory to the Zikronot (see Vol. II, p. 64) is not known, but the ideas of God's all-comprehending knowledge and his perfect justice are both old and familiar; and his annual judgement on nations and individuals was long-established belief.

II, 63 l. 25

An error in this passage was corrected in the second printing: it should accordingly read: "it was transposed to a later hour, in the Musaf prayers," and in the sequel: "It retained this place in the liturgy, but what might be called an anticipatory horn-blowing was introduced when the congregation was seated after the close of the morning prayer and the reading of the law." See Rosh ha-Shanah 16a–b, where the question is raised why the ram's horn is blown when the congregation is seated and (again) when they are standing (in the Musaf prayers); see Maimonides, Hilkot Shofar, 3, 10–12; Elbogen, Der jüdische Gottesdienst, p. 140 f., 142.

II, 64 l. 4

On the significance of these three proper benedictions for New Years, cf. Rosh ha-Shanah 16a, bottom. — It may be noted that the verses selected in the Malkuyot refer to God's goodness to Israel, not to his discomfiture of the heathen.

II, 66 ll. 6 f.

That is, it was treated as a public fast in distinction from a fast of individuals.

II, 70 ll. 3–6

Vespasian converted this into an annual poll-tax on all Jews in whatever part of the empire, to be appropriated to the temple of Jupiter on the Capitoline in Rome, as previously they had paid it to the Temple in Jerusalem, Josephus, Bell. Jud. vii. 6, 6 § 218; Dio Cassius, lxv. 7, 2.

II, 70 n. 1

The portion of the sacrificing priests, defined in Lev. 7, 31–34. According to the Mishnah (M. Ḥullin, 10, 1; cf. Sifrè Deut. § 165) of an animal slaughtered for food (not a prescribed victim) the parts named in Deut. 18, 3 are customarily given to a priest (M. Ḥallah, 5, 9), both in the land of Israel and outside the land, and whether the Temple is standing or not. In the Talmud (Ḥullin 136a) the opinion of Rabbi Ila'i (contemporary of Ishmael and Akiba, early second century) was that these presents (מתנות), like the Terumah, were made only in the land of Israel, not outside of it.

II, 71 n. 1

On the character of some of the high priestly houses of this period see Pesaḥim 57a; Tos. Menaḥot 13, 18–22; cf. Tos. Sukkah 14, 6. In Jer. Yoma 38c the great number of high priests who served in the second temple is accounted for by their getting into office by murder (of their predecessors), "some say that they killed one another by sorcery" (בכשפים).

II, 71 n. 4

On the ratio of the Terumah to the whole, a difference of opinion between the Schools of Shammai and Hillel is reported in Tos. Terumot 5, 3, the former regarding 1/30 as liberal, the latter 1/40. The former is thought to have in view the well-to-do; the latter, the poor. [L. G.]

II, 71 n. 6

The burning of Ḥallah is prescribed in the Mishnah in certain regions in or adjacent to Palestine, where two Ḥallahs are required one of which is thrown into the fire; see M. Ḥallah 4, 5. See Büchler, Der galiläische ʻAm ha-'Areṣ, pp. 255 ff. For modern rules see Shulḥan ʻAruk, Yoreh Deʻah § 322 ff.

II, 71 n. 7

On the meaning and use of the phrase "Mosaic law from Sinai," see Vol. I, p. 256.

II, 72 n. 1

See Büchler, Der galiläische ʻAm ha-'Areṣ, p. 16.

II, 72 n. 2

On the dire consequences of the neglect of tithing, see Abot 5, 8 f. M. Yadaim, 4, 3; the statement in Midrash Tehillim is not found in early sources. [L. G.]

II, 73 ll. 2–5

The Terumah Gedolah of agricultural products (Num. 18, 12 f.) and the tenth of the Levites' tithe (Terumat Maʻaser, Num. 18, 25–28) are the portion of the priests and their households (being in a state of ceremonial "cleanness"); Vol. II, p. 72 (Num. 18, 13–19), and are strictly prohibited to all others; while the remainder of the Levites' tithe is not sacred, and may be eaten by any one.

II, 73 end

Read (as corrected in the second impression): *ʻAmme ha-'areṣ*, 'the (ignorant) people of the land.'

II, 74

On the so-called "dietary laws," and their educational importance, see Josephus, c. Apionem, ii. 17. On the meaning and wisdom of these laws, Philo, De special. legibus, iv. §§ 100 ff. (De concupiscentia, cc. 4 ff., ed. Mangey, II, 352 ff.). Allegorical interpretation, Ep. Aristeae, §§ 143 ff. (ed. Wendland). — On rules attributed to Pythagoras, Diogenes Laertius, viii. 19 ff., 33–35. — Abstinence from every kind of animal food was common in philosophical piety.

II, 74 l. 25–75, l. 3

Such inspection (בדיקה) as is now practiced is of very late origin; it is not known in Talmudic times. (L. G.]

II. 75 l. 4

"Difficult" is hardly strong enough; for a strictly observant Jew it would have been impossible; particularly the cooking utensils used in a Gentile kitchen made anything prepared in them prohibited food.

II, 75 ll. 22 ff.

For a curious partial parallel in Unyoro (Central Africa) see Frazer, Taboo and the Perils of the Soul (Golden Bough, Vol. III, p. 272).

II, 75 n. 2

Cf. Esther (Greek), after 4, 17 (Esther says): *καὶ οὐκ ἐδόξασα συμπόσιον βασιλέως, οὐδὲ ἔπιον οἶνον σπονδῶν* [Perles].

II, 76 ll. 9 f.

Contact with *dead* animals is meant, and should have been said.

II, 76 ll. 13 ff.

See Büchler, Der galiläische 'Am ha-'Areṣ, p. 2 f., n., and pp. 157 ff.

II, 76 ll. 20f.

The purifications here meant are those which required an offering in the Temple. There were rites of purification in which the year 70 was no such crisis, and these may have been observed by scrupulous persons thereafter. For an example see Ḥagigah 25a, and on the question how long they thus continued see L. Ginzberg, Genizah Studies, p. 71.

II, 77 ll. 11–16

See Note on Vol. II, p. 7.

II, 81 ll. 20–22

See below on Vol II, p. 83, n. 2.

II, 83 n. 2

Plato, Diogenes Laertius, iii. 90: *φρόνησις, δικαιοσύνη, ἀνδρεία, σοφρωσύνη*, with brief definitions of their several spheres.

II, 85 ll. 7–9

Numerous echoes and applications of this saying, or of the principles enounced in it, are collected by Kobryn *ad loc.* (f. 25a–27b). — The order, Truth, Justice, Peace, in which the three terms are sometimes found, seems to me to be a transposition, bringing the order into correspondence with Zech. 8, 16, quoted in the sequel.

II, 85 l. 24

בכל מאודך. In Berakot 61b the word is understood of material resources, *mammon*. A different interpretation is quoted from R. Akiba who finds in the word מדה, 'measure'; see Vol. II, p. 253 and n. 4.

II, 85 n. 1

Sifrè, l.c., is quoted in Ta'anit 2a, below.

II. 87 ll. 12 ff.

See King, "The Negative Golden Rule," Canadian Journal of Religious Thought (1928).

II, 95 n. 5

The term בעל חוב, 'creditor,' is used of God in his relation to man; Marmorstein, The Old Rabbinic Doctrine of God, p. 79, citing Shebu'ot 42b, top; Giṭṭin 51b (Rabbah). Other instances in which sin and its penalty are a debt to God are Jer. Shabbat, 15d, הניחו לנבאי שיגבה חובו, and Jer. Ta'anit 66c, where God is מרי חובא. Büchler, Studies in Sin and Atonement (1928), p. 154, n. 2, p. 336, n. 1. On flogging in expiation of offenses against which the כרת is denounced, see Sifrè on Deut. 25, 3 (§ 286): כל חייבי כריתות שלקו נפטרו מיד כריתתן.

II, 96 n. 1

On פרס see Note on Vol. I, p. 35.

II, 98 ll. 6–9

See Vol. I, p. 367. Marmorstein, op. cit., pp. 105–107; though with his surmise that it means "the Father in Heaven" I do not agree.

II, 99

On the service of God out of love or fear, and the obedience of Job, see Büchler, Studies in Sin and Atonement (1928), pp. 122 ff.

II, 101

On the Ḳaddish, see Vol. I, p. 306, Notes **83**, **84**.

II, 102 ll. 4–12

Cf. Ecclus. 33 (36), 1–5.

II, 103 n. 2

In Sanhedrin 74a–b, the offense must be committed with publicity, which is defined as under the observation of at least ten Israelites; but it may be about so small a matter as changing the Jewish mode of lacing shoes for one customary among the heathen, in which the form of the knot had perhaps a magical or a superstitious significance. In the same passage a difference is made between ordinary occasions and a time of religious persecution when the government undertakes by edict to nullify the Jewish law. See Maimonides, Yesodè ha-Torah, 5, 1 ff.

II, 104 ll. 16f.

By an oversight to which Professor Perles has kindly called my attention, number 4 in the text is used twice, and the second of the two notes thus indicated was omitted altogether. The bit of Midrash on Psalm 123, 1 is preserved in the Yalkuṭ II § 548, end (on Amos 9, 6), from which Buber has restored it in his edition of Midrash Tehillim on the Psalm (f. 255a). The last clause in my quotation (l. 16) should read: Otherwise, *Thou wouldst* not be sitting in the heavens.

II, 105 ll. 7–14

The point of the story about Sarah is not the act of charity, but the demonstration that she had borne a child, thus hallowing the name of God. [L. G.].

II, 106 ll. 19 ff.

I. Halevy argues, against Graetz and others, that this conference was held before the fall of Bether (the last act of the war under Hadrian); see Doroth Harischonim, I e (Vol. II), pp. 371 f. For the purpose of the present work this question is not vital.

II, 113 ll. 15–19

Cf. what the Jewish deputation has to say before the Emperor Augustus against the succession of Archelaus, and their request that their country be annexed to Syria under the administration of governors of their own people in Josephus, Bell. Jud. ii. 6, 2; see also ii. 2, 3 § 22 (autonomy under the administration of a Roman governor).

II, 114 ll. 1 ff.

Cf. The Essene oath, Josephus, Bell. Jud. ii. 1, 7: At his initiation "he swears tremendous oaths, first, that he will reverence the Deity, then that he will deal justly with men, and injure no one, either of his own accord or under orders, will always hate the unjust and contend strenuously on the side of the just; that he will ever keep faith with all men, especially with those in power, for without God rule comes to no man," etc. See also Cant. R. (on Cant. 2, 7) and Ketubot 111a, top. — Biblical examples of honor paid to heathen governments and rulers, Mekilta Bo, 13 (ed. Friedmann, 13b–14a).

II, 115 n. 4

References may be added: Josephus Antt. xii. 10, 5 § 406 (for the Seleucid king); c. Apion. ii. 6 § 76 f. (for the Emperors and the Roman people).

II, 115 n. 6

See also the sequel, Bell. Jud. ii. 17, 3 f. (§§ 409–417).

II, 116 l. 8 and n. 1

The name "Vespasian" makes difficulty, for although Josephus (Bell. Jud. iv. 3, 2 § 130) brings Vespasian from Caesarea to Jamnia and Azotus, while Titus, after the fall of Gischala and the flight of John to Jerusalem, moved his headquarters to Caesarea, all this was before the investment of Jerusalem. The strife of factions, however, was already raging within the city as well as throughout the land.

II, 119 ff.

L. M. Epstein, The Jewish Marriage Contract. A study of the Status of Woman in Jewish Law. 1927. With a classified bibliography of the whole subject (pp. 301–304) and an index.

II, 119 ll. 19 f.

That eighteen is the proper age for a man to marry is to be found in Abot 5, 21, where the whole of life is laid off in a comprehensive scheme (Vol. I, p. 320). In foot-note 5 the reference to Ḳiddushin 29b has to do only with the words attributed to R. Ishmael. In the sequel other opinions about the best age for marriage are reported. See L. Ginzberg, Genizah Studies, I. 478. The actual ages most likely varied widely from any mean, with times and circumstances.

II, 120 n. 1

See Ginzberg, *l.s.c.* In Ḳiddushin 29b I have followed the interpretation of Rashi; the contrary explanation is given in the Tosafot.

II, 120 n. 7

One may compare the advice of Pittacus about such an alternative in the Anthology, vii. No. 89: τὴν κατὰ σαυτὸν ἔλα.

II, 121 n. 3

See also S. Krauss, "Die Ehe zwischen Onkel und Nichte," in Studies in Jewish Literature in honor of K. Kohler (1913), pp. 165–175.

II, 121 n. 6

See, however, Ḳiddushin 41a (repeated, 81b, below), in the name of Rab (or "as some say, R. Eleazar"): "A man is forbidden to give his daughter in marriage while she is a minor (*ḳeṭannah*), until she grows up and says, I want so and so." This rule is incorporated in the modern code (Shulḥan 'Aruk, Eben ha-'Ezer 37, 8; but see the Tosafot on Ḳiddushin 41a and commentators on Shulḥan 'Aruk l.c.).

II, 121 ll. 14 ff.

See A. Büchler, "Das jüdische Verlöbnis, u.s.w.," in Festschrift zu Israel Lewy's siebzigstem Geburtstag (1911), pp. 110 ff.

II, 122 ll. 1–3

The expressions used in these lines are exposed to misunderstanding. I did not mean to suggest a religious character in the Ḳiddushin; but the exclusive right of the husband in his wife, just as things and persons in which God has an exclusive right are said in the Bible to be *ḳadosh*, and as such not to be meddled with by others. An equivalent, and presumably older, term is קנה, 'acquire' (property rights). Professor Perles brings to my notice the fact that Rappoport associated the word Ḳiddushin with the Aramaic (and Syriac) קדשא 'ring,' (the man gave the woman a ring), but I should imagine that the ring was so-called because it was an amulet, and of an ancient Jewish ring ceremony in betrothal or wedding I know nothing. (See S. Krauss, Talmudische Archäeologie, II, 36 and p. 455, n. 298).

II, 122 l. 5

Sexual relations of any kind with foreign female slaves are strictly prohibited; see M. Giṭṭin 4, 5. The kind of slavery of Jewish women contemplated in Exod. 21, 7–11 had gone out of use in the times of the Tannaim and Amoraim; the rabbis see in the union of a Jewish female servant and her master a regular marriage, not concubinage (Ḳiddushin 19b). [L. G.]. — The statement in the text that "the rabbinical law corresponds" must be qualified accordingly.

II, 122 ll. 6–10

On polygamy see the article in the Jewish Encyclopedia, X, 120–122, especially for this period, p. 121 A. — "I know of only one case of polygamy among the Tannaim, Abba, the brother of Gamaliel II (Jewish Encyclopedia, I, 29)." [L. G.]. — The nine wives of Herod — not all at once — by seven of whom he had offspring (Josephus, Bell. Jud. i. 28, 4 § 562), are to be regarded as privileges of uxorious royalty, not as examples of custom among his subjects.

II, 122 ll. 16 ff.

For the literature on divorce, see L. M. Epstein, The Jewish Marriage Contract, pp. 302 f.

II, 122 ll. 12–15

On the marriage contract (Ketubah) see Epstein, cited in the last note. That some form of marriage contract is older than Simeon ben Shaṭaḥ is demonstrable (Epstein, *op. cit.*, pp. 17–31); the precise nature of the changes introduced by Simeon ben Shaṭaḥ it is difficult to determine.

II, 123 ll. 6–9

Giṭṭin 90b. See Bacher, cited in n. 3, who surmises that the rabbis here named were the two sons of R. Ḥiyya (third century). It is possible that the two rabbis had in mind different cases.

Josephus' account of his own divorce from his second wife, who had borne him three children (Vita, c. 76 § 426), μὴ ἀρεσκόμενος αὐτῆς τοῖς ἤθεσιν ἀπεπεμψάμην, is indefinite enough.

II, 126 ll. 27 f.

The most significant advance beyond the biblical laws is to be seen in emancipation of the girl who has arrived at the age of puberty (גדולה ,בוגרת) from the control of her father; she is thenceforth completely her own mistress. This is treated in Tannaite laws not as the kind of innovation that is nowadays called a "reform," but as an established principle. See, e.g., Mekilta on Exod. 21, 7 (ed. Friedmann, f. 74b; ed. Weiss, f. 84a).

II, 127 n. 4

The age was not the decisive factor, but the physical evidence of puberty. Since there were abnormal cases both of premature and of delayed development, the rule was that a girl remained under the authority of her father from twelve years to twelve years and six months.

II, 127 ll. 15–17

The earnings of a daughter belong to her father until she becomes *suae juris;* those of a boy in his minority are his own. [L. G.]

II, 128 n. 4

The obligation of fathers to teach their sons Torah and to begin talking Hebrew to them as soon as they began to speak, and that there is no similar duty to teach their daughters, see Sifrè Deut. § 146, on Deut. 11, 19.

II, 129 ll. 14–16

The rule that women are exempt from positive commandments for the observance of which a time is set (Sifrè Num. § 115, at the beginning, on Num. 15, 37 f.) was perhaps first formulated by R. Simeon (ben Yoḥai) who is named there. The Mishnah is frequently at variance with the general rule enounced by R. Simeon; e.g., M. Berakot, 3, 3, quoted in the text. [L. G.]. — The commentators who feel obliged to harmonize these prescriptions with the general rule, are put to some straits.

II, 129 l. 17

The parenthesis (*at Tabernacles*) is accidentally misplaced: it should stand after "the palm-branches."

II, 129 n. 10

These rules affect all the relations of men with women.

II, 130 n. 5

See, however, Ḳiddushin 52b, at the bottom, and Tosafot, *ad loc.* (lemma, וכי).

II, 133 l. 19

This Dama ben Netina lived before the destruction of the Temple; see note 8, and add Tos. Parah 2, 1.

II, 135 ll. 7–10

In Sanhedrin 71a, R. Simeon (ben Yoḥai) is quoted as saying (in regard to some of the specifications of the rabbinical law defining Deut. 21, 20), "Such a case never arose and never will arise."

II, 135 ll. 20–22

The rules found in rabbinical sources about the Hebrew slave are purely theoretical. In 'Arakin 29a it is said that this form of servitude existed only as long as the year of Jubilee was observed, i.e., in the time of the first temple; this is probably an exegetical inference not an historical tradition, but we may safely infer that it had become obsolete long before the age of the Tannaim. See Vol. II, p. 138.

II, 136 ll. 1–4

On the "Canaanite" (alien) slave in Jewish law, see Maimonides, Hilkot 'Abadim, 5 ff. — The legal status of such a slave was better than in Roman law. See, in general, S. Krauss, Talmudische Archäologie, II, 91 ff.; Rubin, Das talmudische Recht, I, i, Die Sklaverei, 1920.

II, 136 n. 1

Whether the slave is real or personal property is in controversy between R. Meir and his colleagues. Baba Meṣi'a 100b. [L. G.]

II, 137 n. 1

The father is here supposed to be a *Gentile* or a Gentile freedman, not a Jew, to whom such relations were, according to most authorities, forbidden.

II, 138 l. 19

See Note on Vol. II, p. 135, ll. 20–22.

II, 142 ll. 13–20

Various kinds of adulteration are named in Eccles. R. 6, 1, along with fraudulent balances, etc.

II, 145 n. 5

The words of the usurer are euphemistically paraphrased in the Talmud. The meaning is "Moses was a *fool*, and his Torah is *not* true." [L. G.]

II, 149 n. 2

Note also the מלשינים in early forms of the Birkat ha-Minim (Shemoneh 'Esreh, 12).

II, 150 l. 7

Read *lishan*.

II, 151 n. 1

On הגיון see L. Ginzberg, Unbekannte jüdische Sekte, pp. 70 f.

II, 152 n. 2

That is, a man should not insist on his rights to the utmost limit of the law, but have regard to the equity of the case and in fairness rather concede something to the other party. The Roman proverb *summum ius summa iniuria* (Cicero, De officiis, i. 10, 33) will occur to everyone.

II, 154 n. 4

Reference may also be made to Yoma 87a. For a form of confession, see Vol. I, p. 512 (N **225**).

II, 156 ff. (chap. vi)

See Bousset-Gressmann, Die Religion des Judentums, 3 ed. (1926), pp. 183 ff.

II, 157 ll. 21f.

In Seder 'Olam (c. 30, ed. Ratner f. 70b) the prophets prophesied till the time of Alexander of Macedon: "from that time on, incline thine ear and hear the words of the learned (*ḥakamim*), Prov. 22, 16 f."

II, 157 n. 5

See also Israel Abrahams, 'Am ha-'Areç, appended to Montefiore, The Synoptic Gospels (2 ed., 1927), II, 647–669.

II, 158 ll. 19–21

"In Tannaite times unclean food is *not* prohibited; men may partake of it if they are willing to take the consequence of becoming impure." [L. G.] See Maimonides, Hilkot Tum' at Okelin, 16, 7 ff.

II, 158 n. 1

The Babylonian Talmud does not lack reported answers to the question, Who is an '*am ha-'areṣ?*, and Babylonian scholars contribute their own (see, e.g., Berakot 29a).

II, 159 ll. 13 ff.

For the texts see Büchler, Der galiläische 'Am ha-'Areṣ, at the beginning; cf. I. Abrahams, 'Am ha-'Areç (above, Note on Vol. II, p. 157, n. 5).

II, 160 n. 1

Jesus son of Sirach was of the same way of thinking. See Bousset-Gressmann, Religion des Judentums, u.s.w., p. 164. In his case one might suspect something of upper-class feeling; but not in Hillel, who was himself a man of the people. For parallels to Hillel's saying, see Kobryn, Catena on Abot, f. 35b.

II, 162 n. 4

It is one of the most important differences between R. Ishmael and R. Akiba; see D. Hoffmann, Einleitung in die halachischen Midraschim, pp. 7–9. [L. G.]

II, 167 l. 5

On almsgiving in secret (בסתר) see Baba Batra 9b. R. Eliezer deduces from two texts that the man who gives alms in secret is greater than Moses.

II, 167 n. 5

Read העבט תעביטנו.

II, 168 n. 3

Hilkot Ṣedaḳah in R. Jacob ben Asher's Tur Yoreh De'ah (14th century) is in many respects superior to Maimonides' treatment of the subject. [L. G.] See also Schechter, Studies in Judaism, III.

II, 169 ll. 16–20

On the ups and downs of human life, cf. Philo, De somniis, i. 24 §§ 154–156, ed. Mangey I, 644 (symbolized by Jacob's ladder).

II, 171 ll. 15 f.

On the almsgiving of Gentiles different opinions are expressed. Johanan ben Zakkai is reported to have said, "as the sin-offering atones for Israel so almsgiving atones for the nations of the world" (Baba Batra, 10b, below; cf. his saying after the destruction of the Temple about the cessation of sacrificial atonement, Vol. I, p. 503; Vol. II, p. 172). The preceding context records the answers which the disciples of Johanan ben Zakkai made to a question he propounded to them, How do you interpret Prov. 14, 34 צדקה תרומם גוי וחסד לאומים חטאת? They took גוי to refer to Israel (quoting 2 Sam. 7, 23), and חטאת to mean 'sin': "Almsgiving exalts a nation (Israel), and the charity of the nations is sin," with various definitions of the nature of the sin — they do it to extend their dominion, to boast of it, to taunt Israel with, etc. After they had delivered these opinions one after another, R. Johanan gave his interpretation of the verse, in effect: Almsgiving exalts a Gentile (גוי), and the charity of the nations is a sin-offering (for them). All agree in taking חסד as synonymous with צדקה. The rendering of the English version, "but sin is a reproach to any people," said to have been anticipated by Symmachus (ὀνεῖδος δὲ λαοῖς ἁμαρτίαι — 'disgrace' as LXX in Lev. 20, 17, taking it as Aramaic equivalent of Hebrew חרפה). Cf. Pesikta ed. Buber, f. 12b (Abin bar Judah; see Bacher, Pal. Amoräer, III, 759).

II, 172–173

For a similar distinction attributed to Plato see Diogenes Laertius iii. § 95 f. (Εὐεργεσία . . . ἢ χρήμασιν ἢ σώμασιν, κ. τ. λ.)

II, 172 n. 7

On this interpretation of Psalm 89, 3, cf. L. Ginzberg, Legends of the Jews, VI, 145, n. 42. — The words are quoted in Sifra on Lev. 20, 17, apropos of Cain's wife (his sister).

II, 181 ll. 24–26

On the duty of giving evidence see also Tos. Shebu'ot, 3, 1 f.

II, 183 n. 1

Into the numerous and various cases in which excommunication could be pronounced — Maimonides, Hilkot Talmud Torah, 6, 14, enumerates twenty-four — and into the forms and degrees of excommunication there is no occasion to enter here; the important thing for us is that a court had power to excommunicate for contumacy of any kind.

II, 184 n. 4

Sifrè Num. § 161 and Tos. Sanhedrin 9, 4 refer to the witness *pleading* in behalf of the accused, not to *testifying*. [L. G.]

II, 187 l. 14

More exactly "eight rows back" (from the front, where God was); Akiba belonged to a later generation. See Vol. I, p. 256.

II, 188 ll. 18f.

On the order of these three things, see above, Note on Vol. II, p. 85.

II, 189 l. 7

That is, make up some *false* answer. Others understand תתבדה "be given the lie."

II, 189 n. 4

For הן as an affirmative particle see Mekilta on Exod. 19, 20 (ed. Friedmann, f. 66a; ed. Weiss, f. 73b); Ishmael and Akiba.

II, 189 n. 8

The equivalent biblical phrase is גנב לב (the heart as the seat of intelligence, the mind).

II, 191 l. 8

In the second Epistle of Clement, c. 12, this saying is attributed to Jesus. [L. G.] — See the prayer of Socrates at the end of Plato's Phaedrus: *Ὦ φίλε Πάν τε καὶ ἄλλοι ὅσοι τῇδε θεοί, δοίητέ μοι καλῷ γενέσθαι τ'ἄνδοθεν.* (The resemblance is rather verbal than real; the "*ἔξωθεν*" here are external circumstances) *ἔξωθεν δ' ὅσα ἔχω, τοῖς ἐντὸς εἶναι μοι φίλια.*

II, 193 ll. 15 ff.

On the bad Pharisees, see the advice of Alexander Jannaeus, when dying, to his wife (Soṭah 22b): Do not be afraid of the Pharisees, nor of those that are not Pharisees, but of the counterfeits (lit. "dyed") who resemble Pharisees (outwardly); whose deeds are like the deed of Zimri but claim a reward like Phineas" (Num. 25).

II, 194 ll. 20 ff.

On God's Truth see Marmorstein, The Old Rabbinic Doctrine of God, pp. 179–181.

II, 195 ll. 5 ff.

Cf. Josephus, Contra Apionem, ii. 22 § 190, *ἀρχὴ καὶ μέσα καὶ τέλος οὗτος τῶν πάντων.*

II, 196 n. 1

Read ed. Horovitz, pp. 248–250, as in the second impression.

II, 196 n. 4

In the names of synagogues the singular is usual, Oheb Shalom, etc.

II, 202 ff.

See Marmorstein, The Old Rabbinic Doctrine of God, pp. 56–61, 109, 121 f., 136. — The earliest use of Abinu as an invocation in prayer is 1 Chron. 29, 10 (David): אבינו מעולם ועד עולם, 'our Father from eternity and to eternity' (forever and ever). [Perles.]

II, 204 l. 20

On these substitutes for the Name see N 113a (on Vol. I, p. 373).

II, 204 l. 25f.

Read *from* Hellenistic Judaism, as in the second impression.

II, 204 n. 4

Seder Eliahu Rabbah contains a good deal of older material.

II, 205 n. 3

Read Vol. I, pp. 451 f., as in the second impression.

II, 206 l. 13

The "sextons" (חזניא) probably in their frequent occupation as (elementary) teachers, assistants to the school-masters. See Bacher, Tannaiten, I², 105.

II, 210 n. 5

Bousset 3 ed. (Gressmann, 1926), p. 376.

II, 212 l. 22

See David de Sola Pool, The Old Jewish-Aramaic Prayer, The Kaddish, 1909, especially, pp. 10 ff. (Language and Date of the Kaddish). — Another view is that the "Kaddish contains some old phrases but is not an old prayer." [L. G.]

II, 216 ll. 17f.

Read (as in the second impression): "R. Eleazar (ben Pedat), contemporary of Johanan." — This R. Eleazar lived in the third century.

II, 217 ll. 19 f.

Vol. II, pp. 84 f. S. Krauss, Synagogale Altertümer, pp. 96 f.

II, 220 n. 2

Also Gen. R. 68, 8. On the way in which these origins were arrived at see S. Krauss, *op. cit.*, pp. 36–38.

II, 220 n. 4

Jer. Berakot 7b, above (R. Tanḥuma); cf. Gen. R. 68, 9. — The איברים ופרדים which were left burning on the altar all night furnish the desired correspondence with the sacrificial worship.

II, 220 ll.16–19

See Vol. I, p. 292. The differences recorded in Tos. Rosh ha-Shanah 4 (2), 11, between the schools of Shammai and Hillel presume a fixed order in the daily prayer before the destruction of the Temple; cf. also Tos. Berakot 3, 11 (R. Eliezer). The point in dispute between R. Gamaliel and his colleagues was the obligation of the *individual* (מתפלל אדם) to conform in this point exactly to the form and order of the prayers in the synagogue. [L. G.]

II. 221 n. 3

The passages cited refer to the repetition of the Tefillah. [L. G.]

II, 223 n. 1

The general rule about sacrifices is M. Zebaḥim 1, 1; every sacrifice must be offered under its specific name; cf. M. Pesaḥim 5, 2; and, of course, with observance of the ritual particularly prescribed. The priest must therefore have definitely in mind the particular kind of sacrifice he is making.

II, 225 n. 4

If the "hour" is taken literally, it would be hard to see how such pious men found hours enough in the day for other occupations. The word is frequently less definite, "a while."

II, 234 n. 4

On the harmony between man's will and God's, see the more general counsel in Abot 2, 4: "Make His will as thy will," etc. Herford, Pirkè Aboth (1925) *ad loc.* quotes Abot de-R. Nathan (Schechter, second recension, p. 36a): "If thou hast done His will as thy will, thou hast not done His will as His will. If thou hast done His will against thine own will, thou hast done His will as His will," etc.

II, 239 n. 3

Cf. Abot 6, 5 (Knowledge of) Torah superior to priesthood or royalty; the forty-eight excellences by which it is acquired.

II, 240 n. 1

For Johanan *read* Jonathan. — חובה is a measurable obligation; in contrast to such an obligation מצוה is used of an action by the performance of which a man acquires merit, though it is not specifically commanded. The whole discussion in Menaḥot 99b is about Josh. 1, 8; all would agree that the study of Torah is one of the greatest, if not the greatest of מצוות in the sense defined above.

II, 240 n. 4

For a different application of the principle, great things or small, see the story of the two rabbis on the way to execution, in Mekilta on Exod. 22, 22 (ed. Friedmann, f. 95b; ed. Weiss, f. 101b).

II, 241 n. 2

Rosh ha-Shanah 35a very likely means that Rab Judah, instead of saying the prayers himself, attended the public service and listened to the recitation of the leader in prayer (שליח הצבור). On Tannaim who gave study the precedence over prayer see Shabbat 11a and Jer. Berakot 1, 5.

II, 242 n. 1

Others take the reference to be to the angels who preside over the heavenly bodies and the elements of nature; Jer. Rosh ha-Shanah 2, 5 (f. 58a, middle); cf. Peṣikta, f. 3a–b, where Michael and Gabriel are mentioned, both of whom are patrons and guardians of Israel. Abot de-R Nathan, ed. Schechter, p. 48 f.

II, 242 ll. 23 f.

The metaphor, 'fire-law' (אש דת, Deut. 33, 2), is developed in detail in Sifrè Deut. § 343 (ed. Friedmann, f. 143a–b; on the text see Friedmann's note 35). It is a deadly fire to those who abandon their studies: כל זמן שאדם עמל בהם חיים הם לו פירש מהם ממיתים אותו.

II, 248 ff.

With the chapter on Chastisement compare that on Expiatory Suffering (Vol. I, pp. 546 ff.). See also Marmorstein, The Old Rabbinic Doctrine of God, pp. 185–196.

II, 249 n. 3

The disease is noted as especially fatal among children, but not confined to them. It is probable that the ancients did not distinguish it from quinsy (acute suppurative tonsillitis).

II, 249 n. 10

On "measure for measure," see also Mekilta on Exod. 13, 21 (ed. Friedmann, f. 25a; ed. Weiss, f. 30a) and on 14, 4 (Friedmann, f. 26a; Weiss, f. 31a); cf. the anecdote of Hillel and the skull floating in the water, Abot 2, 6. Cf. L. Ginzberg, Legends of the Jews, V, 427, n. 172.

II, 252 n. 4

The Megillat Ta'anit was written by Hananiah ben Hezekiah and his associates, as a memorial of deliverances, שהיו מחבבין את הצרות; as Rashi explains it, the afflictions from which they had been delivered. The words of R. Simeon ben Gamaliel are taken in the same sense, the interventions of God to deliver his people in our time have been so frequent that we should not be able to record them. (L. G.] See Shabbat 13b.

II, 253–254

See Mekilta Mishpaṭim 9, end (ed. Friedmann, f. 85b; ed. Weiss, f. 91b) on Exod. 21, 27. See Vol. I, p. 547 with notes 1–3.

II, 257 ll. 18–22

On the penitence of Reuben (and Judah), Sifrè Deut. § 348 (on Deut. 33, 6 f.; cf. Gen. R. 84, 18; Pesiḳta ed. Buber, f. 159a–b (in connection with his return to the pit into which, at his instance, the brothers had put Joseph, Gen. 37, 29).

II, 258 n. 3

On the penitence of Adam see L. Ginzberg, Legends of the Jews, V, 114 f.

II, 258 n. 5

For a Christian parallel, see Hermas, Sim. 5. 3, 7 f. See also 2 Clement, 16, 4 (almsgiving as a mode of repentance is good; fasting superior to prayer; almsgiving to both).

II, 260 n. 4

See also Abot de-R. Nathan, c. 1 and the parallels cited by Schechter. [L. G.] Cf. Bacher, Tannaiten I², 383, also 380 n.

II, 261 n. 2

The services were held on these days because they were the market-days on which the country people came to town (Vol. I, p. 29, n. 2).

II, 262 ll. 14–16

On the date of the destruction of the Temple cf. Josephus, Bell. Jud. vi. 4, 5 § 250. — "Tenth of Lous" (Jer. 52, 12 f.).

II, 262 ll. 22–25

See Büchler, Priester und Cultus, u.s.w., p. 22.

II, 268 l. 8

Read Isa. 1, 15, and correct n. 4 accordingly.

II, 268 n. 4

Cf. Martial ix. 41 — a kind of murder ("istud quod digitis, Pontice, perdis, homo est"). Nocturnal pollution (Deut. 23, 11 f., Sifrè § 255 f.) has as its consequence serious uncleanness for the בעל קרי. He is forbidden to read in the Scriptures or to study any of the branches of the unwritten law (Tos. Berakot 2, 13; Berakot 22a. About the unwritten law certain exceptions are made, in which there is no unanimity). On the ordinance of Ezra see Note on Vol. I, p. 29, N 3. Inasmuch as the bath of purification could not be taken until toward evening, the disqualification lasted through the daylight hours of the day following the pollution.

II, 271 n. 1

Those who thus indulge in thoughts of sin are not admitted to the mansion (מחיצה) (of God) — the part of heaven where He abides.

II, 272 ll. 11–18

Cf. 2 Peter 1, 5–9.

II, 280 l. 25

There is a strong presumption that the language of the apocalypses written towards the close of the first century was the Hebrew of the times, "the language of scholars." Against the opinion formerly entertained that the original language of 4 Esdras was Greek, see Wellhausen, Skizzen und Vorarbeiten, VI, 234 ff., who operates, however, with Biblical Hebrew, e.g., p. 237, the frequency of the Infinitive Absolute with a finite verb, a use which has disappeared in the later Hebrew (Segal, Mishnaic Hebrew Grammar, p. 165). Perles contends for a Hebrew original for Enoch (Orientalistische Literaturzeitung, XVI (1913), 481 ff., 516).

II, 280 n. 2

With the esoteric books of the Essenes may be compared what is told of the Pythagoreans, Iamblichus, Vita Pyth. § 253.

II, 284 ll. 19 f.

The Georgian version is published by R. P. Blake in the Harvard Theological Review, XIX (1926), 299–375.

II, 287 n. 2

The burnings for kings furnished precedent for the burnings for Patriarchs (נשיאים) — the parallel is not without significance — not for private persons. Tos. Shabbat, 7 (8), 18; cf. Abodah Zarah 11a. The question what was burned is asked, and answered, "his bed and all the articles he had in daily use." But the following anecdote shows that others might contribute: "When Rabban Gamaliel the Elder [this appears to be an anachronism] died, the proselyte Onkelos burned for him more than seventy minas," i.e., things mounting up to that value — one may imagine costly gums and spices. The Talmud, l.c., guards itself against the suspicion of a heathenish custom.

II, 289 n. 4

On later Greek notions see Rohde, Psyche.

II, 289 n. 7

Virgil, Aeneid, vi, 425 (the *irremeabilis* unda, cf. ib. 436–439).

II, 290 n. 6

Read עמיו (his kinsfolk).

II, 291 ll. 9–11

Cf. Wisdom of Solomon, 5, 1. Grimm, in his commentary on 4, 20–5, 2 (p. 111), similarly finds in the verses, not the resurrection and last judgement (Böttcher, al.), but "eine *Dramatisierung* des Gedankens . . . , dass Gottlose wie Gerechte im Jenseits Bewusstseyn und Kenntniss von der durch Gottes Richterspruch erfolgten gänzlichen Umwandlung ihres beiderseitigen Schicksales haben," u.s.w.

II, 292 ll. 28 ff.

The speech put into the mouth of Eleazar, addressed to his followers at Masada (Josephus, Bell. Jud. vii. 8, 7 §§ 341 ff.), notwithstanding the appeal to the Scriptures (§ 343), is completely Greek in conception and expression.

II, 294 n. 4

Cf. ἐξετασμός, 4, 6.

II, 295 ll. 4–12.

See Vita Mosis, ii. 39 § 288 (ed. Mangey II, 189); Quod Deus immutabilis, c. 10 §§ 45–50 (Mangey I, 279 f.); De mundo opificio, c. 23 §§ 69–71 (Mangey, I, 15 f.).

II, 296 n. 3

For other references see L. Ginzberg, Legends of the Jews, V, 119.

II, 298 ll. 24–27

Cf. Dan. 11, 33.

II, 298 n. 5

On this commentary see Malter, Saadia Gaon (1921), p. 404.

II, 299 n. 1

With 2 Macc. 7, 9 (ἀναβίωσις) cf. Josephus, cited in Vol. II, p. 317 (ἀναβιοῦν).

II, 301 l. 26

In 45, 3 the judge is "the Elect One"; cf. 69, 27. See Vol. II, p. 333.

II, 302 l. 5

That the name Raphael may originally have been derived, not from רפא, 'heal,' but from רפאים, 'shades' (of the dead), so that he appears quite in character in 22, 3 ff., is conjectured by Ginzberg, Legends of the Jews, V, 71. He would accordingly take Tartarus away from Uriel and give it to Raphael, supposing that the translator mistakenly connected the words with the preceding clause instead of the following.

II, 302 l. 19

Why this category of sinners should be neither punished in the day of judgment nor raised up out of Hades is not manifest. Gunkel, Berliner philologische Wochenschrift, 1903, p. 203) would insert a negative before the second clause in the description, so that it would read, ἀλλ' οὐδ' ἁμαρτωλοὶ ἀσεβεῖς, they are not ὅσιοι, but also not godless sinners and accomplices of the wicked (heathen), and fittingly they do not share either the torments of the altogether bad or the resurrection of the righteous. This plausible emendation removes the main difficulty, but comparison of the Greek and Ethiopic shows that the text is otherwise not in order. — The rabbis had their opinions about the fate of the 'middling class'; see Vol. I, p. 495 f.; Vol. II, p. 318, and Note on the latter place.

II, 311 ll. 1–3

Cf. Exod. R. 44, 6.

II, 315 ll. 24 f.

The notion that the fallen angels are the authors of the corruption of mankind is almost entirely unknown to rabbinical sources. [L. G.]

II, 315 n. 4

Bousset, Religion des Judentums, 2 ed. p. 383, n. (3 ed. p. 333, n.) cites Clem. Hom. viii, 12 ff.

II, 316 ll. 24–26

Commonplaces about the universal and inevitable lot of man from the beginning, in the consolation of mourners, with prayer to God, the great comforter (בעל נחמות), closing with the benediction, "Blessed is He who comforts mourners," Ketubot 8b.

II, 317 ll. 10–13

When and where Ecclesiastes was written are questions which I have seen no reason to discuss. I do not find in Sirach any evidence of acquaintance with the book.

II, 317 ll. 20 ff.

Reference may be made also to Josephus, Bell. Jud. i. 23, 2 § 650, cf. § 653; iii. 8, 5 § 372; Contra Apionem, ii. c. 30 § 218.

II, 317 n. 3

With ἀναβιοῦν cf. 2 Macc. 7, 9 (ἀναβίωσις); Vol. II, p. 299, n. 1.

II, 318 l. 16 and n. 3

In Mekilta Mishpaṭim 14 (on Exod. 22, 5) מצפצפת is used of fire running along the surface of the ground, in distinction from a fire that jumps from point to point, and might perhaps be rendered 'scorching' or 'charring.' In Mekilta de-R. Simeon ben Yoḥai on the same verse (ed. Hoffmann, p. 141), though not in the same connection, ספספה occurs in a context where the meaning 'scorch' or 'singe' seems to be required. In M. Nazir 6, 3, a Nazirite who shaves or singes his hair (סיפסף), no matter how little, is accountable; see also Tos. Uḳaṣin 2, 16. אע״פ שסיפספן באור, "though one singe them with fire." Professor Ginzberg, to whom I owe this suggestion, with an etymological and critical discussion of the words in these and other passages, understands the opinion of the School of Shammai to be that these "betwixt and betweens" will go down to hell and *be singed* by its fires, and after this experience arise thence and be healed. It is evident that this figure for their fate is more appropriate than that which I dubiously employed in the text.

II, 319 n. 2

See Note on Vol. II, p. 321, n. 3.

II, 321 n. 2

See Origen on Matt. 15, 14.

II, 321 n. 3

In Beṣah 15b (cited on p. 319, n. 2) the contrast is between the fulfilment of a commandment (keeping the holiday festively, which belongs to חיי שעה) and the study of Torah (חיי עולם); see on the same page, below, on the division of time, etc. In Ta'anit 21a in the same phrase the current editions erroneously read חיי עולם הבא, the old editions simply חיי עולם. [L. G.]

II, 321 n. 4

Other examples, R. Eleazar ben Azariah, Gen. R. 93, 11; R. Ḥanina ben Teradion, 'Abodah Zarah 17b. Compare also the attitude of the author of 4 Esdras throughout. The relatively early date of these utterances may be observed.

II, 323 ff.

On the Messianic expectations of the Jews the most recent comprehensive monograph is that of Joseph Klausner, רעיון המשיחי בישראל מראשיתו ועד חתימת המשנה, 2 ed. Jerusalem, 1927, pp. 346 ff. — In three Parts: I. In the Age of the Prophets: II. In the Apocryphal and Pseudepigraphic Literature: III. In the Age of the Tannaim. The Third Part is a revision of Die messianischen Vorstellungen des jüdischen Volkes im Zeitalter der Tannaiten, Berlin, 1904.

In Strack-Billerbeck, Kommentar zum Neuen Testament aus Talmud und Midrasch, the subject is treated in long excursuses (nos. 29–33) on "Diese Welt, die Tage des Messias und die Zukünftige Welt; Vorzeichen und Berechnung der Tage des Messias; Scheol, Gehinnom und Gan 'Eden; Allgemeine oder teilweise Auferstehung der Toten?; Gerichtsgemälde aus der altjüdischen Literatur. Vol. IV (1928), pp. 799–1212. The index, s.v. Messias, should also be consulted.

See also Bousset, Religion des Judentums, 2 ed. (1926), pp. 213–301.

II, 326 n. 6

See Strack-Billerbeck, Excursus 28 (IV, 764–798), Der Prophet Elias nach seiner Entrückung aus dem Diesseits; Louis Ginzberg, Legends of the Jews, IV, 195–235, VI, 316–342.

II, 326 n. 7

Ekah Rabbati, ed. Buber, p. 45b.; Jer. Berakot 5a, above.

II, 327 ll. 15 ff.

See Torrey, The Second Isaiah (1928), pp. 5–19.

II, 329 ll. 10–12

In the Amoraic passages of the Talmud *ben David* is rarely used; more frequently in the Midrashim, where, however, *Messiaḥ ben David* is the common form. [L. G.]

II, 329, n. 3

See Vol. II, p. 347.

II, 329 ll. 20–22

In Lam. R. on Lam. 2, 2 a pun on this name is attributed to the Patriarch Judah: in Num. 24, 17, אל תקרי כוכב אלא כוזב read not "a star," but "a liar." In Buber's edition (1899), this piece of wit disappears; see the editor's note, f. 51a, n. 57.

II, 329 n. 2

On this constant usage see Jackson and Lake, The Beginnings of Christianity, I, 348, 353 f.

II, 333 n. 7

In the Talmud also there are several passages in which it is supposed that the Messiaḥ will appear after the so-called "Messianic work" (the gathering of the dispersed and the punishment of sinners.) — See L. Ginzberg, Unbekannte jüdische Sekte, p. 347, n. 2.

II, 333 ll. 21 ff.

Judgment by the Chosen One, Enoch 45, 3, cf. 36, 1 ff. (Vol. II, p. 301, and Note there).

II, 334 ll. 11 ff.

Reference should be made to Enoch 62, 7, the "Son of Man" hidden from the beginning. A Christian hand may be suspected in this passage, at least by way of expansion. — For literature on the "Son of Man" see Bousset, Religion des Judentums, 3 ed. (1926), p. 266.

II, 337 l. 18

The contrast between the peaceful prince and the militant Asmonaeans, John Hyrcanus and Alexander Jannaeus, may have been in the author's mind.

II, 337 ll. 26 f.

Cf. Enoch 62, 7 (Note on Vol. II, p. 334).

II, 341 l. 27

The book of life, see Vol. II, p. 297.

II, 342

Christians who took the Revelation of John literally held that there would be a millennium after the resurrection of the dead, when the kingdom of Christ was to be established in material form on this same earth (Eusebius, Hist. Eccles, iii. 39, 12 — Papias, not recognizing, as Eusebius says, that the Apostolic descriptions are to be understood mystically); Euseb. iii. 28, 1 ff. (Jerusalem his capital, Cerinthus); Justin Martyr, Dial. c. Tryphone, cc. 80–82 (for himself and many others of the same mind, c. 80, 2); the Montanists, *et al.*

II, 344 ll. 8–12

See Vol. II, p. 337, and Note above, p. 200.

II, 346 ll. 13 ff.

On the Messianic notions of the Tannaim see Joseph Klausner (titles above, p. 199.)

II, 347 ll. 20–23

See Note on Vol. II, p. 329.

II, 347 n. 2

Another Hillel was a brother of the Patriarch Judah (II), and it is thought by some that he is meant by Origen (on Psalm 1) when he speaks of Ἰοῦλλος πατριάρχος. "He may have been prompted to this declaration (Sanh. 98b) by Origen's professed discovery in the Old Testament of Messianic passages referring to the founder of Christianity." — Jewish Encyclopedia VI, 401. — In the preceding context (Sanhedrin 99b, top) a מין (perhaps a Christian) asks R. Abbahu when the Messiah will come; and to such a question the answer of Hillel would be apposite. The identification with a contemporary of Origen is, however, very dubious.

II, 348 ll. 1f.

A different explanation is preferred by Ginzberg: Hezekiah was the scholar on the throne, and R. Johanan ben Zakkai may have thought of Hezekiah as coming to meet him at his entrance on the better life; cf. Baba Kamma 111b, where Raba hopes that when he dies R. Osha'ya may come to meet him because he has explained a tradition of that rabbi.

II, 348 n. 3
Ekah Rabbati, ed. Buber, f. 45a f.

II, 352
That Daniel misunderstood this revelation, see Megillah 12a, top (Raba). [L. G.]

II, 352 ll. 25–30
When the kingdom of the house of David will be re-established is one of the things that no man knows, Mekilta Wayassa 5 (on Exod. 16, 32), ed. Friedmann, 51a, below; ed. Weiss, 59b. [L. G.]

II, 353 ll. 1–5
One of the things which God adjured Israel not to reveal was "the end" (Levi). Ketubot 111a. Rashi understands this as an injunction laid particularly on the prophets; and probably this is what Levi had in mind.

II, 353 n. 3
See also Vol. I, p. 368; Vol. II, p. 390.

II, 354 n. 2
"Persian" (for Roman) is a favorite substitution of the censors, and is found here only in censored editions of the Talmud. [L. G.]

II, 355 ll. 5–9
On Jose ben Ḳisma's prognostications also Tanḥuma ed. Buber, Wayyishlaḥ 8 (f. 83b). Here the reference to Tiberias is explicit; they were staying in that city, and he said "this gate." Caesarea Philippi is suggested by the "sign" (אות) he gave his disciples — the waters in the grotto of Paneas should turn to blood.

II, 356 l. 8 ff.
On this and the following utterances see Klausner, רעיון המשיחי, pp. 284 ff. Klausner thinks that they had their origin in the experience of the generation which lived under the decrees of Hadrian after the Bar Kocheba war; the authors of these Baraitas are of the school of Akiba.

II, 356 l. 20

Nehorai is said to be equivalent in meaning to Meir ("he enlightened the eyes of scholars in Halakah") and is taken for the name of the well-known disciple of Akiba. 'Erubin 13b. See Vol. I, p. 95, n. 4 and Note *ad loc.* In 'Erubin *l.c.* the true reading is not נהוראי but מיישא or מיאשא; see Bacher, Tannaiten, II, 6, n. 1.

II, 356 n. 7

The patrial גבלאי may be from n. p. גבל Byblos, in Phoenicia for which Assyrian inscriptions have Guubli.

II, 357 n. 5

Later sources have רעש (or רעם), perhaps the rumbling sounds, precursors of an earthquake; and this may be the meaning in Sanhedrin, l.c. [L. G.]

II, 358 ll. 27–29

See Vol. I, p. 46, ll. 15 ff.

II, 358 n. 3

Cf. Mark 9, 12 ἀποκαθιστάνει πάντα.

II, 359 n. 3

See Büchler, Priester und Cultus, p. 20, n. 3.

II, 359 n. 4

For a complete collection of passages in which doubtful cases are reserved till the coming of Elijah see L. Ginzberg, Unbekannte jüdische Sekte, p. 304.

II, 362 n. 6

Also Pesiḳta ed. Buber, f. 50b.

II, 363 l. 2

Read *ḥamūshīm.*

II, 363 n. 2

Also Pesiḳta de-R. Simeon ben Yoḥai, ed. Hoffmann, p. 38, end.

II, 364 n. 5

The Messianic banquet is perhaps meant in a saying of Akiba, Abot 3, 16: והדין דין אמת והכל מתוקן לסעודה.

II, 365 n. 3
Cf. Enoch 62, 14 f.; see also Note on Vol. II, p. 364, n. 5 (Akiba).

II, 368 n. 7
The name of this land is *Arsareth* in the Latin version of 4 Esdras, 13, 45; cf. ארץ אחרת, Deut. 29, 27, quoted M. Sanhedrin 10, 3; Tos. Sanhedrin 13, 12. The Syriac version has Arzaph and the other Oriental versions otherwise. See Hilgenfeld, Messias Judaeorum (1869), p. 101, n. (v. Gutschmid, Zeitschrift für wissenschaftliche Theologie (1860), p. 76, compares 'Αρσαράτα, Ptolemy, v. 13, 11 (name of a city in Armenia Maior). See Violet, Die Apokalypsen des Esra und des Baruch in deutscher Gestalt (1924), p. 185, for other conjectures, among which "Ararat" may be particularly mentioned. See also Klausner, רעיון המשיחי, p. 305. — On "Sabbatical" rivers, see Josephus, Bell. Jud. vii. 5, 1 § 99 (in Phoenicia); Pliny, Nat. Hist. xxxi. 2, 18 (In Judaea rivos sabbatis omnibus siccatur), cf. R. Akiba in Sanhedrin 65b; but neither of these, of course, is the river beyond which the ten tribes were in exile.

II, 369 n. 1
Return of the Ten Tribes from beyond Sambation, Yalḳuṭ II § 469 (on Isa. 49, 9) quoting Pesiḳta R. (ed. Friedmann, f. 146b–147).

II, 370 ll. 12 ff.
On the Ephraimite Messiah see Klausner רעיון המשיחי, pp. 313 ff. On the origin of the notion see also L. Ginzberg, Unbekannte jüdische Sekte, 337–340.

II, 373 n. 3
Cf. Vol. I, p. 434.

II, 378 n. 5
It should also be noted that in repetitions of the same saying in different sources the terms sometimes interchange, being equivalents in the mind of the scribes, as in the instance cited in note 5.

II, 379 ll. 28–31
The resurrection in Palestine, Midrash Tannaim on Deut. 12, 10 f. (ed. Hoffmann, p. 58). — "Some say forty days before other lands, some say forty years."

II, 380 n. 1

See also Pesiḳta Rabbati, ed. Friedmann, f. 147a (from beyond Sambation).

II, 381 l. 15

"From the Torah" is here a late addition not found in correct texts. [L. G.]

II, 381 n. 1

See also Pesaḥim 68a, end, where Deut. 32, 39, "I kill and I make alive; I have wounded, and I heal," furnishes an answer to those who say that the revivification of the dead is not in the Torah.

II, 383 l. 20

In Talmudic sources Parashah is never the "weekly lesson," but "section." [L. G.]

II, 384 n. 1

A Christian parallel is Athenagoras, De resurrectione, c. 18 f.

II, 386 ll. 2–6

Instead of "he had formerly held the same view," etc., the words of R. Joshua should be rendered: "If the verse had said,' 'The wicked shall return to Sheol, all the Gentiles,' and stopped there, I should have interpreted it as you do; but now since it says, 'who forget God,' there are righteous men among the nations who have a lot in the World to Come."

II, 386 ll. 9–11

The "nations of the world" with whom Maimonides was acquainted were Christians and Mohammedans.

II, 387 ll. 9 ff.

The translation reproduces the Tosefta. In the parallels, Seder 'Olam, c. 3 (ed. Ratner 9a) and Rosh ha-Shanah 17a, the clause "and those who stretch out their hands against the Temple," is not found. The Seder 'Olam has in place of it, "and those who deride the words of learned men" (*ḥakamim*); cf. 'Erubin 21b, where this class is promised a particularly offensive punishment. It may be suspected that the clause in the Tosefta had its origin in the desire of a haggadist to do something with the last words of Psalm 49, 15 (מִזְּבֻל לוֹ), as had been done with what went before it (וצורם לבלות שאול).

II, 388 l. 7

On the words "from the Law" see Note on Vol. II, p. 381, l. 15.

II, 388 l. 9

"Extraneous books" (חיצונים, cf. Baraita). Akiba's damnatory sentence is probably aimed at reading from such books in the synagogue. See Krochmal, Moreh Nebukè ha-Zeman (1851), p. 101 f. (הקורא בהם בצבור וגו').

II. 391 ll. 8–12

With this conversion one may compare the story in Eusebius Hist. Eccles. ii. 9, told of the martyrdom of the Apostle James.

II, 394 ll. 16–25

See E. Meyer, Ursprung und Anfänge des Christentums, II, 58–120; Bousset, Religion des Judentums, 3 ed. (1926). Das religionsgeschichtliche Problem, especially, pp. 501 ff.

II, 394 n. 4

See Pettazoni, Zarathustra, p. 106, n. 5.